Quentin van Marle is a f
writer. The cycling trip forming
Boomerang Road was featured in a weekly slot on BBC Radio 5 Live. His first book, *Marooned*, published in 1995, was based on his 31 isolated days spent on an uninhabited tropical island, an ordeal undertaken for the *Sunday Times*. The author has had a lifelong fascination with travel to difficult and far-flung places.

His most recent cycling effort took him across South Africa from Durban to Cape Town, a decade and more since Nelson Mandela's acclaimed walk to freedom. Based on that trip, his book *Ride the Blazing Rainbow* will be published in 2005.

BY THE SAME AUTHOR

Marooned

Quentin van Marle

BOOMERANG ROAD

A Pedalling Pom's Australian Odyssey

Troubador Publishing Ltd
9 De Montfort Mews
Leicester LE1 7FW, UK
Tel: (+44) 116 255 9311
Email: books@troubador.co.uk
Web: www.troubador.co.uk

ISBN 1 904744 24 9

Cover illustration and line drawings by the author's sister, Daphne van Marle

Typeset in 11pt Minion by Troubador Publishing Ltd, Leicester, UK
Printed by The Cromwell Press Ltd, Trowbridge, Wilts

t² is an imprint of Troubador Publishing

To Jeremy Willis – occasional travelling companion
and an outstanding friend

Acknowledgements

My grateful thanks to the very many people who helped turn this Australian cycling odyssey from an idle thought into a demanding reality. They include: BBC Radio 5 Live and the *Western Morning News*; Brian Stanleick and his Oggy Oggy Pasty Company; the Australian Tourist Commission, both in the UK and Australia; Garuda Indonesian Airlines; Best Western; Simon Day, webmaster at Clear Blue Media; and not least, to Len Little and to all the cordial everyday Aussies who made the long journey such a rewarding and eclectic experience.

Contents

Prologue
Backpedal

I had made up my mind to do it. Ride a mountain bike from Australia's far north to its deepest south. A distance of 4000 kilometres, or two million turns of the pedals. What a hero.

It would be in part-effort, you should know, to relive a long gone and fairly misspent youth. More than 40 years had passed since I'd first departed British shores for youthful employment as a jackaroo on the sheep and cattle stations of the Great Outback – a time that marginally pre-dated the Beatles. It was 1961 and I'd just turned 16.

I have been to all corners of the world since; as a journalist, a yachtie, and as an optimist with good ideas at the time. I married once, twice, and then not at all. Finally came a point where perhaps I wanted to make a little sense of things; to take stock and go back somewhere near the beginning. Australia seemed as good a place as any; certainly better than the once smog-filled midlands where I grew up as a kid, and even the blackbirds woke up coughing.

And where I first learned to ride a bicycle. It was a rickety machine belonging to my sister. It had mismatched tyres and one brake. I've a notion that all of us recall this early triumph – one minute wobbling and falling, the next speeding along on two wheels, grinning with the confidence of a Tour de France Pro. I was seven years old.

Back then of course, there was no way of knowing that so many years on I'd be putting the experience to work in this manner. Back then, if you wanted to get to some far off place called Australia, disparaging adults said you first had to dig a tunnel.

Fast-forward to November 2002 and England's westcountry. There is no telling when, where, or why ideas suddenly hit the brain. This one came while strolling towards the local pharmacy. The thought was still there at the end of the day and what's more, had grown considerably by the following morning.

I bought a map and planned the route. I called a potential commercial sponsor, then contacted a newspaper and a radio station; all were interested. And I got in touch with the Australian Tourist Commission which obliged with partial accommodation and helpful contacts. And finally, I set up a website, *PedallingPom.com*. Within three weeks the whole project had been wrapped up and cleared for takeoff.

The erratic life of a freelance writer does have its finer moments.

The ride itself, we all agreed, should not take longer than three months: which reminded me – the one thing I still didn't have was a bicycle.

Neither did I have much time for reflection, and just as well. Dwelling on the task ahead, with all the questions it raised – fitness, middle age, daily distances, heat and humidity, to name but a few – would persuade any logical person that there is but one answer.

Get a life, sure; but for Chrissakes, not this one.

Trouble is, I'm not always logical. Nor is life itself. If it was, we'd know the meaning of it. Besides, by now I really wanted to do this thing – even if it was just to find out if I've still got what it takes.

Thus, with agreements secured from BBC Radio 5 Live and a leading regional newspaper, a modest sponsorship budget, and a brand new Trek 450 mountain bike, I boarded a series of airplanes which finally deposited me and my machine in the North Queensland city of Cairns on New Year's Day, 2003. Ahead lay endless roads which, I now know, promise the cyclist a good number of near-death experiences. For me, they also spelled adventures, plural; a few of them along memory lane, though most in new and unfamiliar territory.

The media brief was simple enough: to find original human-interest stories along the way and file them back once a week. My personal brief seemed less straightforward. There was only one way of learning if these ageing bones could still pedal all that distance in under three months – and that was by getting on the damn bike and going for it, up the hills as well as down. As for making sense from a lifetime of rather different ups and downs, well that remained an imponderable. I only reiterate that Australia was as good a place as any to try – on what had now, for sponsorship reasons, been dubbed the *Oggy Oggy Ozzy Odyssey*.

All of which brings us back to Cairns, and the present. From here I still have to travel 75km north, to the idle coastal town of Port Douglas. There, the ride starts, the odyssey commences, and understanding – for good or bad – begins its slow seepage from the soul.

Join me now, from the outset. Jump aboard the hi-speed catamaran *Quicksilver* on which I'm hitching a 90-minute ride up a short stretch of the Coral Sea to Port Douglas. Then get ready to pedal your imagination along the highways of what some people around here call God's Country.

And if that be so, then the first truth is already out. God does indeed work in strange ways.

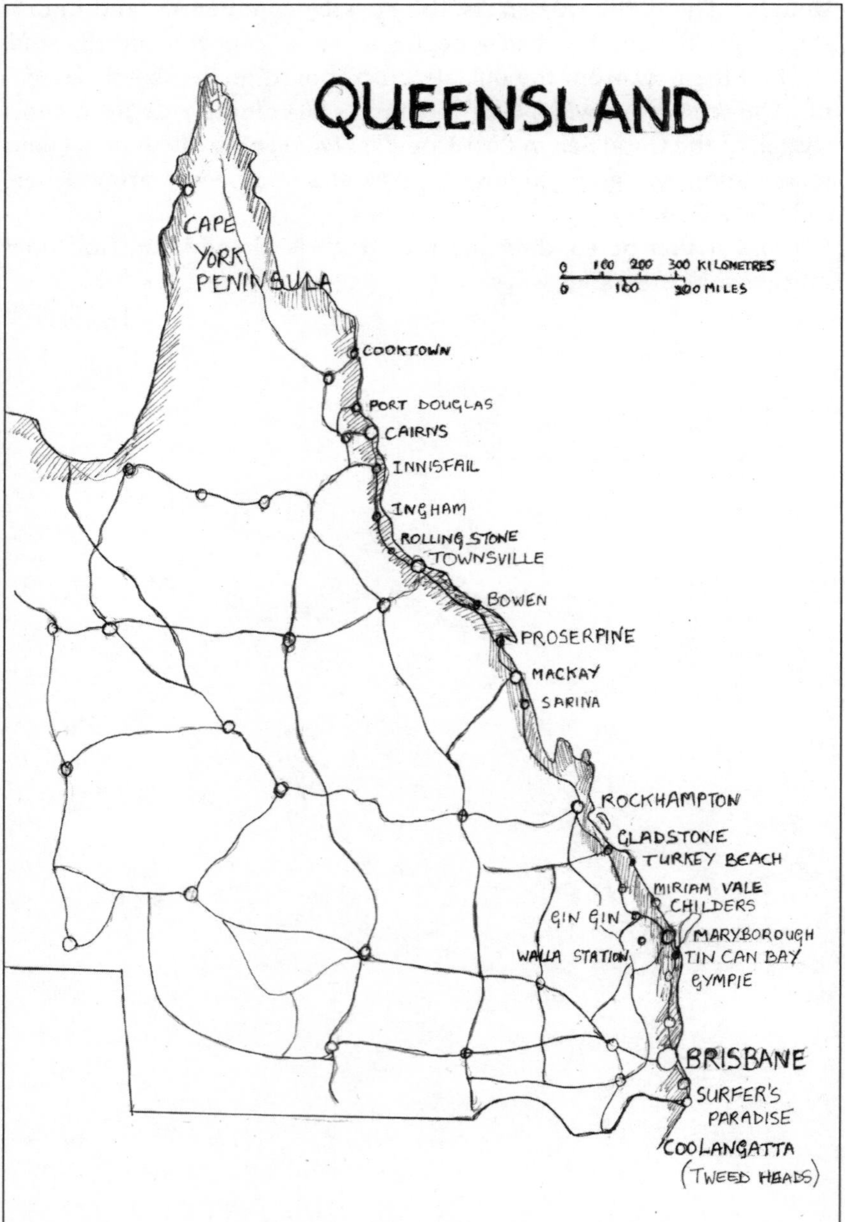
QUEENSLAND
0 100 200 300 KILOMETRES
0 100 200 MILES
CAPE
YORK
PENINSULA
COOKTOWN
PORT DOUGLAS
CAIRNS
INNISFAIL
INGHAM
ROLLING STONE
TOWNSVILLE
BOWEN
PROSERPINE
MACKAY
SARINA
ROCKHAMPTON
GLADSTONE
TURKEY BEACH
MIRIAM VALE
CHILDERS
GIN GIN
MARYBOROUGH
WALLA STATION
TIN CAN BAY
GYMPIE
BRISBANE
SURFER'S
PARADISE
COOLANGATTA
(TWEED HEADS)

ONE
Surface Paradise

Massive twin jet-propulsion units churn up a steamy tropical waterfront. The giant wavepiercer tourist boat gathers pace, and soon the city of Cairns disappears altogether as *Quicksilver* reaches a nearby headland and swings north towards Port Douglas.

Rays from a sultry morning sun glint on a dead calm sea. Twin aluminium hulls with needlepoint bows cut through the water, like switchblades tearing up layer upon layer of soft silk. They swallow up the nautical miles at 35 knots. Far beyond the horizon lies the Great Barrier Reef, 70 or so kilometres offshore. Somewhat closer, perhaps 1000 metres away, is the palm-fringed coastline of the region they call Tropical Queensland. Vehicles are clearly visible on both lanes of the Captain Cook Highway, a coast road with views to die for.

My bike, assembled and ridden for the first time the day before, lies shining and unperturbed against the sterndeck's guardrail. It is gold and black, has 24 gears, a set of road-friendly intermediate tyres, and an air-filled saddle. For the time being, a single rear panier will suffice to carry my total luggage – one canvas rucksack and a canvas briefcase, one on top of the other and held in place by four taut bungee cords. Other items include water bottles, a mini-pump, and a digital distance recorder euphemistically called a computer. Everything about this machine is new, except for its rider. By the time this thing is over, everything will be worn, battered and shattered – especially its rider.

I drift into trance-like thoughts, the way you do sometimes while staring at the sea. They involve another ocean passage, the one that brought me out here way back in 1961, when jet travel was for an unseen elite. It was a time when emigrating Europeans intended to settle Down Under for all time, and when families left at home were resigned to the possibility of never laying eyes on them again. The widespread vision of the day still placed Australia and its rugged outback as roughly equidistant to, and almost the same as, the back-side of the moon.

But for a 16 year old straight out of a neo-Dickensian boarding school, the thought of exploring all those exotic en-route ports was thrilling: Gibraltar, Naples, and Port Said in the Mediterranean; Through the Suez Canal and up to Aden; next on to Colombo and Fremantle in the faraway Indian Ocean; then along the upper rim of the Southern Ocean towards Melbourne and finally Sydney – from where I'd be heading for some remote sheep and cattle station deep in the Australian bush. There were no regrets about turning my back on A Levels or university life, not then and not now. Anyway, this was enrolling into the University of Life, and I couldn't wait.

Quicksilver makes short work of my voyage into the past. In no time it seems, the tourists are filing down the gangwalks into the smart, palm fringed confines of the Port Douglas 'Marina Mirage' – a name suggesting that Cheltenham-type tweeness has somehow found its way to this raw corner of the earth. I wait until the tried-and-tested magnets of tourism draw these new visitors into the marina's shops, cafes, and clothing stores before wheeling the bike ashore. Here, the trippers will switch boats onto a Barrier Reef special; a day out on the water under strict supervision.

I cannot travel that way. If I could, maybe life would have been easier. Anyhow, now I'm in the saddle, my own boss again, riding cheerfully along broad, colourful streets and relieved to be here at last.

A few kilometres from here, on the coastal route north to Cooktown (the last outpost-style town of the true far north), the road runs out of tarmac. It becomes a track of reddish dirt – and right now, in the midst of the rainy season, it can be wet and wild country, the real face of tropical Oz suitable only for 4x4s. I heed both the map and some expert advice; Port Douglas, just a tiny way south, is the spot to kick off from.

The route will take me from here, all the way down the coast to Sydney, where I'll swing inland and head southwest into sheep and cattle country before coming to a close in Melbourne. For me, it's a bit like the return flight of a boomerang. In the 1960s, I had travelled the other way, from the sheep stations of New South Wales, to Sydney, then up to Queensland. So any revisiting I do en-route will be in the reverse order of how it actually was.

Pedalling slowly down a main street lined with gently waving palms, I very soon realise that what had once been an idyllic retreat for up-market dropouts has now gone Big-Time Tourist. I note an undue number of estate agents nestling alongside expensive boutiques with names like *Blokes Up North* and *Jungle Road*; pavement cafes, menus partly written in French; interior design stores; a plethora of one-hour photo shops; and a smart 4x4 with jazzed-up signwriting blaring out the services of a landscape gardener.

Yet I see why first-time visitors are smitten by the town; it has the surface ingredients of a tropical Utopia, readily comparable to Key West – a blurred vision of paradise set in a distant somewhere at the far end of the line. If you can imagine Australia as a toughly-worded business contract then you're sure to find Port Douglas neatly tucked into the Escape Clause.

"Yer bloody lucky, yer know that mate?" The assertion comes from a broad antipodean drawl belonging to the barman of the Central Hotel. His lined face goes well with the bare wooden floors and unpretentious furniture. It is the only surviving old-style Aussie pub in town: the last bastion of the *Ocker* – where this down-to-earth, beer swilling, hard swearing, gambling mad, and semi-extinct Australian male can take refuge from an encroaching world that appears to be stamping on his traditional values by the day.

I'm on a barstool nursing a cold beer, wondering why the barman had said that. Outside, it is a humid 31C, and I've already told him about the long, arduous bike ride ahead.

He puts a cluster of dirty glasses through a pump-wash, talking as he works. "If yer tried to do what yer doing this time last year, forget it. It was 40 degress all day, every day. And the same the year before that. Yer couldn't walk ten metres before needing a wring-out". Then he adds ominously, "Under the most cancerous sun in the world".

That one hung in the hot, still air. On a boat like *Quicksilver*, travelling at 35 knots, you stay cool. I am hoping the same will apply to cycling at ten knots or thereabouts. If, as he says, it is several degrees cooler than the past couple of years, I see that I'm lucky indeed. As for the cancer, well that crosses my mind every time I roll my own.

I buy him a beer and we chat about this and that. Something I say triggers off a question. He suddenly cocks his head, giving me that sly, grinning look of man who knows something you don't.

"Where were you on September 11?" He doesn't have to add the year and my response is instant.

"Southwest England. I heard about it in a cafe".

He nods his okay – then asks the impossible. "Where was Bill Clinton?"

How the hell would I know? Three men are sitting at the bar, bemoaning the result of the day's first horse race somewhere down in New South Wales. It is on the TV bolted high onto a wall. One of them mourns the loss of $50. It's lunchtime, and there's maybe only ten customers in the place. This does not deter the barman from sweeping a proud arm around his domain.

He leans forward, clandestine fashion, with eyes darting left and right before settling on mine. "He was in here, mate. Drinking. In this very pub".

I am deeply suspicious. What, for God's sake, would the former Most Powerful Man in the World be doing in a spit n' sawdust bar in Port Douglas – at any time of year?

Yet it turns out to be true, and I realise I've got my first radio story of the ride with barely a turn of the pedals. During the latter part of his presidency Clinton had made an official visit Down Under – an occasion on which for some reason he was whisked from the capital city of Canberra to a secluded Port Douglas retreat. Just like the tourists disembarking at Marina Mirage for the first time, Bill, if not Hilary, was hooked. He threatened the town with a return visit.

Late one night during that subsequent private trip, and when no longer president, he meandered into the bar of the Central Hotel. The Ockers, not prone to any form of deference, were welcoming in their own way. The punter who moments before had lost $50 on a nag, picks up the tale.

"Yeah, I was in here at the time" he recalls. "He seemed an okay kinda bloke, willing to have a beer with us. Came in alone – or we thought he was alone – when, wham, suddenly in jumped this guy in a suit with a mobile phone in his hand and a real twisted look on his face. He said something to Clinton and passed him the phone. Then a weird look came over his face as well".

The punter takes a serious gulp from a schooner-size beer glass, belches, and wipes a hairy arm across his mouth. "Next thing, about ten of these guys stormed into the pub and surrounded him. Bodyguards in suits, all yelling down mobile phones. One of 'em was cursing Australia 'cause the government wouldn't allow 'em to carry guns. He screamed something about Mr President's life being in mortal danger 'cause now they've got no fucking weapons to defend him with. It was like '*Hey, now see what happens, you smart-asses. Thanks a bunch for nothing*'. All that bull".

The barman nods. "Too bloody right. It was mayhem in here – ending up with Clinton being manhandled into the night by this tidal wave of crewcuts. All of 'em in suits". He shakes his head sadly. "We're not used to that kind of stuff up here. Nobody wears suits".

He grins at his quip, then turns contrite. "A while later we heard about the Twin Towers on the TV. A subduing experience I remember".

It was that alright. I muse aloud my own thoughts of Clinton seeming under more threat from his home-team of hapless U.S. Secret Service agents than some faraway terrorist group. Besides, he was very much an ex-Mr President on vacation in one of the world's great sleepy resorts, where the need to lock your car or shining new bicycle apparently doesn't exist. A place where only washed up bodyguards from a warlike, Zippo-flicking culture could possibly ignore its tranquility, half a world away from where the bullets fly, and loudly rue their empty holsters.

I emerge from the bar, my disdain for megalomaniac politicans intact, and ask someone the way to my hotel, the BreakFree Reef Club. I pedal to the end of the main street and swing right at a turnoff before the beach, where commercial buildings bow out in favour of tidy single-storey houses, sprinkled lawns, and lush vegetation. Away from the business district, this part of town is wrapped in that strange silence unique to hot tropical afternoons. Yes, it could almost be the Florida Keys.

My hosts at the reef club are Wendy Casey and her live-in man, Keith.

She is an ambitious thirtysomething blond who started work at the hotel as a secretary – yet somehow became its manager by nightfall of the same day. Keith, well, he's a bit different. He is mad about golf, not quite so mad about work, and not at all mad about being part white, part Aborigine. This is a syndrome I expect to encounter more than once along the way.

The architectural style of Port Douglas is low slung. Few buildings rise higher than the treetrops. The view from my top floor balcony is that of a steaming jungle postcard. The polite breeze of earlier has dropped, and the touchable palm fronds hang utterly limp as darkening clouds begin to gather in the distance. My teeshirt is clammy. Shortly, I reckon, there'll be an almighty clap of thunder and a powerful downpour. When it comes, the hotel guests lolling down by the pool scuttle for cover from businesslike streaks of lightning.

I take an unworried nap, sprawling out on an oversized bed. Sleep. It's the answer to everything.

Later, as twilight falls, I join my hosts for a sundowner in their split-level apartment above the office. The rain has gone, and for a brief while has taken much of the humidity with it. The air is fresh, if not cool. Wendy is slightly irritable. For her, it's been a long day.

"Had a small problem this morning" she tells me. "Five guests, all Poms, booked wake-up calls for five a.m. They were going on the *Raging Thunder* whitewater tour. But our phone system isn't automated. I had to crawl out of bed to make the calls".

Yes, quite. Most upsetting.

"Of course" she scowls, "The electricity chose that precise moment to go down. No lights, no phones, nothing. I fumbled around for the torch, but...." She glares accusingly at Keith who is busy knocking the cap off a fresh beer bottle.... "Good old Basil Fawlty here had moved it from its usual spot, hadn't he? So I groped around in the dark and eventually found a box of candles".

"Ah", I say. "That's alright then".

"You think so? Is that what you think?"

The voice is stiff and I'm sensing danger. "Well, what I mean is –".

"No, you don't get it. It's the *knock-on effect*. Okay, so I went upstairs and woke these five guys up by hammering on their doors and giving them each a candle to get dressed by. But the problem then was – ".

"Ah" I unwisely interject, "The noise you made awoke the other guests?"

This time I receive a look that would freeze a pizza oven. "What noise? There wasn't any – and you want to know why?"

I nod. It proves to be the best move, seeing Wendy's eyes spin into a kind of optical victory roll. "The *air conditioners*!" she exclaims. "There was no electricity, so they all fell silent!". She looks at my blank face, sizing up an IQ one number down from my shoe size. Sighing, she adds "That's where the knock-on effect came in, don't you see? One by one, the other guests woke up in a drenching sweat, picking up the phones for an explanation. But the phones weren't working, and neither were the lights. Some of them got dressed and stumbled downstairs in the dark –".

"What Wendy's saying" interrupts Keith, "Is that she got out of bed the wrong side". I've already guessed this much. I'm sure he's had an all-day earbashing about this incident.

Wendy snaps, "It's alright for you! You didn't have to face them at 5.30 in the morning".

"If I had" he retorts, "You know *exactly* what I'd've told them, don't you?"

Wendy, ambitious and thrusting, is not going to be outdone. "Aha! That's why I'm the manager around here and you're only the handy-man".

Keith looks my way, shrugs, swigs, grins, and finally slumps into a chair, putting his feet up with a satisfied grunt. "Don't mind us, matey. We tend to have these... discussions".

Wendy is glowering at her man, but there's a discernible shaft of love in there. I stretch to go, but neither will hear of it. "Keith will phone for a takeaway" she announces. "There's plenty of wine in the fridge".

At some stage in the evening the BBC phones to arrange a time slot for the next day. By now I'm having trouble speaking coherently, which is not the start I had in mind. I tell the guy in London that it's all to do with jet lag. He says not to worry, he deals with pissed reporters all the time.

Finally I lurch off to bed. My bike stands obediently against the bedroom wall. "Sunday" I hiccup, patting it's soft air-filled saddle. "We'll get going Sunday, after tomorrow's radio piece". So why not talk to my bike? We're in this thing together.

Saturday morning dawns. Wendy and Keith aren't talking much, if at all. I feel undeservedly fit and cheerful, and ride into town for a light breakfast. Soon I'm back at the Marina Mirage and in casual conversation with marine biologist, Shawn Depper.

Shawn works for Quicksilver Connections, owners of the wavepiercer that I sped up here on yesterday. The company also operates seven other boats and I soon glean that it all but runs this place I've tagged Surface Paradise. For sure, it has the squillion-dollar Barrier Reef business pretty well sewn up, and the town would fall apart without its presence. Hardly surprising that the company is quite touchy about out-of-the-blue journalists like me.

Shawn, 31, is one of a new breed of oceanographers. Half scientist, half tour guide, he accompanies visitors out to the reef, though sees his job more as an educational mission than nautical hand-holding. We sit out in the warm sunshine as the day's passengers, hundreds of them, stream from a sophisticated fleet of air-conditioned buses: Americans, Europeans, Orientals, and Aussies from way down south. They are expertly shepherded into the bustling company store before boarding their reef boat. Clothes, books, bric-a-brac, maps and memorabilia are on offer. What they don't buy now, they will later, when the boat gets back from the reef. Quicksilver people know how to go about this slightly unsubtle business.

Like reefs everywhere, this one, the world's largest, is in calamitous peril. Increasing water temperature from that invisible foe called global warming, causes bleaching of the fragile coral – which in turn is condemning the reef to a slow death by poison. Shawn is in no doubt where the blame lies.

"In a word, politicians" he snorts. Ah, right, them again.

"There are 400 different species of coral out there" he says, pointing far out to sea. "They support the 1500 species of fish which give this coast a decent seafood industry. But it goes beyond the obvious. Living coral is an important research tool into cancer-fighting drugs and other antibiotics. Did you know that?"

No, I didn't. But what I actually do know by now is that every day of the year, the Great Barrier Reef attracts members of the human race in their thousands. And that the human race – not just its politicians – is responsible for just about everything that is bad in the world.

"Our tours are eco-educational" Shawn argues. "We drive home the need to *protect* the reef, not destroy it". He is not used to dealing with the media and is displaying recognizable signs of discomfort. "It's the politicians" he repeats. "If they'd stick to international agreements and do something about the pollution and global warming, we can start to buck the trend – though it's already too late for some coral species to ever recover".

He has a good, strong point; but by now I'm shuffling through a wad of company fact-sheets, noting just how PR minded this Quicksilver group is. In the year when Sydney hosted the Olympic Games, they shipped the burning Olympic Torch out to the furthest offshore station, Agincourt Reef, submerging its waterproof flame down into the full televisual splendour of the coral canyons. God knows what the fish thought. Then they brought it up again, still burning brightly, and took it back to Port Douglas for continuation of its long onward journey to Sydney. The PR blurb claims this televised stunt greatly raised international awareness to "*the beauty of our World Heritage listed asset*".

In other words more business, and then some: and oh, Bill & Hilary took a trip as well, "*to the great delight and satisfaction of the Quicksilver crew*". Also, I assume, to the satisfaction of whoever wrote this drivel. Nowhere in these pages of corporate purring is there any mention of the annual billion dollars or so raked in from reef tourism.

Call me a cynic. And a flawed human being. I'll buy both.

But I am willing to be persuaded, and wish to take up Quicksilver's offer of a trip to the outer reef. In fact, I'd really like to do today's broadcast from the reef itself, but the ship's phone system won't make or take overseas calls. Neither will the vessel be back in time for the programme. Alas, I give it a miss.

I idle the time away until my designated mid-afternon slot, wondering just how many listeners are tuned in at 4am, GMT. A great many by all accounts; dedicated earlybirds, routine nightowls, cab drivers, nightshift workers, and an alarming number of habitual insomniacs.

The system is to work like this: each week I'll call the BBC in London to give the *Up All Night* programme a contact number and a rundown of the week's stories. It then schedules a time slot and calls me a few minutes before going on air. The presenter has all the necessary info on cue, so we're able to chat comfortably back and forth for a few minutes, live over the telephone. This initial broadcast goes off easily. We talk about the reef, the weather, the bike, the intended route, and of course, Bill Clinton. While the presenter is wrapped in headphones and surrounded by studio gadgetry, I'm flopped on my pillow-stacked bed at the Reef Club with the phone to my ear. What a way to work.

Well anyway, tomorrow is the off, 75km back to Cairns, the first stop. I'm anxious to be gone from the intense tourism culture of Surface Paradise in favour of the big open road. And I make this promise – an organised tour it is not.

TWO
Kangarooted

On this glorious morning, Sod's Law rises before I do. It lurks down at Wendy's office in the shape of a good looking lady from Yorkshire, seeking fresh towels from the management. A notice on the door says Sunday's opening hour is a few minutes yet, so we while them away on a veranda, chatting easily. This woman is single, out here on her own for a three week holiday. By the time Wendy shows up, some kind of spark has ignited between us, with a tacit understanding that fun is on the cards. The testosterone may not be at quite the level it once was, but it's around alright.

Of course, what's not going to be around is me.

I hate it when this happens. But it's a minor irritation, soon forgotten as I load up the machine, say a warm farewell to my squabbling hosts, then head for the Captain Cook Highway and the freedom of the open road.

The day is warming up fast. For the first hour, I pedal contentedly along a flat, tree-filled landscape into a slight breeze. Port Douglas is soon well behind me. I'm wearing a colourful teeshirt and blue shorts; wintery-pale arms and legs make a striking contrast.

Sometime later, the first aches begin. Already, the cushioned saddle is beginning to feel like a jagged souvenir from the Berlin Wall, and my thighs are putting me on notice to quit. Maybe I should have trained a little harder back in England; those long daily walks up the steep hills of South Devon, coupled with a sporty kind of diet – not forgetting 100 press-ups a day – were evidently insufficient. I stop for a few minutes, taking long mouthfuls of water and feel the sweat roll down face and body.

Then, a few kilometres further on, just where the hills start, the road runs out of shoulder – that spacious, wonderful, metre of width separating a cyclist from all the hurtling, motorised, tin cans. Not even Wendy could have fixed a wake-up call like this. In this near-empty area of the world, the sheer volume of cars building up along the Captain Cook Highway is alarming; the speed at which they travel, even more so; and the sudden merging of a lone bicycle into stampeding one-lane traffic, utterly harrowing. When an 18-wheeler truck thunders past, all but greasing my hips, it is downright blood-freezing.

After a while of this, I find solace from the traffic by turning down an unsurfaced lane leading to a small, empty beach. I fling the bike against a stark, upright *achtung* surf-warning, and find a suitable piece of driftwood on which to sit, roll a cigarette, and ruminate over this unexpected foe.

If ever I'd hoped this land Down Under to be more or less as I left it, then such an ideal is now blowing way out to sea. As clear as the sparkling blue water in front of me is the plain fact that even this far north, the automobile has aggressively conquered all, through sheer force of numbers.

I am a fast learner. Up there on that single lane highway, the Sunday driver does not see things my way. He is running with the flow of the road and views the cyclist as a lumbering obstruction – astride of which must be the very oddest of human beings. He reasons that no sane person would be out cycling on this road in this heat, and I suddenly worry that he might be right. I've not seen a single other rider all morning. It strikes me that were I to advertise my nationality with, say, a small Union Jack fluttering from a pannier-pole, it might inspire some resigned sympathy in the Aussie behind the wheel – *Oh God, another mad Pom out in the midday sun.*

There's something else. In the space of a few hours, front seat passengers of three passing cars have thrust their heads out of the window, yelling at me and tapping their heads. Am I really that bonkers?

I need to get to grips with this, and fast. There's as much room for bathos and pathos on this venture as there is for vital centimetres of road error. I get up from my piece of driftwood – and instantly realise another problem. In the space of a cigarette puffed from one end to the other, I've gone as stiff as a 12-hour corpse. Not only that. The sun is beginning to fry my vulnerable bald patch and I've forgotten to bring a cap. After years of globetrotting in hot places, how dense can you get?

I draw on the experience from a similar project undertaken in America four years previously; 5000km and more, Los Angeles to Key West. No need for headwear on that occasion, riding through a southern winter. But the aching legs I remember well. I also recall the remedy – to simply get back on the bike and pedal. After a while the stiffness will go away. No, the real difference between then and now is while most of the U.S. roads were wide and empty, this Australian highway I'm now on is hazardously narrow and, as seen from the saddle, psychopathically frantic.

Before long, my ears become attuned to the impending whooshes of passing metal. Whenever that menacing hum of bunched-up vehicles drones up from behind, I pull into the roadside scrub and let them pass. It makes for a tedious stop-start passage but truth be told, I use these mini-breaks to gulp water. I am getting through my twin bottles in copious gulps. Oh, and then comes this hill, a steep three kilometre crucifixion, that just drains it all from me. On my right, forested land rises up to a blue sky. To my left, a boulder-strewn woody incline slants precipitously down to the rolling swells of the South Pacific Ocean.

It is early afternoon and a cloudless 32C. My hair, or what's left of it, is soaked. Yet each time I round a bend, the skybound hill keeps rising to the next curve, and the one after that. The bike and its 24 gears are doing precisely the job they're designed for. But the rider is starting to think that if he's been designed for anything at all useful, it cannot possibly be this.

Mercifully, the apex of the hill comes into view. At its top there is a sizeable lay-by where dozens of sightseers are gathered. I wheel towards it in a gasping sweat. Someone tells me this is as high as it gets around here, and I'm extremely glad to hear that. The view, I have to say, is stupendous: a wild, sandy coastline at the very edge of all the fabulous shades of blue which make up the sheltered side of the Great Barrier Reef – a sight made all the more grand by the imminent prospect of a long, breezy downhill run.

The same guy also tells me I need to put something on my head. A helmet. "It's the *law*" he stresses, matter of factly. I did not know this, and I'm suddenly cross. Whatever plus-points they may have, there is something about cycling helmets that gives the impression of a freshly-hatched alien clutching to your skull.

"The law is an ass" comes my cliched retort. He is a youngish man, early 30s, with wavy dark hair and even darker eyes. His face tightens a fraction. I think he may be familiar with argumentative types, and I'm not wrong.

"I'm a lawyer and I'm local" he asserts. "You are neither, I know that. It'll be $30 on the spot, every time the cops haul you over – which you believe it, they will".

This is not good news. I understand now why there's been this jabbing of heads from car windows. I shrug. "I can hardly buy one here on top of a hill. It'll have to wait".

The lawyer climbs into an expensive 4x4. "Probably see you in court then; metaphorically speaking".

I offer a limp wave. "See ya, Sheriff".

I'm as much irked by the obedience-factor as the actual helmet issue. That lawyer makes four unofficial watchdogs in as many hours. I cannot imagine anyone telling a domeless motorbike rider to get himself a hat. The guy knows the rules and besides, they'd likely get a couple of choice Anglo Saxon words in return. And while I'll not willingly break the laws of my host country, I've a stubborn resistance to having this ugly appendage on my head.

I concede however, that in the absence of a cap, a helmet might be useful for a bit of shade. The bald patch can do with some of that. So can my brow and the back of the neck. While not prone to sunburn, symptoms are already coming on. Whizzing downhill, a slight shivering kicks in that has nothing to do with the rush of air.

At the bottom, the road flattens out and runs directly alongside a virgin seashore of small bays and sweeping beaches. Strange, but there is hardly anyone on them. In England, this would be a panorama of reddening faces and chiming ice-cream vans. Shortly I come to the beachy outskirts of Palm Cove and stop at a busy outdoor bar/cafe to gratefully sink a bottle of cold beer. On the other side of the road is a recreation green with swings and slides. It leads onto a beach – and this one is buzzing. I think of the empty sands a few kilometres back and wonder why the human species so needs the safety of numbers, the more the better. In near-misanthropic fashion, I am of a directly opposite nature.

It is mid-afternoon; less than 50km have been covered. But I'm not in mood nor shape to carry on. I'll find a cheap motel a kilometre or two further on in Palm Cove.

Ahem. The hotels and apartments standing just back from the quiet, palm-lined beach scream money. My budget is modest and I'm not prepared to blow the $100-minimum demanded from the few vacancy signs. Also, this little place has got a really weird atmosphere that I cannot quite put my finger on. Maybe it's to do with the rainy season. In the past half-hour it has turned grey, overcast, and heavy. Another storm is on the way.

I finally spot a small motel hidden away in a back road, but before I get there a loud voice shouts from across the road. "Off yer bike, mate. Now!".

Two cops in a prowl car. "No helmet, no-can-ride" says the elder of the two. "If we weren't on a call out, you and me would be into the paperwork by now. So put a helmet on – or walk the bike". The car takes off with a tyre screech, hurtling around a corner. I dismount, just in case they're going around the block.

There is no room at the inn, but the motelier tells me of a place at Clifton Beach, three kilometres further on. This means pedalling, which might or might not cost me $10 per kilometre. Fortunately, it doesn't.

When I get to the Clifton Palms Motel, the slight shiver is now a fever and I really don't care about anything except bed: not food, not a shower, not even the lady from Yorkshire. A whole lot of use I'd be to her right now. I'm shown to a basic unit, swallow almost a full litre of cold water, and wrap up between the sheets with the fan going full blast. Odd, I know. The sheets are to stop the shivers, the fan to cool a boiling head.

I slide into that feverish comatose state – partly awake, yet semi-absorbed in a crazy dream that's going on in my head. Don't ask me why, but amid the 'dream' comes a deep voice uttering the word *root* – that earthy Australianism for the sex act. Just as the more universal four letter word applies to all manner of unwanted disasters, so too does this. For *worn out, had it, all in, shagged, stuffed* – read *rooted.*

"*That's what you are right now, mate*" booms the voice, coinciding with a crash of thunder. "*Not just rooted, but K-a-n-g-a-R-o-o-t-e-d, haw, haw, haw*!". It's mad, resonant laughter has dark apocalyptic echoes.

In such a way, Here Endeth Day One.

And now comes Day Two. Sleep, or whatever passed for sleep last night, has done its job. The fever's gone, leaving only a few burns from the world's most cancerous sun. I rise early and take a cautious shower, dissolving any residual stiffness. The morning air is humid, but the sun is out and the very sight of Clifton Beach, with its long stretch of empty golden sands, uplifting. Last night's Voice of Doom is back in its own murky dimensional pit. Kangarooted I am no more.

The owner of the General Store stares curiously at my bike. I'm in there to buy a cap. He sells everything from fresh milk to industrial batteries. I tell him the final destination, Melbourne, and he puts his hands on hips and whistles softly. "Good on yer" he says generously, "Bloody good on yer, that's what I say". After a brief hesitation he adds, "Wish I'd done it myself. Travelled and that. Clifton Beach....it's yer know, beautiful but limited".

Yes, I do know. So is everywhere after a while; even the great cities, the finest resorts, and the most spectacular sights of the world. In the end, it all becomes more of the same. Here, in this cluttered North Queensland store, I get sudden confirmation of a personal truth that I've long believed to be damagingly probable – yet have lost every single battle against.

A boredom threshold of dangerously low proportions.

Wearing my brand new cap, I ride away thinking about this. The road is now as flat as an airport runway. Not only is there a hard shoulder on the highway itself, there are civilised cyclepaths running parallel to it – a sure sign that a major town is not far off. I remain bemused at the weight of traffic, though yesterday's chilling moments are, for the moment, over. I should be glad of that, but for some reason I'm not. It is as if I actually need an ongoing personal War

Zone; one that keeps me fully alert to its deceptive, constantly changing ways of attack.

This must have been why I came out here in the first place, back in 1961. Not merely from premature itchy feet, but something stronger. No doubt it is why I eventually became a journalist. For the travel, the variety, and sometimes the risk. Maybe there's one great big self-destruct mechanism ticking away inside, counting down the moments to some kind of showdown with my own shadow.

An easy 25km to Cairns takes two hours, impeded by a slight southeast blow. Roadside billboards begin way out from town. They plug real estate, reef tours, camping grounds, motels & hotels, restaurants, bars, airlines, even law firms. Helmeted locals pedalling the other way up the cyclepath nod in mutual acknowledgement; one taps at his head disapprovingly. *It's the law.*

Cairns International Airport looms up on the left. A billboard catches my eye. I stop to write down the phone number, thinking the advertisement might not only turn into a great little story, but offer a temporary antidote against this morning's psychiatric self-diagnosis.

Even from the outskirts, it is impossible to ignore the full-on Americanisation of this metropolis. It could be Culver City, California, or Corpus Christi, Texas, with row upon row of pizza parlours, burger grills, and other dime-a-dozen fast food joints; there are tyre depots, used car dealers, hardware stores, neon-lit motels, and low-rise office blocks. Vehicles park in the same sensible American manner, nose-on at an angle to the kerb. And like Average City, USA, the streets form tidy squares and rectangles. A blind man cannot get lost.

I locate my lodgings, the Bay Village Resort, one kilometre north of downtown Cairns. Three storeys of red brick built surround an adequate swimming pool, itself fringed with coconut palms, banana trees, parasols, and deck furniture. An oasis in the midst of concrete. I take a splash, listening to the potpourri of languages and accents criss-crossing the pool: Japanese, Malay, Canadian, UK – and some boisterous Russian coming from a group of extremely fat and blindingly pale poolside boozers.

Back in my self-catering room, I fish out the number of Cape York Air, a small charter airline I'd seen advertised on the billboard. The very name tells me that it must surely fly right up to the very top of Oz, to Cape York itself, beyond which lie the Torres Straits, next stop

Papua New Guinea.

During the 1960s, the very first thing I did on returning from this part of the world was to enroll for a residential flying course and earn myself a UK pilot's license. I've had an on-off love affair with aviation ever since. Now something in my journalist's instinct is prodding me to give this outfit a call and see where it leads. For the moment, mind, I'll omit any mention of the bike ride. Apart from having one's sanity questioned, it tends to perplex the other person. The image at that end of the line is of a BBC reporter with a Pommie accent, clear and simple. If we throw in the incongruous image of a dusty unshaven cyclist, it may upset the balance. Best leave it be.

"How can I help?" asks Arthur Williams, Managing Director and Chief Pilot. Good question.

I introduce myself, tell him I'm keen to do an aviation item for the BBC, something like the Flying Doctors or a Day in the Life of a Bush Pilot. Arthur catches on fast. He says to hold it right there, don't go away, he may have just the thing.

I wait for him to come back on the line. "You're in luck" he chirps, "How do you fancy playing postie for a day?"

"I'm sorry?"

"Yeah, you know, postman".

Now it's my end of the phone that's confused. Is he asking me to deliver letters? "We operate mail routes most days of the week" Arthur explains. "Tomorrow we're on the Heathlands run – that's the most northerly cattle station in the entire country, right up near the cape itself. There's room on the plane if you want to tag along".

I snatch the offer. Further dialogue with Arthur reveals that we'll be leaving Cairns about dawn, back around dusk. Inbetween, there'll be 14 deliveries at Australia's remotest cattle stations and wildlife reserves. This is strictly dirt-strip stuff, one-up from flying by the seat of the pants. I further discover this to be the longest scheduled one-day airmail run in the world, and feel the first fix of necessary adrenaline.

"Okay" goes Arthur. "Report in at 6.15am. Tomorrow's pilot is a bloke called Max – he's got stories that'll make your hair stand up. By the way, the plane is a single-engine Cessna 206". He pauses a moment, and in different tone says, "Not a bad old bird, on the right day".

I pick up a copy of the *Cairns Post* from the lobby, perusing it from under a poolside parasol. The city has just experienced it's first drive-by shooting, carried out by a carload of airgun-toting youths firing random potshots at pedestrians. A Dutch girl is to be flown home immediately for 'muscular remodelling': her arm has been savaged by a Hammerhead shark two kilometres offshore. A young British student from the Newcastle area is going to jail for a month after a Cairns court convicted him of terrorist-type behaviour aboard an internal Qantas flight; something to do with a threatening remark he made to a flight-attendant while in an alcoholic stupor. He is going to an inland prison on the nearby Atherton Tablelands, where I know there's a vacancy because the *Post* reports that an inmate was found hanged in his cell last night.

This last item brings to mind a previous encounter, that in its way relates to all these stories in the newspaper. Or what we're to make of them.

A while ago, when residing in the USA for a brief period, I visited a morgue in Jackson, Mississippi. On three separate slabs directly opposite the mortician's desk were the naked bodies of a car crash victim, a messy shotgun suicide, and a woman with multiple stab wounds from an enraged ex-lover. And lying inside an unzipped body-bag was the blue/grey face of a young man – he had hanged himself just three hours before with a length of electric cable, still bound tightly around his neck. I asked the mortician – a gruff individual with a dim view of the world – if he lost much sleep while travelling down his chosen road.

His reply, delivered through clenched teeth chewing on an enormous unlit cigar, was as blunt as it gets.

"These stiffs" he said, nodding towards the assorted corpses, "Mostly they're people who couldn't cope; losers, if you know what I'm saying. This and that went wrong with their lives. What you're looking at is the result of the shit they came up against. But I can't give any thought to that, because I see the same goddam thing coming through these doors every hour".

He stared fixedly at me through horn-rimmed glasses, ready to add final touches to a potentially profound statement. "I see life as an ongoing card game. The deck is shuffled and the cards are dealt. At some crucial point in the game, you draw an ace or you draw a dud". This time he pointed a sharp finger at his motionless subjects, all shortly to be cut up with the surgical equivalent of a chainsaw. "They got lousy cards at the wrong time, and I'm sorry about that. But it's the way it is. All you can do is get on with life – until the cards dictate your own turn for the fridge – which one day they surely will".

He's right enough about that. Meanwhile back here in Cairns, it seems a few grim hands have been pulled from the pack. Tomorrow I'll see what a bush pilot makes of it all. As Arthur Williams says, Max has got stories to make my hair stand up. And, I'm informed, the aircraft I'm to be flying in is not a bad old bird... on the right day. If anything sounds like a shuffle of the cards, this does.

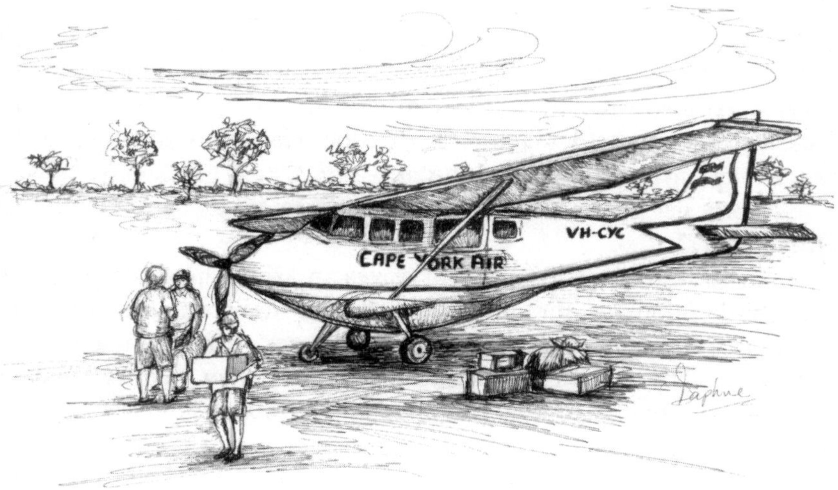

THREE
Angels of the North

Max Davy is a stout man, late 50s, still with a good pile of dark hair on top of a round, ruddyish face. He's from a time when sweaty khaki shirts and oilstained shorts was the general attire for bush pilots, accompanied by spanners and spare parts stuffed into belts and pockets. Nowadays, we live in a daft age, when garbage collectors wear uniforms and bus drivers sport epaulettes. This morning Max is rigged out in neatly pressed navy blue trousers and a crisp pale blue shirt with winged emblems.

We are in the airline's very own departure lounge – half a dozen hard chairs lined up opposite a counter behind which is the very nerve centre of Cape York Air – an elongated desk running alongside a wall, stacked with sideband radios and navigation manuals – and where Max is rummaging through load factors, passenger lists, fuel calculations, and all the pre-flight paperwork that goes into every commercial flight in the world, no matter how small the aircraft or how short the route.

Two other people are sitting in the silence of the hour. A lady of late middle age, wearing a floppy bush hat with a bulging rucksack beside her feet; and a thin, red-bearded man with a baseball cap and a pile of luggage held together with rope. He seems agitated as he shoots up and strides to the counter.

"Gotta get up to Wattle Hills" he says to Max's back. "Gotta get there today".

Max doesn't turn around, but waves an arm behind his shoulder. The body language shouts *bugger off*, and his words are stiff. "See what I can do" he snaps without enthusiasm. "Wait until I'm done with this". The restless man slumps back into a chair, folding his arms with a loud sigh. The lady briefly scowls at him from over a newspaper.

Outside on the apron sits our not-bad old bird: a white Cessna 206, otherwise known as the Cessna Caravan. It has a single prop-jet engine and broad fuselage. Protruding between non-retractable wheels is a hefty cargo pod. In flying parlance, it's called a workhorse. Today's flight is absolutely no-frills. Max advises me to carry a bottle of water on board.

Wattle Hills – somewhere way up north – is among our destinations. Even so, the man with a beard is told to try his luck elsewhere. The plane is so loaded with freight this morning, it won't stagger into the air with him and his luggage aboard. Or that's the excuse he is given.

Max Davy slowly shakes his head as the laden-down figure trundles off. "That bloke's on the dole" he growls. "Hitched a ride with one of our pilots down here to the big city, spent his money on God knows what, and now expects a free ride back. We're not a bloody charity".

He can say that again. Only governments and Hollywood gobble up more dollars than aviation.

We're ready to fly. The one other passenger is the curator from a Brisbane museum on her way to Heathlands, today's northernmost airstrip. She's a friend of the couple who run the place. So in addition to all the mail and freight, on board is just Max, myself, and this lady called Jeanette.

Then, surprisingly, a second pilot emerges. Max grins. "I'm new to Cape York Air" he says easily. "We're using today's flight as a type-rating run. You know, get the 206 stamped onto my license. I haven't flown this thing before".

Great. Tell that over an EasyJet intercom. Yet I know from his whole demeanour that Max Davy can pilot anything from a kite to the space shuttle. All it means is that today, a pilot utterly familiar with the airplane will be fine-tuning our captain to his new machine. Were it not for strict aviation regulations, co-pilot Mark Dormand need not have bothered to get out of bed.

The 206 takes only a short stretch of runway to roar upward. No-nonsense seating equipped with shoulder-harness safety belts allows for up to eight passengers; plus extra freight space at the rear, now piled high with mail sacks. We're soon at 8000 feet, following the coastline beyond Port Douglas then turning inland over the Daintree River Valley just before Cooktown. The first stop of this great northern wilderness will be an outpost called Laura Township.

A photocopied brief tells me that the township once had four hotels, several stores, and a rail link to Cooktown. That was in the goldrush days, when dreams of unimaginable riches drew bold prospectors up here in swarms – until, that is, the bubble burst. More than a century on, Laura now acts as a supply settlement for nearby ranchers, a few 4x4 tourists, and the Ang-Gnarra aboriginal community, whose local cave paintings provide the focus for an annual riverside festival. I stare down at this ocean of flat, green, empty acreage, strewn with rivers snaking this way and that. Up in the front office, Max and Mark are talking through headphones. This is one noisy bird.

A long brown strip of earth looms up on the horizon and Max begins the first descent of the day. The 206 whooshes down over a few huts then rolls dustily along the uneven runway, as if sliding across a lumpy mattress. The plane brakes to a halt by a Land Rover parked next to an unpainted shed. With engine running, Mark opens the rear door and says that if anyone wants the loo, now is the time. I am the only taker, and I soon see why.

The shed *is* the loo – a homebuilt receptacle standing atop a deep hole in the ground, entrapping offensive elements to both sight and smell. But what the hell should I expect out here – a flushing system? This is how it was back on the sheep and cattle stations of my youth. I must have gone soft in the interim years.

With Laura Township's mail and goods soon aboard the Land Rover, we're aloft again and heading for Lakeland Station, a former cattle property and now one of the biggest national parks in the state.

This is swampy territory, inhabited by wild pigs, snakes, and man-eating saltwater crocs. And kangaroos. About 40 of them are leaping and bounding on both sides of the landing strip.

The Park Ranger, dressed in a grey shirt and blue shorts, emerges from a 4x4 parked under the shade of a gum tree and greets the aircraft hungrily. He makes a stooped dash to the open door, utters a polite "*Owyergoin*", grabs his goodies and hurries back to his vehicle. He is replenished with mail, newspapers, food and beer. For him, this is company enough until Max & Co drop in for a couple of minutes next week. If you ever want to become a salaried recluse, apply for a posting with the Queensland Parks & Wildlife Service.

At 225kph, we are now moving well towards the cape; Lockhart River next stop. Mark Dormand leaves his right-hand seat and comes back for a brief, noisy chat. This, he says, is one of his final runs with Cape York Air. He's leaving for bigger planes and bigger money, flying miners and equipment to and from Papua New Guinea; three weeks on, two off. Mark is a slim, competent 28 year old with strong Oriental features – the result of a Malay mother and an Aussie father.

Day turns to night as we thrust into a dark tropical cloud. Heavy rain envelopes the ship and it begins to buck savagely. Mark falls temporarily silent as he casts a cautious eye towards his older colleague in the captain's seat. Max seems about as worried as a grazing cow. We soon emerge from the worst of the gloom, swooping down on another landing strip. This one has a tarmac runway, and there is one other light aircraft on the ground, alongside a fuel bowser. Furthermore, I spot a concrete shed with three men milling around its doorway. This is big-time stuff. I learn that the tarmac has been there since WW11, when the strip was a base for Air Force bombers in combat with the Japanese. Every now and then, someone in a cement truck comes by to fill in the potholes.

We roll up to the apron and disembark. Lockhart is a refuelling stop. It is damp, overcast, and muggy. The men by the shed are uniformly dressed in long white jeans, elastic-sided boots, bush shirts, and wide-brimmed hats. I just know them to be cattlemen of some sort because I once wore the same gear myself. It is a timeless dress code, of the same tradition that keeps Threadneedle Street awash with pinstripes every Monday to Friday.

The three men turn out to be regional vetinary inspectors, checking out the cattle from station-to-station. They very patiently wait for the pilot of their chartered Piper Commanche to finish his cigarette, which he seems in no hurry to do. Their captain is stretched out on a bare wooden bench, legs crossed, deeply immersed in thoughts of his own. I muse that the airplane really is the only way to get about around here; indeed, for some it is the only way to get around a single cattle property. Further inland, where every drop of rain is worth thrice its weight in gold, stations spread to several million acres apiece.

Stop Four, Wattle Hills, puts both pilots into a touchy mood. It is 90,000 acres of extinct cattle station, now aparently home to a community intent on its own form of lifestyle – and our aviators are thinking about using the dicey weather as an excuse not to land there at all.

"This community is supposed to be a government-sponsored experiment in self-sufficiency" Mark sneers. "Grow their own food, milk their own cows. It's why they got the land for nothing. Fine, if that's what you're actually doing. The reality however, is they live on welfare and whatever their dole buys them". He shakes his head. "From what I can see, the only thing they grow....." He tails off, maybe remembering that I'm a journalist.

"Cannabis?" I suggest.

"Something like that. I see it as a colony of useless dopeheads living off the taxpayer". With a sigh he adds, "But I suppose we better drop in".

We land on a kind of plateau, and I notice that few words are exchanged between our co-pilot and the hippyish residents awaiting their cargo. While Mark unloads, Max turns his ample neck towards Jeanette and me. "No-bloody-hopers, this lot" he states earnestly. "That bloke trying to bludge a ride this morning, he's one of them".

Rightly or not, the Wattle Hills lifestyle isn't going to get a good press around this airplane. I put it out of mind as we again soar into an utterly vacant sky, and bank northwest towards Heathlands. As with other flights I've made over such sparsely-habited terrain – Canada's Labrador, the Brazilian jungle, the Sahara Desert among many – the vast emptiness of the land below serves as an edged reminder to the insignicance of we mortal human beings; and in particular to some of our ridiculous ideals. This raw, awesome, magnificent wilderness has been around for millennia – and it will still be around on the day when some future breed of archeologist digs up a personalised number plate and other telling artefacts from the fall of mankind.

The 206 labours on towards high noon. The sun is out once more and the sky is now a deep blue. Down on the ground, the steamy day is coming to a sweltering boil. The northernmost station on the Australian continent finally comes into sight, with Cape York itself somewhere just beyond the horizon. In the space of a morning, this little one-engined plane has covered almost 800km. We are much closer to Papua New Guinea now than to Cairns. Effortlessly, Max puts his new charge down onto the reddish-brown strip and taxis towards a tired looking long-wheelbase Land Rover waiting to take us to the station homestead and lunch.

It is hot outside; by God it is.

By some miracle, the homestead is an oasis of red and green flowering shrub. A cluster of palms stand sentry at the driveway, next to which is a powerful satellite dish linking the world to this far-flung outpost. I note a keenly-angled bank of solar panels absorbing torrents of invisible sunrays, instantly converting a free cosmic source into clean electricity.

Several support-posts keep the homestead raised about one metre from the ground. It is surrounded with a broad, shady veranda. We amble inside, through a flyscreen door, into the ample kitchen and living area. Shelley Lyon, our hostess, greets Jeanette with big hugs. Our pilots get beaming smiles, while I receive the dictionary-definition of a pumping handshake. Shelley is dressed in the now-familiar tunic of the Park Ranger – grey shirt with badged sleeves and dark blue shorts. It turns out that Heathlands is no longer an actual cattle property. In 1968 it became a 'Pasture Research Centre' – but then went the same way as the others by reinventing itself into yet another national park. Heathland's half-million acres is apparently no longer of sufficient size to make it a paying proposition.

Shelley is a friendly, enthusiastic soul somewhere in her 40s. She's got a good length of wavy-blond hair and a round, suntanned face. Her husband is presently on the way back from Cooktown where they keep their main home. He's in a 4x4, negotiating some of the roughest roads in the land. His bump-filled, rock strewn, backbreaking drive takes 15 hours each way. Shelley sits us down at a large dining table covered with a red vinyl cloth. Across a flyscreened window hangs a long row of greeting cards supported by a length of cord. The Twelve

Days of Christmas haven't crossed my mind since Gatwick Airport.

She serves up scones & jam, coffee and iced tea. The talk is of a new born baby only 100km away, and of other close neighbours; of bush politics; and of the drought and resultant bushfires. The drought is not quite as bad up here in the tropics, but down south there is a major crisis. For me, this is as if the Cessna 206 is my personal Time Machine for the day. I have been here before – in this kitchen, in on this very type of conversation, during my teenage time as a jackaroo on a sheep & cattle property down near Cootamundra, New South Wales. I cannot believe that all these years have passed. It's like I've never been gone from this tough, tight, remote way of life – even though my passport tells a very different tale. Much later on, I'll be pedalling through Cootamundra, and I'm definitely going to call in.

After a pleasant hour, we drive back to the station's airstrip. On the way I ask Max for a few stories to make the hair stand up. He seems oddly reluctant, only muttering something about vital bits & pieces falling off the plane in mid-air. He thinks I ought to ask Mark instead.

I get it. Max is new to this outfit and worries about blotting his copybook with the management. These mail runs are lucrative business for Cape York Air, subsidised by the federal government. He is bothered that a foreign journalist will misuse his stories to write barnstorming wing-and-a-prayer copy that might attract the wrong kind of attention from the government pen-pushers in Canberra. At 58, Max Davy is unlikely to find another job with great ease. I think I may need to get him inside a bar.

Mark is happy for me to sit up front with Max for the next two or three landings. We put on the headphones but stay off hair-raising topics. It's a 20 minute hop due-south to Moreton Telegraph Station, during which time I discover that Max gets to see his wife in Brisbane roughly once a month. Bush flying, he says, means a nomadic lifestyle. And "Yeah, you're right. There are stories. Bloody good ones. Maybe I should write a book". Then he says, "I'll tell you about them sometime. Not right now".

Gee, thanks Max.

At Moreton we pick up a young lady called Angela. She's coming down to Cairns for a short break from the trails & trials of the outback. Then it is up, down, and up again, every ten or 15 minutes, in and out of working cattle stations on the western side of the cape.

They've got names like Batavia Downs, Merluna, Watson River, Picaninny Plains. Station workers await each arrival, such is the clockwork of their week.

Older hands are dressed traditionally, like the three men at Lockhart River; the younger guys not so. At Watson River Station, two young men collecting mail and several boxes of freight are in baseball caps, baggy shorts, and barefoot. Max tells me a good, safe story. This place, he says, is a brand new addition to the route. The two guys outside got very fed up riding their motorbikes across rivers and swamps up to the nearest strip at Merluna Station. Sparkplugs took as much of a bath as they did. So they carved out their very own airport.

I suddenly see Max Davy, Mark Dormand, and that horizontal pilot back at Lockhart River for exactly what they are. These guys, and all the others doing this job, are the very lifeline of the cape. The true Angels of the North. They've got good intentions and better still, they've got wings.

The afternoon is wearing on. We call in at a strip known as Archer River Roadhouse, a wet season destination when the river becomes an impassable barrier by road. Then it's on to the penultimate stop, a refuelling point with the improbable name of Coen. As we sit in the shade of the 'terminal building' – a concrete hut with three chairs, a washbasin, some chipped coffee mugs, and an old electric kettle – I find Mark willing to recount a few anecdotes of his time with this airline. He is, after all, leaving in a couple of weeks.

"I guess the most fun – if you can call it that – is when we get to carry magistrates and lawmen on the monthly Out-Station Assizes. You know, hear all the cases and that".

Bloody hell, I breathe. Is this what I think it is? A few white men inside a ramshackle hut sitting in judgment over aboriginal disputes?

"That's right" Mark nods. "A couple of months ago there was some argument involving two men from separate aboriginal settlements. I forget the details – except that neither side liked the verdict or the penalty. The result was a full-on fight, a real humdinger, between both parties and their supporters. Fists and boots flying, chairs flying, blood all over the place. It was so out of control that the cops and magistrate locked themselves into a Land Rover and would not come out".

Angela, a dark haired woman of about 30, is fully attentive. "Booze?"

Mark nods again. "Yeah. Tanked up to the hair roots".

She looks my way. "It's a problem here. Aboriginals and drink don't mix". I can tell her of a few other people who don't go well with alcohol either. They are in every British city centre, every weekend. But I see what she's saying.

"We get a few weird cargo flights too" Mark goes on. "I've carried live pigs and snakes for the Parks & Wildlife Service. And talking of booze, I've had the 206 loaded to bursting with beer and spirits before now. Mostly for tourist groups. Little by little, they are beginning to find their way up here".

This is why I'm so readily permitted onto today's run. The government is pressing all its mail-run airlines into ways of reducing the huge annual subsidies. *Playing Postie for a Day* is a new idea, and one way of attracting dollar-paying tourists. Who knows, it may even spread to the Out-Station Assizes, with ringside seats to a prize-fight thrown in for free.

We board for the final run back down to Cairns, flying southeast for 90 minutes. Somewhere down in the wilds, a bushfire is smoking heavily. No one knows how it got started, only how it will end. "Looks like it's burning itself out" opines Mark. "It's not exactly a built-up area down there, so nobody worries too much. Fires tend to die out at the first swamp or treeless plain". This one is like a dying match in an oversized ashtray.

Sometime later, the sea comes into view again. We overfly Port Douglas and as dusk gathers, head for home along the coast – the last dash of a 1,600km round-the-houses day trip. The longest one-day airmail run in the world. There is a blaring irony in flying 800km north in order to continue pedalling another 3,925km south. But by the time I reach journey's end, way down in a future Melbourne, it will indeed have been a north-to-south odyssey.

I need to get pedalling again, I know that – though not before keeping an intimate date with a wild and extremly pissed-off crocodile.

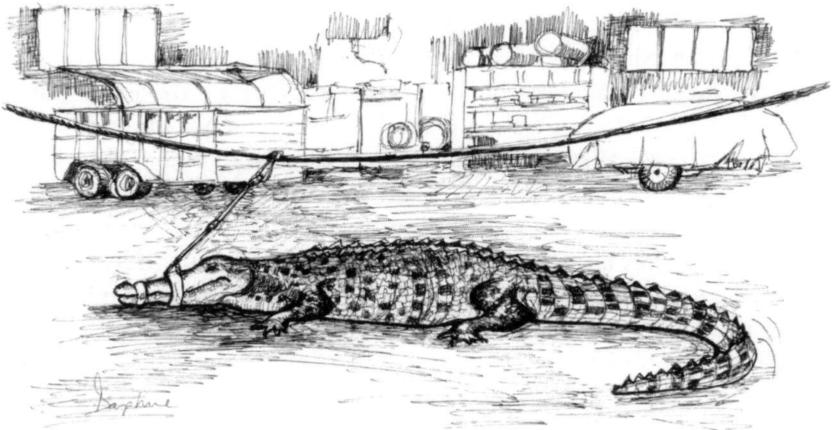

FOUR
So Many Ways to Die

A giant padlock clamps the door of 26 Knight Street. Mark Read, a cheerful 33 year old fair haired Conservation Officer with the Parks & Wildlife service, is struggling with a bunch of jailer's keys. It is another hot, sweaty day and I can already feel the clear blue morning sky threaten another afternoon storm.

Number 26 is a lock-up garage on the western edge of Cairns. In the yard outside are a couple of odd-looking metal contraptions. Mark tells me they are purpose-built crocodile cages, a DIY job. While he engages in a stooped battle with keys and padlock, drops of sweat begin to form small patterns on his uniform shirt.

But this man is of the dogged breed. No task too big or too small. "*I'll have this bloody thing open in two shakes of a dead dingo's donger*" he says determinedly.

I feel strangely nervous of going inside. Somewhere in this suburban lock-up is a three-metre crocodile weighing 140kg. I had heard about the captured reptile from an earlier telephone conversation with the editor of the *Cairns Post*, and thought it would make a radio piece. Eventually our man frees the padlock and the door opens with a loud groan. Mark grimaces at the rusty sound.

"Try not to make any noise" he says contritely. "We don't want to upset him more than he already is". He warns me not to get too close to the reptile because it won't take much to set him off.

It is gloomy inside, typical of any lock-up. This one is larger than most. There's a skiff with a 75hp outboard sitting on a trailer. In one darkened corner is a second trailer loaded with some different sort of cage; in another corner, there's a stack of outdoor equipment. And in the dark, uncluttered centre is one motionless crocodile lying on the concrete floor with his short stubby legs hunched up. Even in the murk, his dotted blue-green-grey skin pattern is as striking as the spikey design of his sharp, powerful, prehistoric body.

His mouth is shut tight by a tough strip of industrial tape. A second strip covers the animal's eyes. Looped around its neck is a metre of chain, itself attached to heavy-duty cord hanging between the concrete walls like a washing line. From the background comes the sound of piped music.

"The music has a calming influence" whispers Mark. "So does the eye tape". He spreads an arm around the shed. "This is hardly a croc's home patch. The sight of four walls and the confines of a place like this agitates them unneccesarily".

He tiptoes me towards the equipment corner, then rummages through a box and pulls out a spearhead. It has a sharp harpoon-like tip surrounded with steel claws. "This chap" he says nodding towards the croc, "Was nosing around a place where he shouldn't have been, near the mouth of the Barron River where there's a beach". With a small sigh, he adds, "Wherever there's a beach, there are humans close by.

"We hunted him down in that boat over there during the wee hours" Mark continues. "In the dark you spot the lazer-red of their eyes as they float on the river surface". He holds up the harpoon tip. "We fired this thing into the back of his neck".

He dismisses any suggestion of pain or cruelty. "Croc's have skin thicker than a stack of bricks. They might feel a thud when it penetrates, nothing more. But it's enough to tell them that something is up – and then they'll put up a fight so ferocious that it sometimes lasts for hours. It's like fighting a Great White Shark with rod-and-line, only far more dangerous. You've got to let them thrash around until they are *completely* worn out. This one took three hours".

"And then?" I enquire.

"We pulled it in and carefully wrapped the tape around its mouth. The croc has no upward-strength in the mouth when it's shut. The tape will hold it down securely". He gives me a grinning wink. "It's when it's wide open and snapping down on you that the problem starts....".

There are many ways to die. Few of us know how or when it will happen; only that one day it will. A friend in England has a daughter living in Australia. Her own best friend came out here for a holiday and was eaten by a crocodile – an unexpected and horrific way to go.

This particular creature was injected with an anaesthetic while being hoisted aboard. In such a small open boat, I have little difficulty in seeing that sedation makes for an easier passage home. But what is now to become of the reptile? It obviously cannot stay where it is.

"I'm quite envious" Mark enthuses. "He's a full-blooded teenage male, and still growing, so our friend here is in for a treat. He's gonna go to a crocodile farm – where he'll re-start his life as a stud".

As we get ready to leave, the conservation officer passes close to the croc's nose. Whether it is from sound or smell I know not, but the animal stirs and hisses angrily indeed. Ah, if only he could know what I now know, he might be a little more accepting of his circumstances. Very soon he'll be shagging his toughened hide off.

It is high time now for my own hide to get tough. There are 340km, or nearly four days riding between here and Townsville, the next major stop. Though I've spent fruitful hours picking up a few reasonable stories, I fret over the undeniable fact that only a pathetic 75km has been cycled so far.

This is a schizophrenic project. In one incarnation I am a probing hack (with all the vices); in another, I'm a long-distance cyclist. It is probably fortunate that I'm a Gemini. Those who come under less-erratic signs of the zodiac might experience trouble with the dual personality aspect. Not me. I am able to dart from one role to the other like a greasy fox.

I go back to the Bay Village Resort and call the BBC before loading up the bike. Tales of bush pilots and crocodiles has the programme planner all excited and she presses me for a broadcast today.

I let the weather decide. The blistering day is marching on, and ominous clouds are forming in the southeast. I opt for the airwaves, vowing to leave in the morning, first light. The programme planner says great, thanks, and from now on we'll broadcast every midweek, promise.

Later, I pedal into town and call in at a cycle store. A range of helmets hangs from a wall and I tyre-kick a few of them. A guy with a German accent asks if he can be of help. No he cannot, because I can't yet bring myself to buy this piece of loathsome headgear. I'd rather wear a silly French pompom or a wartime *Luftwaffe* cap.

Then I meander into a downtown sports bar. Cricket is on the giant-screen TV, Australia versus England in the Ashes series. England are batting, and for a brief spell it looks as if the Poms might be on an unlikely winning streak. Marcus Trescothick is making short work of the Aussie pace bowlers with some classy boundaries. The Aussies are getting decidedly rattled, and so is the bar clientele. A statistic I recall from somewhere claims that wife-beating around here skyrockets whenever the Baggy Caps go down to the Poms. I gulp my beer, choosing to watch the game from my room at the Bay Village. There I can whoop-and-holler without concern of lynch mob reprisals. Or, depending on how the game goes, commiserate alone, free of the inevitable jibes. International sport brings out the best and the worst of us, I guess.

I finally get moving again in the relative cool of early morning. It is no longer called the Captain Cook Highway, but the Big Green Way. The town of Innisfail is 90km south, where I'll head for today. There is a firm blow coming from the southeast, creating an unwanted headwind; but the land is tabletop flat with acre upon spreading acre of sugarcane on both sides of the road. Every hour, I stop for a few minutes. It doesn't take long for the first water bottle to empty. This is hot, thirsty work. Late morning I call in at the pub of a one-horse town called Fishery Falls, and sink three small bottles of chilled apple juice in quick succession. The barman and his two bush-shirted customers sit and watch in suspicious silence. As I leave, a posse of leather-clad bikers roars up outside, the chromework on their big, powerful machines glinting in the sun like blinding disco strobes. Hollywood makes the occasional movie about towns like this.

I mount my human-powered machine just as one of the posse removes his helmet. Correction; *her* helmet. The short-cropped blond stares at me curiously, then taps her polished black bonedome. "Cops are about today. Better put your helmet on".

"Can't, it was stolen" I lie, pedalling off.

There must be a price for inane untruths like this. The first installment becomes due a few kilometres down the road: a dark, two-metre snake lying directly in my path. It is very likely dead, but there's no time to debate that aspect because my front wheel is almost upon the still 'S' shaped creature.

An instinct that has obviously not left me since earlier days in this land flashes into gear, and I swerve like a lurching drunk to avoid the serpent – knowing that if it is alive, it will rear up on impact and entangle itself into the spokes. That is what a snake does. Dizzy or not, its next lightning move is a strike. And another way to die.

Good thing I avoided it. I stop and turn around about ten metres further on. The snake has vanished into the roadside undergrowth.

I knew a man back in those days who'd been bitten by the common and simply-named Brown Snake, and recall his words as if it were yesterday. "*It was like two red hot needles going into me ankle*" the station-hand shrugged. "*Not much fun at the time. Nausea and shit. But yer know... yer get over it. Maybe I was lucky. I got to the medico in time*".

Yes, lucky. The alternative is to flick open a penknife, grit your teeth while carving a bloody circle around the bite, and then cut deep into the poisoned area to attempt an extraction of the deadly venom. As the man said, not much fun. This is the first snake of the journey and my heart is pulsating abnormally. By no means will it be the last.

Late afternoon I wheel into the cane-cutting town of Innisfail, happy that the ride has now started in earnest. I discover a small motel tucked away on a sidestreet, operated by a friendly middle-aged couple named Peter and Denise. She tut-tuts as I sign the guest register and tells me to get a helmet from a bike shop just across the road. For Peter, the motel is a moonlighting thing; by day he is Chief of Staff for a maverick state politician. He too, suggests a helmet. I am feeling the pressure.

I take a quick look-see around the town. There's an aggressive game of pool going on in a noisy bar, a place clearly for younger people than me. At the entrance to another, a passed-out drunk blocks the way. Anyway, all I want is a takeaway of some sort and my bed. Within the hour, I've scoffed the former and am deep inside the latter.

The next day I cross the road and very reluctantly purchase my nemesis. It is electric blue with air-ventilation and a peak. When I see how it looks in the mirror, a frightening intergalactic creature stares back at me. As an eye-catching work of art, these helmets are so awful they must surely be in line for first prize at the Tate Modern. I decide to hang it from the handlebars and wear it only when absolutely necessary.

I've got a 100km ride today to the town of Cardwell. It is a grey morning and a little cooler than usual. Pedalling against southeast gusts makes for some occasional tough going, exacerbated by short downpours. An arrowed sign suddenly catches my attention. It points to a place that a psychotic hit-man or a commission-only debt collector might consider for his calling card. It has the intriguing name of *Murdering Point.*

The woman behind the counter of a local service station – or 'servo' as they're called – knows the story. Sometime in the early 1800s a British ship went aground on one of the inner barrier reefs. At low tide, it is possible to walk out to this reef – which is precisely what the warlike indigenous inhabitants did. They butchered the crew and, it is said, ate them to the bone. Both the name and story reinforce today's thought on there being so many different ways to die.

By early afternoon I reach the town of Tully, a.k.a. the *Golden Gumboot*. Tully has the distinction of being the wettest place in Australia, and is living up to its reputation as I ride into a 'servo' for some shelter from the rain.

And for a pee. Inside the gent's loo an angry trucker stands over the only washbasin, vigorously scrubbing his arms. He is a short, tubby man with a dark moustache, fired-up eyes, and a grim expression – yet one of those few people who knows how to swear without intent of, or indeed giving, any offence. I have not heard such expert cursing anywhere.

The tirade is directed at the emotionless lead-couplings of his truck and trailer. They have covered him in oil and grease and he's none too happy about this. The washbasin is black with oil. He tells me to pay him no heed as I stand at a urinal with my back to him, but it's difficult not to. By the time he's railing into the second minute of an invective that would make a lumberjack cringe, I am laughing so hard inside that I give up all thoughts of a pee.

"*Bastard fucking things! I'm splattered all over in this bloody shit, from arseholes to breakfast time*!". That's the repeatable bit. Outside, I lean back against a wall and then slide all the way down it, creased up with laughter as the torrent of abuse continues unabated from inside the loo.

The rain eases and I carry on towards Cardwell, a coastal town I've never heard of. Two dead snakes later, and deeply immersed in thoughts of God-knows-what, I am taken by surprise somewhere far along the highway. The last thing I expect to hear on a bicycle is a human voice coming from just behind my right shoulder.

"How ya doin'" it mutters gruffly.

Then it's alongside me, another cyclist, American by the sound of it. He wears black shorts, red shirt, and a red helmet. Dark spikes of stubble line his face. Without another word, he speeds ahead, and I see that his machine is loaded down with long-distance gear. In America, where I came across half a dozen coast-to-coast riders, we tended to stop and compare notes. Though not this guy. He seems to be on an urgent mission. Before long, he is a small unsociable dot a long way further up the road.

Cardwell looms up, and I strike another 100km off the tally. It is a spread out, rather nondescript place; a few motels, garages, tyre depots, stores, and rundown cafes & takeaways line its broad main street. Behind, there's an unremarkable beach with marshy edges. A billboard invites investors to sign up for forthcoming waterside apartments; another announces the site of a proposed yacht marina. My impression is of a slightly dilapitated town the world has passed by; a place to pass through quickly, then drop from memory. And where a couple of Mr Bigs have spotted real-estate business opportunities because today, the trend down south is to move to the coastal north.

I find a reasonable motel and am told by Shirley, the plump manageress, that I'm the only guest. So if I want dinner tonight, go find it elsewhere. The cook ain't coming in. How about a beer then? Yeah, the bar is open, but only until eight. The two other customers are over yonder, young men playing pool at the far end of a large room furnished with empty tables.

The barmaid, Mary, is an attractive brunette of early middle age. I introduce myself and receive a handshake that belies her femininity. It suggests *No Brawling* and a hard outdoor life. I make some comment or other.

"Bananas" she says.

"Bananas" I say back, with no idea what she's talking about.

"I had my own 20-acre banana plantation until the government forced me and Shirley out of business" she snaps, almost slamming my beer onto the counter. "It favours the big growers. Independents cannot afford the taxes that we're hit with – a deliberate government ploy to force us out of the game". There is acid in her voice. "So now me and Shirley are down to running this place".

Which, apart from me, is empty. At the height of Australia's holiday season. All the same, 20 acres doesn't sound like a lot of land to make a living from. Not out here.

Mary bristles at my ignorance. "Mister, that's enough to produce *one helluva lot of bananas*". I am put very firmly in my place, and I see where her toughness comes from. I think hard about what she's telling me. In this incredible Land of Plenty, she's saying that big Australian hearts don't extend to big Australian business, nor to the Australian government; that the people down in Canberra have adopted the well-tested *George Dubya* Theory: that the Big and the Dirty make better bedfellows than the Small, the Unknown, and these days, the Annoying.

Even from the short ride to date, I'm spotting a big shift in attitudes since my previous time out here. Pioneering and individual efforts were once rewarded with grants and other assistance. Such benefits now go to the big corporations. From this unspoken government dictum, the small and disaffected have taken on a slightly bitter and inward-looking stance that I suddenly realise is personified by this decaying North Queensland seaside town. It will take Mr Big and his developers to smarten it up and put it on the map.

Townsville is now about 150km away. Early morning, I press on through more unsettled weather. One almighty hill between Cardwell and Ingham gets me sweating and cursing, but after that the going becomes flat and easy. On the southern side of Ingham – a clean, pleasant little place that is the heart of the sugarcane industry – I call in at Andy's Roadhouse. A hard faced woman takes my order for a cheese sandwich and coffee.

Eyeing the bike, she barks "Don't you have a car?"

I need to give some kind of polite reply. There's a sandwich to worry about. "No car. But I've got thighs like rock if that's any consolation".

As she moves towards the kitchen, she calls out with her back to me, "Yeah, that'd help in the bedroom. But you'd have to get a car to get me. No way I'm going with a guy who's only got a bicycle".

I think I'm playing my cards right.

The weather cheers up a little as I pedal on south. The map tells me of a place called Rollingstone 50km further on, where I'll bed down for the night. High ranges roll out to the west but the road remains even. It is strangely empty today, and I've got a whole two-metre width of shoulder to cruise along, which I only have to share with broken glass, blown truck tyres, dead snakes, and a growing number of dead kangaroos.

The 'roo is as much a nocturnal as daytime creature. At night, truck lights will dazzle and mesmerize it as it eats away at roadside pickings. The driver of an 18-wheeler will feel only the slightest of bumps as he carries on down the road. For him, it's all in a night's work. The farmers and ranchers say he's doing them a favour.

I reach Rollingstone late afternoon. The township, for want of a better term, has a police station and a General Store doubling as a two-pump petrol station. Further along is the Rollingstone Hotel, a single-storey building with an unpainted tin roof. A few locals are drinking at the bar, which is also the reception. The woman behind it says that $23 will buy me a room, that dinner is at eight – and by the way, is there a sudden epidemic breaking out? One cyclist is unusual enough around here, but I make the second in the space of an hour. An American on a laden-down mountain bike checked in a short while ago.

Seems like the Man on an Urgent Mission didn't get away from me after all; and in this lonely little world of mine – just me, my bike, and the open road – I look forward to our encounter this evening.

FIVE
The Women of Rollingstone

In my tiny room at the rear of the hotel, grey metal slats fill the window in lieu of glass, spoiling the view of a rusty water tank standing amid a rough chicken patch outside. The fan slowly cranks into life, long after the flick of the switch. It sounds like a groaning ghost, wobbling precariously from the yellow-flaked ceiling, and baring all its wires and naked electrical mechanisms.There's a lopsided dark brown wardrobe in one corner, a bed in another. The bed is of the iron variety, and it's hard to say which is older – the iron frame or its mattress. The shower and loo are communal, yet seem to function well. At $23 a night, I do not mind any of this. Once the day is scrubbed off, I wander cheerfully into the bar.

No problem in recognizing the other cyclist. He's a beefy character, mid-30s, and still in his red shirt. The chin stubble is even darker with an added day's growth. He eyes me knowingly as I walk towards him, and puts down a weird looking drink before taking my outstretched hand.

"Joseph Fay, Washington DC".

"You overtook me yesterday between Tully and Cardwell".

"I passed some Go-Slow. Was that you?"

"You seemed in a hurry".

"Things on my mind". His cocktail glass contains a swampy-green liquid. "Wanna try one of these?" he asks.

It looks like frogspawn in a laboratory test. "What is it?"

"Dunno" he shrugs. "The bar tottie won't tell me. It kicks, I know that".

The 'tottie' comes over. "Don't ask" she rules. "It's a secret recipe, speciality of the house". She pours me a test-shot from a jug. Some kind of white rum and lime juice is my guess, but apparently I'm way off. Do I want it or not? I say yes, just as the shot delivers a delayed opening blow. Strange to find such a potent cocktail in the middle of hardened beer swilling country. But there is something strange about this hotel anyway that I cannot yet tap into.

The drink seems to be oiling Joseph Fay's tongue. Before long I know him to be an advertising man with his own agency that relies heavily on a small contract from a government department. Like me, he is pedalling south. Except that Joe is not going to get very far. He's only got ten days vacation and cannot extend it because the vital government advertising contract is up for imminent review. It is curious that he's doing this at all. Washington to Cairns and back is a very long haul for the sake of a brief solo bike ride.

"It's a bet" he grunts. "There's this guy in DC who figures I can't ride the 750 kilometres from Cairns to Mackay in seven days. Well I've studied the map and reckon I can. I've got $1000 and a lot of pride riding on it".

Joe and this other guy have cycled together before, through Ireland, where they developed an ongoing bitter-sweet rivalry. He says they'd arranged to make this tour together, but his companion pulled out at the last minute – saving face by turning the whole thing into a wager. Both men are seeking opposite results and one or the other has to lose. Joe doesn't think it should be him and I'm naturally sympathetic. He really is a Man on a Mission.

"If I lose this one, I'll find some other way to shaft that asshole".

Joe needs to average over 100km per day, which in theory is attainable enough. The problem is not of actual distance, but of elements and obstacles; hills, heat, headwinds, rain, punctures, injury, tiredness, and other unseen permutations. It's tough to keep up an average like that for long. We are not Tour de France riders.

Joe is on the fluffy side of the media business, but we've something in common other than cycling: a lingering cynicism that prevails throughout the industry. I see it as soon as he spouts off his agency's motto. '*If it ain't true, don't print it*". He speaks these words with a sideways glance – and a slight curl of the lips that might be more accurately described as a 50% down payment on a sneer.

My suspicion is affirmed when he adds, "I always ask a new client one simple question. '*How d'ya like your bullshit served, buddy? With or without extra balls?*'".

I am getting to like this game American. He signals for another round of the strong but palatable secret concoction. While refills are being seen to, the odd feeling that there's something not quite right about this hotel returns. And yet there is nothing especially abnormal. I mention this to Joe and he shoots me a glance.

"Funny. I've been thinking the same thing".

It is 7.30pm. Around the oblong bar are five customers: Joe and myself; a tipsy young couple heavily into themselves; and a quiet man of about 25 who is staring intently into his beer glass, as if it contains the answer to it all. There is a small restaurant area beyond the bar with five tables covered by patterned green cloth, candlesticks on each, like some cosy mini-bistro that seems a thousand miles from my room 10 metres down the hall.

The barmaid thrusts menus into our faces. A larger, older woman emerges from the background, looking as if she's overslept from a long afternoon nap. "Any problems, my sweet" she yawns at the help, then kisses her cheek. She's late 30s with short dark hair and a broad face. A loose-fitting yellow floral dress does not disguise large thighs and buttocks.

Gambler Joe is fast on the uptake. "Those two" he says under his breath. "Ten dollars says they're a couple of dykes".

I don't know why we take an instant interest in such things. Maybe we have some inner need to understand our surroundings in order to know when to speak, what to say, and where to walk on eggshells. For whatever reason, I begin to look for the signs – which are quick in coming. Body language and eye contact tell their own tale and it soon becomes clear that the two women have indeed got something going.

The barmaid – she is obviously more than that – takes the dinner orders while her companion refills our glasses. She chats pleasantly, revealing that she and her other half came up here a year ago from somewhere down south, bought the lease on this hotel, and are hoping to make it work. It's touch and go, she says bluntly.

"This was a real run-down dump before we took over" she says in a particularly heavy '*strine* drawl. She asks if our rooms are okay, and we automatically reply yes, fine, thank you. This one is the dominating partner and it shows. In fact, now that I've got the lay of the land, everything falls into place. It is as if the two women are acutely aware of any in-built discomfort their sexuality might create among strangers and have decided to shout it out loud into every new face that walks in. That way, everyone can get on with the business of being themselves.

For some reason they won't open the bistro area, and neither will they allow us to eat at the bar. Women. These two anyway. Our plates and cutlery are put on the top of a waist-high freezer next to the exit, to which we drag over a couple of barstools. But the steaks are tender and excellent. I share a bottle of wine with Joe. Such moments of relaxation are often the best in a cyclist's day.

The hotel owners are having dinner by themselves, over at a wall counter. They share just the one plate, taking turns to delicately pick at it with their fingers while gazing intently into one another's eyes throughout the meal. I idly wonder what brought them to this tiny settlement of Rollingstone. Prejudice seems improbable, since they'd be more likely to find that sort of persecution up here in right-wing Queensland. They certainly would have 40 years ago, though from all accounts contemporary Oz has a large and expanding gay sector cruising amid a mostly-tolerant society.

I rise early the next morning, grab some coffee, and load the bike. Townsville is only 56km away but there's a strong headwind that is going to be tough on the legs. The two women are up and about. Seems that something has come up and they too will be going into Townsville later on in the morning. They have a minibus outside and offer me a lift – which I very politely decline. Were I caught out in a violent thunderstorm, that would be another matter. But the day is bright and sunny, if windy. Besides, by leaving now I'll probably get there before they do. Joe is nowhere to be seen, still sleeping they think. No matter, I'll likely run into him somewhere further down the road. Or not.

Phew, this wind is something else today. So is the increasing roadside debris of smashed glass and ripped-up truck tyres. It's everywhere. Traffic densens as the morning ticks on. Trucks roar past on the nearside lane, but I'm well protected by a decent width of shoulder. I catch the backdraft from their slipstreams and get a few brief moments of easy pedalling.

It takes nearly four hours to reach Townsville's northern outskirts, where already it has the feel of a big and busy place. I strap my helmet on. Police cars are prowling around in a way that indicates a no-nonsense approach to life in the nation's largest tropical city. Industrial estates and business parks feed the way downtown, and traffic lights appear every few hundred metres. An impersonal ambience of urban sprawl comes into play.

Approaching a red light, a vehicle passes me with assorted hoots and shouts. I pull up beside it. The women of Rollingstone are in the front; behind them is a grinning Joseph Fay, his bike and luggage lying in the back of the minibus. He pokes his head through a window. "Told ya I'd find a way to screw that bastard in DC!" he whoops. "Gonna cream his thousand, man. You'll see!".

It would appear that Joe's gambling adversary in Washington DC is soon to be spoon-fed a platter of bullshit piled high with lashings of extra balls. But in a city where the telling of giant whoppers comes naturally, and in a country where the dollar bill forms the basis for an entire national culture, any which way you get through the day is seemingly okay.

I find my way to the Ridgemont Executive Motel, at the top of what must be the city's only hill, and very possibly the steepest one in the State of Queensland. Even the cars are struggling with its sharp gradient. At the top, I overlook the downtown district, with views of a sizeable island a short way out to sea. Today, the sea is a dazzling mixture of various blues, looking so warm and clear that it might almost have been run as a luxurious bath for God Himself.

An illusion of course. Down in the deep, it's business as usual. At the high end of the food chain, the sharks and barracuda go about their predatory raids on smaller prey. There are wriggling sea snakes, moray eels, giant clams, poisonous stonefish and pufferfish, and a whole array of species looking for protection and survival in a silent, continuous war zone where suspicion and death lurks at every jagged coral corner.

I doubt that fish fall in love.

With the sea in mind, I wander downtown in search of Reef HQ, the administration centre for all matters pertaining to the Great Barrier Reef. I walk along Flinders Mall, the pedestrian-only main shopping thoroughfare with a line of shade-giving trees running down the middle. Clothing stores, outdoor cafes, pharmacies and one-hour photo shops abound. McDonalds claims the mall's most prominent site.

A short stroll towards the port area leads me to Reef HQ – a walk-through labyrinth of man-made subsea tunnels designed to simulate the Barrier Reef itself. To call it an aquarium would be like comparing a Rolls Royce to a plumber's van, for this, I think, is the world's most intelligent shore-based marine attraction. There are no leaping dolphins, hand-fed by gawping crowds; nor will you see the fibreglass dorsal fin from a remote-controlled Great White slicing the water alongside a tourist pier. Reef HQ may be an undersea theme park, but it's got a learning-zone culture.

The architect's brief was easy. *Take the whole of the Great Barrier Reef, then reproduce it as a living, scaled-down entity inside a city building*. I mean, what could be simpler? Anyway, the result is a remarkable piece of engineering that has created a simulated environment of exact ocean temperatures, currents, surface waves, and living coral in which almost every species of the reef's regular inhabitants are represented, from large black-tip sharks down to tiny angel fish and seahorses. There is even a built-to-scale version of the wreck *S.S. Yongala*, a mail and passenger ship that went down off Townsville in 1911 taking 121 lives with it. As I walk through silent passageways immersed in three million litres of seawater, with the living reef on either side of me, everything I view is explained by information boards. And if that won't do the job, there's a giant IMAX theatre upstairs continually screening educational reef-related themes.

But the cycnic in me is never far from the surface. I cannot fault the display – it is good; really good. Nevertheless, the visit is marred slightly by the suggestion that you not only reflect on the experience in the HQ's waterfront cafe, but on the way out you should '*Shop until you drop in our award winning souvenir store*'. In this otherwise first class attraction, where adults have already paid a $19.50 entrance fee, the effort to squeeze the last possible cent from each visitor comes into 20/20 vision. It is as if the HQ's own watchful sharks are circling everyone's thinning wallet.

Okay, so it's the way of the world, everywhere. Sometimes it's a necessity, though always tacky. And it triggers off another personal truth.

A deep yearning for that elusive somewhere of the soul; a place where the spirit has bypassed every call centre, profit target, balance sheet; all corporate greed, and every government promise.

But where, in a world centred on the economics of mass consumerism, is that ideal to found? In a religious or self-sufficiency commune? On a desert island? Via some passionate love affair perhaps? Or maybe aboard a yacht on a calm, empty ocean?

I think not. They offer only temporary respite. Somewhere, the word *simplicity* begs to be heard.

Even if it seems otherwise, this ride is uncluttering my own jumbled mind. The bicycle is a very simple machine.

Bowen Beach at sundown

SIX
Handbrakes and Headshakes

Townsville is screeching. It is 6.30pm and I cannot believe the din along an almost empty Flinders Mall. It is the piercing shrill from thousands of Lirokeet Parrots, high up in the trees. They are laughing, squabbling, debating, and generally going mad in a ridiculous, amplified cocophony of sound – a kind of vocal foreplay that will soon lead to a mass exodus towards some nocturnal adventure or other. I learn this from the cab driver taking me back up the big hill to my motel and an informal date with my hosts, Neville and Marie Brookes.

Neville is Crocodile Dundee. In the kindest possible sense, he belongs out there among the snakes and the dingoes – not here, standing in as relief manager for the Ridgemont Executive Motel. The bush and the swamps practically gush from the pores of a tough lived-in face that sports a proud dark moustache. He's mid 40s, with a clear penchant for Bundaberg Rum and roll-your-owns. His arms are scarred from "*more than 60 cancerous extractions caused by the sun.*".

He waves that off as a trifling matter, far too boring to talk about.

It is going on sundown. From our bar table we clearly see the offshore lump of real estate known as Magnetic Island – so named by Captain Cook because something in the island's mineral properties played havoc with the ship's compass during the explorer's voyage of discovery along this coast in 1770.

Marie is a big, competent woman with blond hair and cheerful eyes. They make an honest, uncomplicated pair, no flies on either of them as they drift from motel to motel, filling in for absent management. Like the Port Douglas couple at the Breakfree Reef Club, Marie is management material while Neville kind of tags along in an accepting way. But this is not where they want to be. They've got plans.

"Cardwell" he says, surprising me. "That's the place where things are gonna happen. And it's still affordable. Marie's got good ideas for a waterside restaurant, and I'm looking for a new boat to take the tourists fishing. We've got it all worked out. I'll catch the little sods, and she'll serve them up. The fish, that is. Tourists will foot the bill on both counts".

Perhaps he's right about Cardwell. The only way it can go is up.

We are joined by another guest, a consultant engineer of some description. Mike Rutherford is a globetrotting Aussie. He's lean, dark haired, fast talking, and he keeps saying something about a handbrake.

"The wife" he complains. "I call her the Handbrake. Every time I put a new idea to her, she slams the stoppers on it".

Marie is setting a row of tables. A gathering of 12 is due in for dinner. One by one they drift in, all smartly dressed professionals equipped with glitter minded 'handbrakes' who are each fairly dripping with gemstones. Neville gets up to serve behind the small bar. The contrast between them is like a swearing sheep shearer mingling with a group of fine-art critics.

I chat with Mike Rutherford. His job seems to have taken him almost everywhere, including a stint of improvement-making to the London Underground system. He and the handbrake are now living back in Oz, a place called Noosaville further down the coast. But Mike is restless and talks of moving to Cornwall for a while.

I know how he feels. Home is an elusive place if you've spent your life in and out of foreign parts. Home lies somewhere in the ideals of the mind, not in bricks & mortar solidly embedded into one miniscule dot of the earth's surface. In the early 1960s, when

Australians were a tightly inward-looking breed, I was hard pressed to find anyone who wanted to venture beyond these shores, not even on holiday. Now, in a much more open era, I'm hard pressed to find anyone who hasn't. Home as you once knew it is never the same for anyone after long periods away.

The group of 12 settles down at their table. Neville returns with a brimming glass of rum. He takes a cigarette paper from its folder and lets it hang from his lower lip while he pulls tobacco strands from a pouch. He handrolls the smoke with the natural ease of a woodsman.

"Them people" he says, nodding towards the group. "They're members of the Porsche Owners Club. Go take a look at the car park. There's a million dollars of metal out there".

I glance over at the noisy table. The men are probably wealthy lawyers and accountants, mostly in middle age. But despite the jewellery and the make-up, not one of their handbrakes is likely to get past the reception desk of a photographer's studio. Maybe a Porsche makes you look or feel a little better, I wouldn't know. And I really do not care.

Neville is soon into his favourite topic, the great outdoors. He tells the story of his encounter with a King Brown, a fast and highly venomous serpent. The snake was trying to wriggle forward, but Neville had grabbed its tail, pulling it backward. The creature suddenly obliged him with a mighty whiplash – at which precise moment our hero let go and scrambled to within a split-second of his life.

I ask just why the hell he was tugging at the snake anyway. He merely shrugs and grins. "Just to see how it would react. I noticed its tail lying under a bush and couldn't resist. Big bastard, I'll tell you that. Going on three metres".

I shake my head. I'm none too crazy about snakes: nor sharks, Neville's other pet tease; tiger sharks, big ones, four or five metres in length. For some reason, he derives pleasure from luring these ill-tempered maneaters right up close to the beach, then provoking them with a long pole until he gets his pretty much guaranteed action-packed response.

I somehow doubt that similar topics are under discussion at the Porsche club. I notice that the guy at the head of the table has their undivided attention, like some sort of guru.

Next day, I carry on 80km to the town of Ayr, accompanied by a thick head – the result of too much leftover wine from the Porsche table, whose wasteful members had roared away into the night, perhaps fearing the breathalyser. If something is going to catch the midnight eyes of a prowling cop, the Porsche is always a fair bet. By this time, Marie had joined the party with Mark, Neville, and me – as had the guru, a Swede called Otto, whom I gather is Australia's roving Porsche expert and something of a legend among Aussie owners. What he says goes.

Otto had thought it criminal to leave the wine to waste. Nobody got to bed before 3am. Tonight, I'm out for the count by nine in a small, nondescript motel somewhere in a town that's taken its name from a large Scottish shire.

Feeling better from a long sleep, I ride another 100km through canefields and flatlands to the seaside town of Bowen The headwind turns to a sidewind, blowing from the east. Rain starts and stops and I shelter under trees when it gets too heavy. Low clouds sweep across the unchanging scenery of what has now become The Bruce Highway. I look upon today as a chore, to be performed as efficiently as possible.

Interesting little place, Bowen. At water's edge is a sandy beach curving around a broad bay. Natural palms are scattered here and there. It is sunset and there's nobody else in sight. Behind me, tidy wide streets lead up to the quiet town centre, which rises up a small hill and then dips down again. Colourful murals on several downtown walls intrigue me. They are superbly done.

One depicts a four-engined Catalina seaplane. Bowen, it seems, was a busy base for these hybrid aircraft during WW11. Another has ships of every description anchored in the bay, suggesting serious port activity at one time. A third shows two tradesmen working the original 19th Century printing press of a local newspaper, the *Bowen Advocate*. There are 24 such wall murals adorning the town's history, all of them alluring works of art.

Not quite so alluring is my overnight room at the edge of town. The run down Pearly Shell Motel is operated by an unshaven, overweight chap called Frank. He wears a stained white teeshirt and a grubby pair of crimson shorts. Frank delivers a small jug of milk to the room – a standard courtesy here, which goes with the teabags and coffee sachets – and lives up to his name by informing me that I'm off my rocker.

"S'not so bad 'tween here and Mackay" he states. "There's places to break the journey. But matey, the patch 'tween Mackay and Rocky...

hell, that's more than 300 kilometres of zilch, zero, nothing. If yer brains ain't already fried, they bloody well will be along that stretch of road. It's a fuckin' graveyard for blokes like you".

For Rocky read Rockhampton.

"Something to look forward to" I mutter defiantly, knowing it's going to be tough. Others have said the same thing.

The ceiling fan won't work, so he switches on an ancient air conditioner. It booms and shakes and drips water. There's an old TV standing on a dark brown desk. Frank switches that on too and it crackles like popcorn in a cinema, flicking weird electric patterns across the screen. Frank scratches at his stubble, then says "Best yer only have one or other on at a time. The telly don't like it when the air conditioner's on".

I care more about staying cool than watching television. Australian TV is on a par with America's worst. Imported soaps and serials which have been screened elsewhere as long as a year ago, vie with home-grown programmes which are too awful to watch. This is dumbed-down television in the raw. On a scale of one-to-ten, it scores the Mick Jagger Fidelity Rating, 0/10.

Frank asks, "Where yer gonna ride tomorrer?"

I stab the map. A town called Proserpine is only 60km away. That'll do for the day. This is not a record attempt.

Frank whistles, seeing it from another view. "That's a bloody long way in one go".

"Not to me, Frank. It's like taking the dog for a walk". Sometimes you've got to act the tough guy.

He shuts the door behind him, shaking his head, muttering.

Next morning, Frank grudgingly wishes me luck as I ride off. Something makes me stop about a hundred metres on, and I turn my head. Frank is standing there, hands on hips, still shaking his head, as if making absolutely certain that I disappear. I wave, and he waves back. In some way that I cannot fathom, my presence seems to have briefly unbalanced his life.

Just out of town, at a Caltex servo on the left, there's a young man standing at the roadside with a rucksack. He's got an outstretched arm and thumb. I smile and say, "Sorry, mate. It'd be a bit difficult".

"Hey, wait!" he exclaims. "I'll sit myself on your luggage. I've done it before".

"You must be kidding" I reply a little sourly.

"No, c'mon. Let's try it" he begs desperately. He must have been standing there all night.

I'll try most things once, but not this. "Good luck" I say with a wave.

"Yeah, you too" he calls out in a voice that is behind me now.

More flatlands and canefields. All the way from Port Douglas there has been a lack of shade. The trees stand well back from the road, seldom stretching their precious commodity onto the highway. The hours between noon and two are the worst. My cap and electric-blue helmet give some relief, but within minutes the sweat builds up inside and finally becomes intolerable. I am learning to control my thirst however, sipping from the water bottles instead of gulping.

About 15km from Prosperpine, I come across a roadside fruit vendor. He is an Indian Seikh, with a fierce beard and a spotless white turban. But his accent is pure *'strine*, broad and heavy. He's got pineapples, mangoes, bananas, nectarines, everything tropical, in a neatly-arranged display inside his lean-to. It is covered with a white canvas sheet propped up by bamboo poles. This is a lonely part of the highway. Hazy mirages bounce off the distant tarmac. It seems an odd place for a fruit stall; and an even stranger spot to find a Seikh, even one of his accent.

"Not my stall" he drawls. "I'm just paid to sell that banana you're eating".

He doesn't seem like an ordinary employee to me. We're able to spot the difference between those who can and those who teach. Something tells me this man can.

I prod him with a few questions. He resents the sudden intrusion into his life from a total stranger, but I view everyone I meet on this ride as a potential radio piece.

"It's a very long story" he snaps bitterly. "My business went bankrupt. Skullduggery and backstabbing from a rival. Look, I don't wanna talk about it, okay? Because I'm plotting my revenge and a big comeback". His eyes are flashing now.

There is silence for a moment as he points to a wastebin for the banana peel. "This road is quiet and away from it all. A good place to avoid creditors and to work out my next move". He sounds deadly serious. Seikhs, to my certain knowledge, can be a fearsome and unforgiving tribe. Whoever this guy has got it in for should tread carefully.

He's right, though. There's nothing like an empty highway to think things through. Just now I'm thinking that it matters not where you are in the world – a big city, a tiny village, a shanty town, a paradise island, or even in a roadside fruit stall – personal vendettas and human conflict will always be hovering somewhere nearby. Sad, but true.

I ride into Proserpine, an attractive little place with a lone commercial street, and check into an old-style hotel, $30 for the night. I wonder if Joseph Fay is here too, but the woman at reception shakes her head. "You're the first cyclist we've seen for a long time. Where are you going anyway?"

"Melbourne, eventually".

There's a very long pause, verging on the uncomfortable. She stares at me through thin wire glasses without expression or a single blink of the eye. Then, with another shake of the head, she says very slowly, "*Holy buggery, you must be mental. Quite, quite mad*".

Later, I cross the street to a renovated pub for something to eat. There is something familiar about the two bespectacled women sitting at the bar, and they've got the same thought about me. One of them says, "Didn't we meet in Cairns?"

Yes, I remember now. A tall, thin pair of Dutch lesbians staying in the room next to mine at the Bay Village Resort. We'd spoken briefly, just before they'd set out on some magical mystery tour leading to Ayers Rock and other attractions. But now they harbour a grievance. One of the two fell ill, requiring hospital treatment. The tour guide said her complaint was inconvenient; it was holding everyone up. The two women say they were dumped in some small town off the beaten track. Prosperpine has the nearest hospital, and some kind person gave them a lift. The hospital wants money, but the tour company won't offer a refund. All their plans are in disarray.

I see the dilemma and make sympathetic noises, glad that my own tour through Oz is simply one man and his bike. I buy them a drink, wish them well, and look elsewhere to eat.

I'm just 125km from the city of Mackay. I bed down for the night, resolving to make that distance tomorrow, headwind or not.

The wind relents. Billboards begin to appear, plugging the Whitsunday Islands, a fashionable tropical archipelago that's a short seaplane ride away from Mackay. Another billboard supports a dated political poster. It depicts the national flag and carries the message, *Vote No to the Politician's Republic.*

That is what they did in a referendum. Voted No. Aussies traditionally mistrust politicians and their motives. By and large, they believe there may be something wrong up there in the head with anyone who seeks high office or power over others. The thing about the Queen, says the older generation, is that she never *sought* position; she was born into her role, with no other choice but to get on with it. Better to put up with someone who never looked for power, than the sinister megalomaniacs who yearn it.

It is gone dark by the time I pedal into Mackay, utterly worn out. This is a much smaller city than Townsville and although I'm already booked in somewhere for a couple of nights, tonight I find the nearest motel I can. After a shower, I flop into bed, falling at once into a deep and wonderful oblivion.

The dream is real enough. I'm flying Tarzan-style through the jungle. Below, the snakes and crocs are manifest, waiting for the drop. When it happens, I awake with a shudder just before crashing to the ground.

It is daylight. The dream has a meaning, as I think they sometimes do. I just hope it's not prophetic. Today I am going to sample a new form of jungle sport not much known to the outside world. It's inventor calls it *Forest Flying.*

SEVEN
EcoLand

The tropical north is now behind me, and I welcome myself to Central Queensland. Long before the morning is out, Mackay has become an endearing city with the friendly and airy ambience of somewhere much smaller than it is. Clean downtown streets are set in tidy tree-lined blocks where parents seem relaxed about their kids playing out on its quiet, bungalow-clad roads. It is the region's principal sugar port. With the advent of tourism, Mackay has grown into a coastal centre of 70,000.

I switch addresses to the comfortable White Lace Motor Inn, pleased to be having a day or two off from the pedals, and look forward to the rainforest this afternoon. The invitation to try out Forest Flying will apparently have me whizzing along a highwire through a jungle full of fruit bats. It seems a reasonable BBC story.

Donna Lowe taps on my motel door, a beaming smile spread across a broadly tanned face topped with shortish fair hair. Her

Yorkshire accent is undiminished, despite spending the last 12 of her 38 years Down Under. She has come to take me to the highwire site, which first of all means a 60km drive inland. Donna's bubbling chat is infectious. Enthusiastic people like her give balance from the ever-beckoning call of cynicism.

The drive takes us towards the hilly ranges of the Eungella National Park, a major habitat of the platypus mammal. Translated, this means that the road has emptied out and we're in the boondocks. I ask how she and her husband came to roost so far from anywhere.

"For me, it all started with the usual working holiday. I was in Sydney when I met Dave. He'd been a cabinet-maker in Hull, then one day decided to emigrate – and when Dave decides something, that's it. No argument, and no going back. He arrived out here about 17 years ago with a backpack, a few quid, and his set of tools. Dave hates the big cities as much as I do. But at the time Sydney was....you know, the work and the money thing".

We finally pass through a township called Finch Hatton. It has a General Store and a pub on one side, a church and primary school on the other. Donna turns off the paved road onto a bumpy dirt track rising into the hills. "Dave had spent some time around here before we met. He used to tell me about it, really firing up my imagination. I guess we talked ourselves into coming north and buying our 72 acres of jungle".

She shifts gears as the track gets rougher. "Almost there now".

Her expression drops a notch. "Actually, there's much more to it than that. Better that Dave fills in the blanks". It drops another notch. "It hasn't been easy, you know".

I think I do. Easy Street has always been off my road map too.

We come to a clearing. There's a small caravan under a cluster of trees. Solar panels lean against it at an angle to the sun. "The office" Donna smiles. "Everything you see around here is Do-it-Youself, including the electricity". We climb out of the car and walk down a sharp track into another clearing where a fair haired man and some other guy with a dark beard are explaining the rudiments of Forest Flying to a tall, blond Dutch couple. There are fresh mangoes on a wooden table, expertly sliced into edible cubes; Jungle Airways 'welcome drink'.

David Lowe is nudging 40, with long fair hair spilling onto broad Yorkshire shoulders. He wears a green sports shirt, shorts, and thongs. Above us, up on a ridge, a line of high-tensile cable attached to a post runs about 50 metres down a slope to another post. "Ready to take the test flight?" he asks genially. "We can talk later, back up at the house".

I follow him up the slope, then strap myself into a hang-gliding seat made of two canvas strips suspended from the wire via a pulley system. There is another gadget that acts as a brake when you pull down on it. The brief flight down the slope requires a thick pair of gloves to prevent handburn, because the process also dictates that the free hand grips the cable itself. I think I understand Dave's instructions – this is not quite the sort of aviation I'm familiar with.

I manage to brake before slamming into the lower post, which means I've passed my 'test flight'. Now it's time for the real thing. A solo glide through a kilometre of in-your-face jungle and deep gorges, the daytime bedroom for a giant colony of fruit bats.

We trek up to the take-off point, atop a hill overlooking dense rainforest. I watch as the Dutch couple, one by one, slide away like human cable cars until they are small dots silently disappearing into a lush green ocean. This is such a quiet, remote, and beautiful spot that I wonder just how the hell Dave and Donna Lowe managed to get the mechanics of this cable system up and working in the first place. It is not as if the area is overrun with advanced engineering projects. This truly is virgin territory.

I'll shoot first, ask questions later. Right now it's my turn for the sky.

I've not done anything like this before. I balance on the launch pad – a breezeblock standing on a plank that itself stands on a pair of upside down buckets. Once harnessed in securely, I let go of the brake and glide off into the silence of the sky and the jungle – one moment 30 metres high over a deep stoney gorge, and trying not to think that this may be another way to die, and the next, feeling my face tickled by protruding palm fronds. If the going gets too fast, I tug on the brake; too slow, I give a couple of mighty hauls on the wire.

Eyes should be peeled for the sleeping fruit bats, but on this first run I am concentrating on the flying. For me, this is akin to the first flight of the Wright Brothers. But once relaxed, it is exhilarating, fabulous. But hey, what's this? I'm speeding straight towards a good thumping from a tall tree and apply the brake urgently – in time to see a grinning David Lowe greet me from a tiny treetop platform.

"Charing Cross" he sings out cheerfully. "All Change".

I swap cables for the homeward run, flying through a mixture of thick forest and open sky, face-to-face with black fruit bats hanging in inverted clusters, sleeping the day away. Come nightfall, they'll be off in search of fermenting mangoes. By daybreak, they'll be back, arguing and screeching, drunk on the night's pickings. Donna had told me this in the car.

At one stage, the going slows right down and I'm all but motionless, swaying high above a trickling creek. But some hard tugs on the wire soon has me coming in to land back at the test-flight base. I guess the whole thing has taken only a quarter hour or so, but they've been 15 absorbing minutes, producing a range of emotions: nerves, awe, peace, calm, wonder, and one or two racing heartbeats.

Forest Flying is one of those all-too-brief adventures that makes you *feel good*.

Soon we're up at *Chateau Lowe* – no ordinary house, this. Before moving in, the Lowes lived in a roomy treehouse – yes, treehouse – but the pestilent tropical white ants served an eviction order by chewing it all away. So they came down to earth, and now live in another House That Dave Built. A family home, I should stress. The couple have two young kids, a boy and girl, aged seven and four.

They came down to earth alright. This family home is *underground*.

We'll return to their amazing architectural accomplishment shortly. By now, it is clear that I'm in the company of two inspiring, original, and most extraordinary people – and whose philosophies and values lie on the plus-side of simplicity. Both of them love Australia with a passion, particularly their back garden of 72 wild acres.

Dave says laconically, "We bought the property without a way to keep up the bank payments. Our mindset was to leave the place to itself for a while by making a little money elsewhere". He raises a meaningful eyebrow. "The bank manager helped us to set up shop in the Whitsundays, a place called Dayream Island".

We are out on the patio of their eco-house, glasses of homemade beer in hand. This spot is so heavenly, so cool, as to be almost a daydream itself.

"Daydream Island" Dave repeats. "What does that say to you?"

What it says to me is not necessarily what it does to others. What it says to me is another product from Mr Big, probably influenced by some mass-market Florida resort like Marco Island. Whoever named it is certainly looking for daydreamers en-masse. I've seen roadside billboards for the place.

"Yeah, it's a blatant tourist trap" Dave nods. "Point is, we got the license to own and operate a semi-submersible. Trips along the reef. It was a paying proposition".

A semi-submersible is a sort of submarine that doesn't actually dive below the surface. The undersea viewing area is already submerged below the hull's waterline, so that passengers enjoy a subsea vista of shallow reefs and marine life from a boat that is in fact cruising along the surface.

"For three years, we did alright" Dave carries on. "The boat enabled us to keep up the payments on this place and enjoy a reasonable living. Until one day the management of the island announced it was '*closing for imminent renovations*'. He utters those words with biting sarcasm. Daydream turned to broken dream as business dried up completely, with no indication of when the island was to reopen. Dave alleges that it was a deliberate ploy to encourage him, and others, to drop out of the running.

"My belief is they intended to reissue various concessions to pals and cronies, or to people who'd fork out a lot more money for them".

Alas, not an unfamiliar tale from the dollar-mad tourist business – now neck and neck with oil as the world's biggest industry. I had heard many such gripes during a four-year writing stint on a travel magazine. The dejected Lowe's left their boat where it was and returned to Finch Hatton with no income and no idea of how they were going to cope, let alone keep up payments to the bank.

Necessity, it's said, is the Mother of Invention. This was when David came up with the notion of Forest Flying. Donna is no 'handbrake'. She saw what he was getting at and gave him her total support. She is a most unusual woman.

"I'd seen a Sean Connery movie" Dave enthuses. "It was called *Medicine Man*, about a medic in the South American jungle who had to dream up some way to cross an impassable canyon in order to tend a dying patient. The only possible option was to rig up a cable system – which I suddenly saw as a way out of our own financial hole".

Selling his vision to a doubting bank manager already concerned about a semi-submersible – the bank's rotting asset over on shut-down Daydream Island – was a major feat in itself. Particularly when Dave suggested the use of bows & arrows as a method of firing the cable up into the trees. I chuckle at my sudden vision of an incredulous banker trying to take all this in. But the bank manager might have had a little explaining to do himself had he not authorised a tight, strings-attached go-ahead. The bucks of Daydream Island – or lack of them, rather – stopped at his very own desk.

"It took us a year, start to finish. I mapped out the flying area, pinpointed the trees to be used for cable support and platforms, then set about turning it into reality. We did absolutely *everything* ourselves".

You have to try and picture this. A couple of Poms treading through thick jungle, marking out cable-routes, trees, and taking notes; all in the vague hope that their concept of an aerial jungleway would lure enough tourists to make the long detour from the coast – and that the safety-minded authorities would view their efforts through sympathetic eyes.

Forest Flying? What the bloody hell is Forest Flying? I dunno, sounds dicey to me. Anyway, which construction camp is gonna design and erect the system – Costain or McAlpine?

Er, well actually....

With the surveying complete, they drew up a shopping list that included reels of fishing line in addition to bows & arrows. "What I did" explains Dave, "Was to fire ample lengths of fishing line up into a tree via bow and arrow. Next, I'd attach the fishing line to the cable on the ground, and sort of reel it up to the required position. Primitive, I know. But it worked".

This is pure caveman thinking. But then David Lowe really is a caveman, as we'll see from his house.

Finally the whole system was up and ready to roll, but first it had to be very thoroughly tested. "I've had two very nervous moments with it" David confesses. "The first, when I strapped myself in at the take-off point for the very first time, realising that this was the moment of truth. If it wasn't going to work, we'd be well and properly stuffed". As a grinning afterthought he adds, "And I worried about it supporting my weight. If it hadn't, I would have dropped 30 metres to the ground – and I guess that would have been that. Game of Life over".

Yes, I guess it would. "And the second?"

"Ah. Well that was when it actually *did* drop. During the test period. I think I fell 20 metres". The cheerful grin seldom seems to leave his face.

I get Total Recall from last night's dream, from which I had woken up in time. But what about David Lowe?

"I remember bracing myself for the impact with the ground, but the halt came abruptly in mid-air. I was suddenly swinging wildly from a totally slack line. My heart thumped like a drum-roll. I was scared stiff. One of the supports had come loose, it had to be that. So I just kind of hung there for a while, getting my composure back and trying to figure things out. Anyhow, little by little I was able to pull myself up along the slack and reach safety".

The authorities didn't get to hear that story. Besides which, the authorities have stayed strangely aloof from the project. Which government department would regulate Forest Flying anyway? Aviation, Sport, Tourism, Transport? From what I gather, this go-for-it couple *is* the Ministry of Forest Flying.

The good news for their bank manager is that *Tourism Queensland*, the state's official body down in Brisbane, is taking the concept seriously. Over 1000 paying pilots have flown the forest, and word is spreading fast.

There is now as much media interest in the lifestyle of David & Donna Lowe as there is in Forest Flying. The two seem to go hand-in-glove, for the couple's home life is as close to genuine eco-living as it gets. They grow their own fruit and vegetables, kill their own goats and chickens, pump their own water from the creek below, generate their own electricity, and brew their own beer.

I not only accept the offer of a refill, I strongly hint at it.

From my seat on a patio embraced by palm trees and rock-garden, I stare into the reflections from a huge semicircular window, with a door cutting through the middle. This is the entrance to the Lowes DIY cave which tunnels into a high mound, naturally roofed by earth and grass. Inside, the walls and ceilings are thickly cemented and well supported by heavy wooden beams. The semicircular window draws astonishing light into the dwelling. This spacious kichen, complete with woodburner stove, is also the family room. To the rear, on either side of a subterranean passageway are the bedrooms, two for the kids and one for the parents. The passage leads out to a back yard containing a solar powered shower unit and a compost-making loo.

"We've no need for heating or air-conditioning" Donna says. "The house stays natually warm in winter and naturally cool in summer". She tells no lie. Outside it is high summer. Inside, it is wonderfully cool.

The bloke with the beard whom I'd seen earlier walks up the rise and joins us for a beer. He's a local named Paul, a married man with two kids, no job, and a python living in his attic ("to keep the bloody rats out"). He seems at home up here in Ecoland.

"Yeah, I help out when I can" he drawls. "I really appreciate what Dave and Donna have done with the place. Wouldn't mind living this way meself; wouldn't mind at all, only the missus is too keen on her comforts. Me, I see things a bit different".

So, unfortunately, does a troublesome neighbour, whose property borders the Lowes. He is being obstructive over rights-of-entry because the track leading to the flying site crosses a tiny part of his land. The dispute threatens to run and run.

Yet the Lowes are probably the happiest couple I've met for many a year. They seem totally dedicated to each other and to this very special eco-path they've carved out for themselves. The neighbour might consider them a pair of social misfits, bloody Poms, whatever. But most everyone else in Finch Hatton thinks otherwise. Forest Flying is putting this one-horse town, minus horse, on the map and is a welcome addition to the occasional tourist bus heading through town up to platypus country.

For me, the Lowes have created what I yearn, albeit in different format. This is their particular take on the theory of simplicity, and it is attracting a growing fan club throughout the world, via the media, the internet, and word of mouth. They have become genuine eco-celebrities, showing an alternative way to go – and that anything is possible so long as you've got the guts and imagination to go for it. In a perverse way, the corporate bosses of Daydream Island assisted the Lowes in making their own dream come true.

EIGHT
The Long Road to Rocky

Seems I have no broadcast this week. The BBC's radio coverage of the Australian Open tennis tournament cuts through my time slot. I'm bursting to tell the story from Ecoland, but it will have to wait – as will an unexpected item gleaned from a complimenary local newspaper put into my motel room.

Proserpine, that attractive little place of a few days ago, makes a disturbing front page story. It seems that shortly after I left, the town erupted into violence as gang warfare broke out between rival drug barons. According to the report, it turned into a street riot involving guns, knives, baseball bats, burning cars, a good number of serious injuries, and several arrests. Aggressive driving apart, this is my first real indication that a worldwide social ailment has fed its way into small town Australia.

I am not in the least shocked; after so many years in journalism, it would take an awful lot to do that. But I am surprised.

For all I know, these days there are drug dealers camped out at Ayers Rock. Or on some Barrier Reef tourist atoll. Or doing the rounds of the sheep and cattle stations by private airplane. I do know that the most peaceful English villages with thatched cottages and charming olde-worlde pubs, are all within shouting distance of bigshot dealers. This is no inner-city issue any more. This is utterly global and nowhere is immune.

Pass me the salt and the simple life, please.

From Mackay, there's an easy 32km flip south to the town of Sarina, which I cover in two hours. But after this comes my 300km of nothing – which is going to be anything but a simple life. Rockhampton suddenly seems a rather long way away, and I shall be mighty glad to get that section of the ride done and dusted with.

I check into a $20-a-night Ocker's hotel in Sarina, a town about the size of Proserpine only not quite as surface-pleasant. It has an aura of which I'm unsure; tight and just a little sullen. My room is the size of a shoebox, but I manage to squeeze the bike in too. There's a door leading out to a broad first-floor veranda, and I stand out there for a while, leaning against the railings and puffing on a home-rolled.

The strap on my wristwatch has broken. I wander the town in the hope of finding some place that sells such items, and spot an unlikely looking jewellery store up a sidestreet. As I enter, a big guy with a ponytail emerges from the back room. He offers me a one-or-the-other choice; a blue velcro strap, or a black thing embedded with spikey silver studs. I pick the former.

While he's fiddling with my watch, I peer at the jewellery on display under a couple of glass counters. This is not the sort of stuff to be found in Bond Street, nor your local H. Samuel high street cheapo. This is mean-looking body wear, of which a vicious skull-ring is by far the most sensitive item. In my peripheral vision I see the jeweller eyeing me up and down, smirking.

"Bikers, mate. That's my market" he asserts. "If I relied on necklaces and wedding rings around here, I'da gone outta business in the first two weeks". He thrusts out a big, powerful hand. "John Ward, creative crafsman to the two-wheeled society".

"I picked the right place then" I respond. He lifts an interested eyebrow which drops again as soon as I tell him that my bike comes complete with pedals.

"Dunno about that kinda stuff. I'm a Harley Davidson man

meself". He goes on to say that Queensland's motorbike culture is getting bigger and bigger, and that he's carved out a decent niche for himself in this part of the state. "Say a biker down in Rocky gets himself a new girlfriend, right? He'll think nothing of sticking her on the pillion and riding the 600 klicks to here and back, just to buy a piece of body metal that says she is now his property".

Since he's mentioned it, I may as well get his opinion about the road to Rockhampton. "Bikers may think nothing of it" I say, "But I'm a little more apprehensive".

He draws a sharp intake of breath and his eyes narrow. "You're gonna ride your bicycle to *Rockhampton*? Jesus Christ, listen to me. There was a young Jap who tried that about three months ago. They found him delirious by the roadside, burnt all to hell and back. Ran outta water. He went mad, I'm told".

At least John's version is more encouraging than the one I heard from that scruffy motelier back in Bowen. By his account, they'd found the Japanese cyclist dead on the side of the road, his eyes gouged out by vultures.

"Thanks John" I say defiantly. "But I'm going to try it anyway. The alternative is to settle down in Sarina. Raise a family".

He grins. "Dunno which is worse. Well, good luck. Better you than me".

Later, I go down to the hotel bar. A dozen or so barflies are getting well-oiled and giving the dark haired middle-aged barmaid plenty of lip. It is her 50th birthday, and this is their way of acknowledging the milestone.

"Hey" shouts one Ocker, "Didn't you used to be a blond? I recall a time when you was a good looking piece. That's when you was blond".

"Nah" calls out another. "She's too fuckin' dumb to be a blond. Say, whaddya old man get yuh for yer birthday?"

She is taking it all with a happy smile, and with a few choice one-liners of her own. "Nuthin'" she states. "That bastard bought me nuthin'. Says he's not gonna get me any more presents until I open the box from two birthdays ago".

She is swishing back and forth serving midis and schooners, clearing glasses, emptying ashtrays, and clearly loving all the banter. I ask what it was he'd bought her two years ago that she's still to open.

The barmaid spreads both hands downward on the bartop and

thrusts a mock-scowling face into mine. "Lawnmower" she replies tartly. "*A fucking lawnmower*. There's some very long grass at my place now".

I nod gravely. "An unromantic choice".

"*Romance*?" she snorts. "There's bin no romance for years. Might've bin once, but that was before he began farting in his sleep".

"Nah, nah" says someone else. "Fair do's now. You're the one who does that. I remember the night. Long time ago, but I remember alright. Betcha never told yer old man about us, did yer?"

"Yeah, I told him. He just laughed and told me to think up a better one. Said your own wife told him that you can't even get it up for a porn movie". Chortles and guffaws fill the air.

I slip off for a takeaway pizza and eat it out on my veranda, thinking about the Japanese cyclist who either died or went crazy on the road to Rocky. Before turning in, I re-study the map. Tomorrow, the day after, and the day after that as well, will be like running the gauntlet. The bike is my only friend. Everything else out on that highway belongs to the threatening unknown. But there is some solace to be had from the map. Everyone's been telling me that it's 300km of zero out there – but this, I now see, is because they drive through non-stop. In fact, there are three or four settlements a few kilometres off the highway, about 100km apart from one another. These are my safety nets where I'll find shelter, food, water.

I haven't seen the sea for days. The road is only a few kilometres inland, but it may as well be in the middle of the desert. It is shadeless, empty, quiet, and lonely. The occasional roadtrain thunders by, all 36 wheels spinning so fast they appear to be revolving backwards. Drivers sitting high up in their cabs seem the size of matchboxes. Private cars speed by as if getting the hell through some mythical sci-fi land called *Purgatory*. Dead snakes and a plethora of very dead kangaroos litter the shoulder; the odour coming from the 'roos becomes unbearable as the day heats up to the noontime boil. The flat horizon is exactly the same as the hour before, and the hour before that. There are moments when I check the road markings to confirm that I'm actually moving forwards.

I have extra water bottles and several protein-rich bananas. And I have my own thoughts into which I now travel deeply. It is as good a time as any to reflect on why, at 57, I'm 12,000 miles from home, pedalling down a road that turns cyclists into madmen or corpses. What strange thread running through my life has brought me to this wild, empty freeway?

I'll start at the beginning. It's a long way to backpedal, but then I've got plenty of time and plenty of road.

I was born in the summer of 1945. My father, a major in the South Staffordshire Regiment, was seconded to the Fleet Air Arm serving in the Pacific. Ironically, his aircraft carrier, *HMS Formidable*, was somewhere along this coast on the day that I arrived into the world. He returned to his native Staffordshire later that year, after the Japanese surrender. But life would never be quite the same for him again. His war had been the full six years, 1939–1945, which included a trying time on the beach at Dunkirk where he was responsible for getting everyone to safety at considerable risk to himself. But he was a big man in every sense, with no time for pettiness or small-minded people – both to be found in abundance on the mean little streets of post-war Britain. He took to the bottle and died aged 42. I was 13 at the time

I have inherited much of his make-up. I too have no truck with the ignorance of small minds; and I too enjoy a drink. By the time I'd reached a rebellious, fatherless 16, my despairing mother had consented to me coming out here, where I spent over two years, followed by a further two year period in New Zealand. My work ranged from the sheep and cattle stations through to newspaper printing. Inbetween I'd gone prawn trawling, window cleaning, scrub cutting, dish washing, bulldozer driving, laboured on the building sites, and for a very short period, tried and failed to sell encyclopaedias. I arrived back in England aged 20, viewing my homeland through the analytical eyes of one who has been away, seen and done things.

Actually, England was a pleasant surprise. The drabness of a previous Britain had vanished while I'd been gone. It was the swinging mid-60s when rock music and fashion put colour and zip into an increasingly cheerful society. I moved to London, embracing that magic city for all it was worth. The only downside of the day was Harold Wilson – very possibly the worst Prime Minister that Britain has ever had.

I got myself a pilot's license and tried to follow Dad's footsteps into the Fleet Air Arm – only to be told, sorry old boy, you'll need two A-Levels as well. In the midst of rocking London, I was not going to go back to school. Instead, I went to Canada for a year, where the only educational requirement for a commercial flying license was the 'ability to read, speak, and write English'.

To pay my way through this I had worked at Expo '67 in the wonderful French Canadian city of Montreal. Soon I was joined by a friend, Jeremy Willis, to whom *Boomerang Road* is dedicated. We have been very strong friends since 1966. When the six-month exposition was over, we simply packed our gear and hitchhiked south, down along the Eastern Seaboard of the USA to Miami. From there, we boarded an old rattletrap to the nearby Bahamas Islands, spending three gloriously idle weeks on someone's boat. I caught the island bug very quickly. I could not get the place out of my mind.

Back in Miami, we hitchhiked right across the USA to San Francisco, then up to British Columbia, finding work on a lumber camp and living in a log cabin by a running stream. It finally sunk in that my life was not going in the general direction required by governments, establishments, institutions, or insurance companies. Nor airlines for that matter. That was when I began to think about writing for a living.

Back in London, now aged 23, I joined a Fleet Street press agency as a sort of trainee reporter, ten quid a week, filing other journalist's copy over the phone to the nationals. Finally I got my first reporting break when, on a particularly busy newsday, the *Daily Express* ordered a story on a shipment of gold bullion making its way through London to the Bank of England. I was dispatched down to the Square Mile, no other reporters available. I had no press card and not the slightest idea of what I was doing. So I stood in a doorway sheltering from the drizzle and took meaningless notes, like the Swiss number plate of the delivery truck and its time of arrival.

Swoop. A squad car arrived out of nowhere. Three grim-faced cops bundled me out of the doorway, into the car, and down to Wood Street Police Station. I had an explanation but no press card to prove it. And there was nobody at the agency to back up my story. Everyone was out. The police told me there was a press-block on this story – which explained why the *Express* had thought it better that one of us get arrested instead of one of its own.

So my career as a journalist began inside a police cell. Slowly I realised that this was the way it was always going to be, and I'd better look out for warning signs. You'll get another fine example of this in a minute.

My boredom threshold was stretched. I kept thinking about those three lovely weeks in the Bahamas. And about boats and the sea. More and more about boats and the sea, and freedom from the daily drudge. One afternoon, while reporting a particularly dull story about a double-decker bus that had overturned in the West End, I reckoned to do something about it. I decided that somehow I'd get the money together, buy a boat, and go back to the Caribbean; if not the Bahamas, then somewhere in that region.

I put an advertisement in the personal columns of *The Times*. It went along the lines of *Partner wanted for Caribbean charterboat enterprise. You provide the capital, I'll provide the rest.* Over the next two days I received over 40 replies. I picked the guy who wanted the least from it – just a few weeks a year in the sun – and went about searching for a suitable second-hand motor cruiser, which I shipped out to Barbados on the deck of a banana boat. I named her the *Tropical Tramp*. The hacks at the agency, some of whom went on to become big names in Fleet Street, couldn't believe it. And frankly, neither could I.

But this was to turn into an adventure from hell. The *Tropical Tramp* was a jinxed vessel. Whatever could go wrong did go wrong. Whatever could not possibly go wrong, found a way. It provided me with a living nightmare that finally ended in a dramatic midnight sea rescue off the island of St Vincent. We were in dire peril of sinking – but in the end the boat refused me even that small courtesy, and became the subject of a salvage claim. A wealthy islander offered a modest sum for her that I snatched right out of his hand.

I used some of the money to explore other islands, including the British Virgins. Back then, in 1968/69. they were absolutely that. Virgin. I hired a small skiff powered with a 25hp outboard and went diving over the wreck of the *Rhone*, a mailboat that had gone down a century or more ago. On the way back to Tortola, the main island, the outboard shook loose from its mounting and vanished 400 feet down into the deep. I had no paddle or radio. And the current was taking me back out to sea at an alarming rate.

I am not an unlucky man. Quite the opposite in fact. But I'd not been especially fortunate these past few months. This was my second sea disaster in two weeks – and what happened next, I'll tell you, fitted shape and pattern exactly.

It was late afternoon, a Saturday as I recall, and unless I did something pretty damn quick, I'd be spending the weekend in an open boat drifting across an empty ocean towards Venezuela. Tortola lay seven miles to the north. Other islands in the BVI group were in sight, but out of reach. The nearest land was a hostile, steep, and uninhabited island with the forbidding name of Dead Man's Chest. Legend has it that here was the place where marooned pirates were dumped to serve out their punishments, hence the sea chanty:

Fifteen men on a Dead Man's Chest
Yo ho ho, and a bottle of rum
Drink and the Devil have done with the rest
Yo ho ho, and a bottle of rum

I suddenly realised that were I to lash a diving fin to the boathook, I could create some kind of makeshift paddle. And if I were to paddle like a lunatic on the starboard side only, I could utilise the southwesterly current to get myself onto the dry land of this spooky little island before nightfall. But I'd have to be quick. The sun goes down in the Caribbean like a fiery boulder hanging on some imaginary parachute.

Finally the dory crunched up onto a needle sharp reef on the eastern edge of Dead Man's Chest. I scrambled to the other side, gashing myself in the process, and swam ashore half an hour before darkness. I peeled off the branches from a dead tree, spreading them across two boulders set one metre apart, to form some sort of shelter. It was going to be a long, lonely night – much, much lonlier than this long road to Rockhampton. In a pale moonlight, interspersed with sweeping clouds and occasional downpours, the outline of the sheer grey-slate cliffs of Dead Man's Chest was eerie indeed. The howl of the wind coming off a deserted sea was like an endless wail from the ghosts of pirates past.

It was an abject, sleepless night. The next morning I stared out across my harsh surrounds. To the east was the sharp reef, only no sign of the dory. It had broken free sometime during the night and drifted away. To the north, far across the Francis Drake Channel was Tortola. To the west, another uninhabited island called Peter Island – now an exclusive resort and very much inhabited. In the first shafts of sunlight, I spotted the tall mast of a yacht over there, swaying at anchor in a sheltered bay.

It was two miles away, but I decided to swim for it anyway. About an hour later I was treading water by the side of the yacht, on bareboat charter to a couple of New Jersey doctors and their wives. At first they were wary. My blabbering story of a night marooned over on Dead Man's Chest had made them jumpy. Things like this only happen in movies and novels. But it had happened, and it had happened to me. They finally allowed me on board, where I radioed in for a rescue boat.

A couple of weeks later, back in London, and planning a new boat and another crack at the Caribbean, I attended a house party. A guy in a leg-cast and crutches was holding court to a spellbound audience, giving graphic details of his recent skiing accident in the Austrian Alps. I figured I had a better story, but inside the warm confines of a civilised gathering, where such things only happen in movies and novels, I doubted anyone would actually believe me. I was by then having some trouble believing it myself.

I tell this story because it is all part of a pattern that has weaved in and out of my life ever since. I'll go into a bit more detail during this hot, hard slog down to Rocky. It's a good way to take my mind off the pedalling.

I ride 120km today, and pull in for the night at an off-road settlement called St Lawrence. There is a small hotel, the Sportsman's Arms, and the few people in the bar are curious. All think I need my head examined.

What my head needs right now is sleep, glorious sleep.

Dead Man's Chest

Heritage Hotel, Rockhampton

NINE
Along the Alley of Menace

I wake to another day in paradise. This remote little township is on an inlet that had once been a small paddlesteamer port. Early sunrays dance off the rippling water. I slip into my usual attire of teeshirt, shorts, and trainers, eat a light breakfast, and am ready to hit the road again. There's 90km to cover today that'll take me to somewhere called Marlborough. The map says it is about the same size as this place. Rocky is going to seem overwhelming.

I pedal back along a minor road to the Bruce Highway, where the scenery is just the same as yesterday. The road has a few undulations here and there but is mainly flat, with a shimmering horizon forever in the distance. Trees are set well back from both sides of the road. Shade is at a premium.

So far, I've not had a puncture or any mechanical setback. The Trek 450 – which now I affectionately call Oggy Boy, after the Oggy Oggy Cornish Pasty Company, my sponsors – has been my absolute rock. The only sound I hear right now is of two purring tyres uncomplainingly eating up the distance. I mentioned before that Oggy Boy and me are in this thing together – something I come to understand only too well along a stretch of road like this. The unlucky Japanese cyclist returns to mind, and I wonder if anyone would stop were I to have a breakdown. To have gone mad or died on the roadside, a good number of drivers must have ignored him and sped on by. This is the sort of territory where you could be vulture's prey by sundown.

You probably don't think this way inside an air-conditioned car with cruise-control set and the radio on. But you do think this way on a bicycle. Best to put it from mind. Best to go back to where I left off yesterday, trying to work out what had led me to even think about doing this seemingly-crazy thing in the first place.

Backtrack to the summer of 1969, when I was somehow determined to return to the Caribbean with another boat. But there was a slight hitch. I had fallen in love.

It was an unlikely union. Bridget was three years older than me, working at an investment bank in the Square Mile. At that time, rather than re-enter journalism I took a casual job with a very strange outfit called *Problem?* Bridget shared a roomy flat in Kensington with the secretary of a junior minister in Harold Wilson's government. I shared a dingy bedsit with a colleague from work.

By day we pursued our very different occupations; hers involving millions, mine involving some bizarre stuff. *Problem?* was a 24-hour subscription service whose members could call upon it to solve whatever difficulty they had at the time. Mostly it was dog-walking or cleaning up after a heavy party. But sometimes it got a bit wacky. A washed-up racing driver was among the employees, who's nightly task it was to 'babysit' the wife of a wealthy industrialist whenever he was away on business. She didn't like being alone and was afraid of the dark. Our racing ace paid her liberal attention, and vice-versa.

My previous benefactor from the *Tropical Tramp* had decided to emigrate. He harboured no ill-will over events in the Caribbean and had the grace to wish me luck with a second stab at it. While working for *Problem?* I found a chap in the Channel Isles willing to back a new charterboat venture. This time we'd be heading for the (then) little known Cayman Islands, a British Crown Colony.

The following story almost defies belief. It wouldn't happen today.

I had made several fruitless attempts to achieve prior permission to operate in Grand Cayman, via the Foreign Office and the Caymanian government. Cables and letters went unanswered, as did a good number of telephone calls to the islands. I think someone did pick up the phone once, but the line went into a series of deafening crackles before fading out altogether. In the end, I simply chanced it by putting my brand new 23ft sportfishing cruiser onto the deck of a Fyffe's banana boat, then boarded the ship myself as a passenger, Caribbean bound once more.

Bridget would follow as soon as I'd found a place to live and settled in.

The Chief of Police on Grand Cayman (then an island of only 8000, now more like 38,000) was an Englishman from Croydon known as Captain Pocock. He also doubled as head of immigration. This guy was straight out of a Graham Greene novel, and for some reason became incensed, really livid, that I'd had the temerity to turn up on his patch without prior warning. I tried to explain, but he wasn't listening.

Anyway, I was now on his island and so was my boat. So what was the khaki-clad cop going to do about that?

"Allow you a tourist visa only" he snapped. "You can use your boat, but you'd better not try and charter it out. Not until we get this bloody mess sorted. You should have gone by the book. I've got rules and regulations to observe and as far as I can see, you represent one almighty violation of them all". Not the slightest hint of humour crossed his brow.

I had no intention of failure this time around. Where there's a will, there is a way. Bridget duly arrived and moved in – which only served to exacerbate the situation with Captain Pocock. One evening at the bar of the Seaview Hotel – a rundown colonial bar frequented by expatriates and broken down drunks – the captain stormed in, swagger stick underneath an armpit, and ordered me to report at his office the following morning.

This, I thought, does not sound good. Not good at all. Particularly since Bridget had been snapped up by an offshore bank and had already started work. The bank had real clout with the island government and Pocock could not refuse her a work permit. Next day, I kept my appointment with fate.

His office had louvred window slats. A cannabis plant stood on a sill. Overhead, the ceiling fan clanked and groaned. Outside, it was grey, damp and steamy. The captain barely looked up as I entered. He simply waved to a chair opposite his desk and went on reading some report or other. Finally he turned to me, stretched, and put his hands behind his head, revealing dark patches of sweat on khaki-covered armpits.

"You're a bloody nuisance, you know that?"

"So it would seem. I'm sorry".

"This woman you're shacked up with... *whatsername*? Is it serious?"

I assured him it was. He seemed disappointed.

"I see. Well, there's been complaints from some influential locals".

I was baffled and told him so. We were not a problem to anyone.

"No, you don't get it. You're *S-h-a-c-k-i-n-g U-p*". He said that as if he'd just chewed on a slice of raw lemon spiced with pungent garlic. "It's causing upset. This is a religious island. Couples don't move in together until they're married".

He let that hang in the air. I said nothing, wary of where this was going.

"I'll do a deal with you" he said, now leaning forward on his desk. "*If you marry whatsername, I'll issue a provisional six-month work permit for the boat business*".

Every word of this true. I know of no-one who has ever been given such an option by a police officer or anyone else. The guy was bribing me in return for my agreement to a type of shotgun wedding in order to appease a few prudes. There was of course a slight difficulty. I had never approached the subject of marriage with Bridget, nor her with me.

Pragmatism seemed my best move. "I'll see what I can do. I'll have to ask Bridget, naturally".

"Ah, yes, that's her name. I remember now".

I got up to leave. "What happens if she turns me down?"

For the first time, a small grin twitched at the sides of his mouth. "Then you'll have to live apart. I'm told that her bank takes a dim view of the present situation. Which will bring the whole matter of you being on this island back full-circle". The grin grew by perhaps one millimetre. "Doesn't look too bright; not from where I'm sitting".

I took Bridget to the Seaview Hotel that evening and told her what had happened. She was – still is – a very phlegmatic woman, and after a drink or two asked if I thought we'd make it together. I was 24 years old and useless at this sort of commitment. She was 27 and mindful of the body clock. She agreed to give it a go.

As if in some kind of omen, an American tourist came over to our table asking to charter the boat for a few days. My response left him bewildered. "That depends on how quickly I can get married".

I consulted a lawyer, some Canadian, who said that first of all I'd have to put an advertisement in the local weekly rag, *The Caymanian*. "You know the thing: *has anyone got any objections to Sid Snodgrass marrying Mary Poppins*? The law requires a week's notice".

But the latest edition had gone to press that same day, which meant a further delay at the beginning of a hopefully-lucrative tourist season. The Canadian grinned and said there was another way. He pointed out of his window towards a rough patch of grassland, the main square of the Cayman capital.

"See that tree in the middle? It's used as a public notice board for *Wanted, Dead or Alive* posters. We can tack the notice on that – which means you'll be eligible to marry in a week".

The notice was duly nailed into the bark and the ceremony arranged with the registrar of births, deaths, and marriages. It would take place in the living room of his house on a Saturday afternoon. During the short ritual attended by two witnesses, the registrar's teenage daughter entered the room; she yawned, flopped down onto the settee, stretched out, watched the proceedings with her head resting on a hand, bored stiff. The girl somehow added an aptness to matters at hand. If, at some time in the past, I had ever given some future wedding day any thought at all, this would not have been my vision of it. And I can say with absolute certainty that it was not how my new wife had envisaged what should have been her biggest day. It was over with in ten minutes, no parents, party, or guests. We emerged from the registrar's house into a late, hot afternoon and climbed into my dusty jeep. The mosquitoes were out and biting.

That evening, while having dinner at the *Lobster Pot* restaurant, Captain Pocock came in for a drink. He spotted us, hesitated, thought about walking out again, then plonked himself down at the bar anyway. A few minutes later, a chilled bottle of champagne arrived at our table, and I knew I'd be getting my work permit. For the captain, this wedding had been some kind of triumph, his authority restored.

But for us, the Cayman Islands only lasted a year or so, for all kinds of reasons: not the least of them was the erosion of shine from claustrophobic island living. Yet the marriage lasted 15 years, with two great kids along the line.

Another truth. *It matters not if you say I Do or I Don't. Relationships will run their natural course irrespective of wedding vows. When it's time to move on, the wise will move on. This is a fundamental law of nature.*

I truly believe this to be so.

More on the past somewhere further along the ride. Suffice for now to say that some sort of life-pattern is emerging that doesn't make it altogether surprising to find myself in the here-and-now, pedalling a psychological gauntlet down this long alleyway of potential menace. But I'm moving along nicely towards Marlborough. I am feeling fitter and stronger than for a long while and I know this to be at least one reason for making this semi-athletic odyssey. Even at my time of life, sunshine and the outdoors fill me with a huge sense of youthful wellbeing. And I'm still getting a kick from riding into new places, meeting new faces, eating and sleeping in changing surrounds – and then riding away again towards future horizons.

But that doesn't necessarily mean it's a *sane* thing to do. The list of *what ifs* seems to be growing each time I think about it, especially out on this piece of road. What if I blow a tyre, break a leg, run out of water, ride over a live snake, get hit by a truck or a car, suffer a heart attack – or just get plain unlucky and encounter a carload of bored, anti-cyclist yobbos wanting to play games?

All are possibilities on this tedious highway, where long distance truckies and unwary tourists routinely fall asleep at the wheel. But what if I heed all the *what ifs*? Well I'll tell you what – I wouldn't be here now. I'd be sitting on my backside somewhere in England wondering if there's anything worth catching on TV. Now *that* is negative thinking, which as far as I can tell, never did any good to anyone. Positive thinking on the other hand.....it seems to me that positive thoughts, followed through with positive deeds, will carry us successfully down whichever road we choose in life.

And the plain fact is that I'm enjoying myself. I am alone and I'm happy in a simple freewheeling kind of way. It won't last of course. Happiness comes in small pockets, at certain times and places, when all the right influences and planetary aspects fall into unison. For the moment however, it is there. So I grab it and hold onto it gladly, until the next time around.

With a couple of mouthfuls of water remaining and bananas all eaten, I eventually turn off to the Marlborough Motel & Caravan Park, a short way from the main highway. This empty road is now more than two-thirds done. The billboards are starting to appear again, advertising the Tropic of Capricorn. Rockhampton is slap-bang on its trajectory, and all being well I should wheel in there late afternoon tomorrow.

Which I do, and feeling pretty damn pleased with myself too. And with Oggy Boy. We have successfully negotiated those 300kms of debris, dead animals, angry trucks, a good number of lunatic drivers, and a range of psychological mountains which combine to make up a cyclist's Alley of Menace. As far as long empty distances go, the worst is behind me now.

Rocky is divided into north and south by the rolling Fitzroy River. It is quite some way inland, but has the feel of a port. My accommodation is on the south side of the river, but there's been a mix up and the Regency Motel does not expect me until tomorrow. So I check into a small place called the CityWalk Motor Inn in defiance of a big sign at the entrance saying *Absolutely No Cycling*.

"Nah, you're okay, mate" says the lean, grey-bearded proprietor. "That sign is an *attempt* to stop all these bloody kids riding through our forecourt. Christ, they're on everything these days. Scooters, rollerblades, BMXs, skateboards. The other evening I caught *four* of the little bastards loaded onto one bloody bike; like a flaming circus act they were, wheeling rings around one of the guests. Chased 'em off, I did. One litle shit stuck a finger up in the air at me".

He is re-living that moment, and it would be fair to call him angst-ridden. He is of the old school, rueing the demise of discipline. "No bloody respect, not any more. Bloody kids. But nah, you're okay, mate. The bike's welcome too".

The following morning I ride around the city streets, which are squared off into the same tidy pattern of most other towns I've passed through. Down by the river is a magnificent three-storey colonial building called the Heritage Hotel. It is built of yellow brick, and the upper storeys are surrounded by verandas and white iron railings. It is the product of the 1858 goldrush, which brought prosperity to the region. As has the cattle industry. Rocky is Queensland's hub for the transportation of beef.

I park up by the river and bask for a while in the morning sun. A garbage collector with a pronged stick and a bag ambles by, staring at the bike laden with my gear in readiness to switch motels. He asks where I've come from, where I'm heading. His response is pretty much bog standard.

"Fuck me" he breathes. He is a youngish man, 35 or so, and only too willing to chat. Soon I have his entire life history, which basically amounts to Rockhampton from cradle to now; a marriage somewhere inbetween and apparently intact. And a yearning desire by both he and his wife to "Get out of Rocky for good and always".

"Why so?" I enquire.

He ponders for a moment. "There's a joke about this place that says it all. *What is the difference between Rockhampton and the Titanic?*"

I shrug the obligatory 'dunno'. "*The Titanic was moving forward when it sank*". We both chuckle, and then he adds, "Whenever something good looks like it's going to happen to the city, it fizzles out. It always fizzles out. Never moves forward. Rocky's a city going nowhere".

A part-aborigine in his 40s is chatting up a young girl on a riverside bench. He looks around, then comes up and asks for a pencil. "Need to get her details" he grunts. Both of them look as it they've been up since yesterday. I hand him a plastic pen and he goes away.

The garbage man stares at his back through narrowed eyes. "They're a problem, those guys" he says with complete indifference for political correctness. "Glue sniffing through empty Coke bottles. Stealing. Yeah, they're a problem in a high-crime town".

"And the whites?"

"Oh sure" he comes back, nodding vigorously. "Every Thursday night right through the weekend. *Hooners*".

"*What?*"

"Hooners. Ain't you heard of hooning yet? What these kids do is to meet outside the town hall after dark in their hotted-up cars, then turn the streets into a racetrack. They're a sort of motorised version of Pommie football hooligans. Hooners versus the Police. They outnumber the cops, and it can get chaotic; but they're pretty well organised. The further south you ride, the more you're gonna see it. Hooning's a nationwide youth culture".

I make a mental note of this. His mention of football hooligans reminds me that I've yet to learn anything about Aussie Rules, a game unique to Australia, and which might make a radio piece. My garbage man is utterly dismissive. "This is Rugby League territory, mate. Aussie Rules is a down-south thing, Victoria mainly. A game for wimps and pooftahs. We call it *Aerial Ping Pong* up here".

It has become clear that Oz has its own version of the north-south divide, based on tribal rather than class difference. Victoria has chilly winters; more and more Victorians are moving north and Queenslanders resent the influx, making them the butt of derogatory jokes. They refer to them as Mexicans or Wetbacks because they come from south of the border.

"*The best thing about New South Wales is that it comes between Victoria and Queensland*" quips the man.

This chap needs to get out of Rockhampton, he's right about that. Whether he will or not is another matter. Tomorrow he'll be back at this very spot, picking up the litter – and I'll be moving on. It is as if he reads this thought in 3-D, and for the very briefest of instants his gaze turns intensely hostile.

Just as quickly, he regains an amiable composure. As if in recognition of that rapid flash, he says "You know, 90 percent of Australians would love to do what you're doing, and I'm one of them. It's the freedom, the fucking freedom of it all".

Slowly and deliberately I reply, "*Then do it. What's there to stop you?*"

The Turkey Beach shark net

TEN
Turkey Beach

It is broadcast day, the usual mid-afternoon or wee-hour slot, whichever way you you care to see it. I use these non-cycling days to file copy for the *Western Morning News* and to update the *PedallingPom* website, which is getting an extraordinary number of hits – not only from the UK and Oz, but unrelated places like the USA, Argentina, Brazil, The Seychelles, Estonia, Croatia, China, and Japan. Seems that we really do live in an electronic global village because these strange visits can only be coming from a second-tier audience of the radio station. People the world over are tuning into the BBC on the internet.

Today, among other items, they'll be hearing about *hooning*: a ridiculous name for an even sillier acitvity, but I guess this is the sort of thing youngsters do in a town that's going nowhere. Anyhow, to get a second opinion on this, I can think of nobody better than last night's disconsolate bearded motelier who assures me eagerly that every weekend he listens to the noise of screeching tyres around the city, and to police sirens wailing from all directions – the sure sound of the city's youth expressing violence and rebellion with hotted-up engines. And of bored cops delivering power and authority via flashing lights and snappy handcuffs. I daresay that both sides enjoy themselves in equal measure. The motelier has his own view. "*It's the kids*" he snarls. "*No bloody respect*".

My thoughts fly back to the bush pilots, the Park & Wildlife Rangers, and the cattlemen up there in the wild north. Same country, just a different planet.

Gladstone, 100km south, is next stop. The following morning I ride out of town and into a ferocious headwind. All the same, I make good progress, which probably has something to do with a bustling new confidence after the Alley of Menace. Traffic is heavy, but the road is even with plenty of shoulder width. The sun is out and despite the bluster, it's a hot, dry day.

Towards late afternoon, not far from Gladstone, I stop at a small roadside inn gasping for fruit juice. There is a middle-aged couple sitting at the bar, nursing cold beers. He is short, stocky, mid-50s, dark haired. She is almost strawberry blond, early 40s, amiable and chatty.

"We passed you a long way back" she says. "You've made good time".

She is either being polite, or has been sitting here a good while. What a car makes in an hour, a cyclist like me will do in a day. I smile back and tell her that *Rapido* is my second name. We get talking. Her male companion is affable, though quiet. The woman suddenly turns to him and says, "Ronnie, I want us to take this man home to Turkey Beach".

Ronnie looks at her, then at me, pulls a face, raises his arms and hands in a full-on shrug, and says "Sure. babe. Fine with me".

She turns back to me. "You wanna come home with us? To Turkey Beach, population all of 50 people?"

There is something in my psyche that responds to this. I am not at all sure what is going on here, but after Menace Alley and a fairly clinical time in Rockhampton, I'm ready to try my luck at spotting the ball. I go to the bike and bring back the map. Ronnie puts a podgy finger onto Turkey Beach. It's the other side of Gladstone, and then a further 22km up a rough dirt road to the end of the line: one way in, the same way out. Even in a part of Oz where foreign tourists have been oddly disappearing of late, something tells me to accept.

Half an hour ago I was wheeling along this highway under my own power. Now I'm speeding along in the cab of a utility truck with two complete strangers taking me to their remote beach community. Oggy Boy is in the back, glad of the rest. I too am glad of this diversion into the oddballs ways of humanity.

I told you this is no organized tour.

The lady's name is Sharyn. I am squashed in beside her. Her scent and her bare legs touching my own push my blood temperature up by a degree or two. Ronnie seems deep in thought at the wheel. At some point beyond Gladstone, he swings onto a dirt road and pulls up abruptly. He gets out and messes around with a box lying in the back. Sharyn nudges me, grinning. "It's our little ritual, this. We do it every time we turn onto the track".

Ronnie returns to the cab with three cold beers. "No fucking cops on this piece'a road, matey" he laughs. "Her an' me just love a drink while we drive, don't we babe?" And why not, I ask myself? There's nobody to endanger but ourselves – not along 22km of slow-going dirt road leading to a mere 50 people who choose to live in a faraway cul-de-sac.

I love this kind of offbeat escapade.

The houses of Turkey Beach are in no particular order. They are simply *there*, erected wherever the occupiers have chosen to put them. Ronnie's house is typically tropical; living space upstairs, with a ground-level guest room beside a carport and boat shelter. This is going to be home for the next couple of days, and it very quickly becomes so.

There is a brief emergency though. Ronnie opens my door and steps inside; then very quickly steps out again, breathing hard and shutting the door behind him as if there's a corpse inside that he's forgotten to bury. "Bloody hell" he snaps, "A taipan's been living here".

The taipan is Queensland's deadliest snake. It is small, thin, fast, and lethal. Lying on the floor is a freshly-shed skin of the reptile, maybe a metre in length. An extremely cautious and very thorough search, using poles and shovels to remove bedclothes and furniture, reveals nothing. Thankfully it has slithered off elsewhere, through the air-conditioning duct they think.

Let me tell you about my two unusual hosts. Ronnie Jensen is a

Vietnam Veteran living on an Army payoff. He has been this for *all* his adult life. Hollywood being Hollywood, you'd never know that the Aussies & Kiwis had fought in Vietnam alongside U.S. troops – and that some of their men had also suffered the psychological ailments normally ascribed to jungle crazed GIs or baffled conscripts from Kentucky and Alabama.

Ronnie was drafted into the Australian Army as a kid, and dispatched to a place called Vung Tau, a peninsular port not too far from Saigon (I may touch on Vung Tau later in the journey – I spent time there myself, though it was nothing to do with the war). He saw action, and along with his mates, went through as much hell as any of the American GIs. The end-result of Ronnie's war was a psychiatric unit and a pensioned discharge from the force. He's had three marriages, three divorces, and has seven kids strewn around the country.

Every now and then, Ronnie returns to the psychiatric ward to spend a little time in padded rooms, bouncing off the walls. But he is easy to get to know, and once trust is established he opens up a soul that is twice the size of a barn door.

Sharyn, his lady, has a smile that would melt the North Pole and, when riled, a temper that would freeze it back again. She too has been thrice married, and thinking about braving it one more time with our Vietnam Vet. They make an apt partnership, even if it does exist on high-voltage electric charge. If they haven't got a problem, they'll create one. It takes me all of two sizzling hours at Turkey Brach to work this out, and I see why the taipan has vanished. It feared for its life.

Ronnie escaped to this tiny bayside settlement 13 years ago. He is of quite some misanthropic persuasion. Any more than about five people around him, the panic attacks and the claustrophobia crank into gear. The Vietnam War, without any doubt, has had a profound effect on the man. Nightmares still recur nearly 30 years on. He jumps and twitches in his sleep, screams, lashes out, sweats.

Yes, I'll certainly touch on Vietnam later. It affected me too, though not in the same way; my experience was long, long after the war was over.

Sharyn found Turkey Beach via her last husband. He is elsewhere these days, but she stays on because of Ronnie. They met one evening down at the shark net, which maybe set the precedent for the subsequent toothmarks of this volatile relationship. "I looked at him" she glows, looking at him now. "*It was like, bang, this is it!*".

Ronnie recalls it with a happy grin. "Yeah, same here, babe". Before dark they take me down to the beach to see the shark net, a community project allowing the small population to take a dip in safety. It is a rectangular affair, nine posts on each side embedded into the sand which suport the surrounding meshwire. The net stretches from dry land to about 30 metres out into the water.

"Tigers and bullsharks" Ronnie grunts. "They cruise in real close. Take a fucking arm off in one bite".

It is not by any means a paradise beach; it's more the lapping shore of a broad, mangrove-strewn inlet, mud crabs a speciality. In the twilight though, it is quiet and serene. On the way back we call in at the General Store just before it shuts to buy a few necessities. The *Turkey Beach Kiosk* is the 'city centre', the hub of activity and gossip, run by a Kiwi and his Oz wife. It doubles as the editorial office for a spasmodic local 'newspaper' called the *Turkey Gobbler.*

I peruse the most recent issue, dated Christmas 2002. Six pages of amateur DeskTop Publishing containing remarkably varied items. There's a warning against the menace of dioxins; advice on dealing with venomous snake bites; an interesting tearjerker on bereavement; a be-on-you-guard story over a recent housebreaking; an intelligent Christmas Quiz; and an array of readers' letters – including this one from somebody disillusioned with the Christian aspects of Yuletide.

He writes: *Where is there a God? Where is the God for those millions of little black African children dying of starvation, lying in gutters, covered in flies, and just strong enough to shallow-breathe? I can't see Him. So I choose to stay an atheist; listen to dirty jokes, swear, and gaze at the best things in creation which are beautiful women. I choose to watch porno flicks, drink what and when I want, and think what I like without a guilty conscience. Because it won't be any hotter in Hell than it will be at my own cremation, whenever that comes.*

I chuckle and show the letter to Ronnie who says, "Ah, that's Ian Simmons. He's always going on about something. A Pom actually. Came here years ago. Active on the environmental front". He rubs his chin stubble as if in profound thought. "Come to think of it, he's the bloke who put a stop to a proposed rocket base just up the coast".

This might just make a radio piece and I want to meet him. "No worries there" adds Ronnie. "He's a couple of houses down". In Turkey Beach, I don't suppose he could be many more than that.

Well, not now; but maybe someday soon. This tiny place is interesting a growing number of outsiders: second homes, things like that. It is an empty second home that's the subject of the *Gobbler's* house-breaking piece. Such matters are a contentious bone with locally-born residents and those who settled here to get away from the world; people like Ronnie Jensen. It is only recently that full-time residents have taken to locking their doors.

Later in the evening, as we're having a drink and telling a few lies, in walks a big bearded man who goes by the name of Whiskers Ray. He's early 50s, greying fast, overweight, and on the dole. Ray is a well-regarded firefighting volunteer and an adept mud crab catcher, but other than for the occasional outbreak of flames and a seasonal trawl through the mud, there is no work in Turkey Beach – a situation that seems to suit him fine. He sits down at the kitchen table and brings out some equipment. Pretty soon there's an eruption of bubbling noises as he brings his 'bong' up to a full head of steam. For a while, Ray disappears into a huge grey-white cloud of smoke. When he emerges from the haze, his eyes are bulging and rolling like lottery balls, which miraculously settle into a look of utter serenity.

I make a slip of the tongue. "Interesting piece of kit, your boong".

Everyone splutters. "Yer mean *bong*, doncha?" Ray wheezes. "A boong is a bloody abo, for fucksake. A blackfeller!".

So it is; I now recall the derogatory term. Ronnie says, "You know them bull-bars on the front of my ute? We call 'em *boong bars*, haw, haw".

"Ah" I reply merrily. "All that's missing from this town is the crooked mayor and the drunken sheriff".

"Might be better than the cop we've got" opines Whiskers Ray. "Too bloody straight if you ask me. Goes by the book". Apparently Sergeant Owen Harms is based at Gladstone but comes prowling around town every now and then, always unannounced. Largely though, he leaves the place to police itself. Or did. That too is a'changing.

Ray says with disgust, "I passed a whole bunch of campers setting up their bloody tents just down the road. Tomorrow the beach will be crawling with new faces, cruising up and down, peering into houses, asking about the price of land. More second-bloody-homes, more people. I'm telling you, Turkey Beach has had it; *fucking rooted* is what I say".

This is a long weekend. The trippers have discovered Ray's bolt-hole from the world. Serenity suddenly leaves his face, and the bong toils loudly as he takes solace deep inside another bubbling smoke-screen.

Ronnie's got a 27-foot dayboat ouside with a 75hp outboard on the back. If the beach is going the way that Whiskers Ray dreads, there's going to be a fantastic opportunity for a charterboat operator. When Ray leaves, I tell them about my time in the Cayman Islands and watch Ronnie's eyes light up as he translates these words into possibilities here at Turkey Beach. I've been told that Ronnie is an excellent fisherman.

The man not only has a boat, but an emerging area to operate in, like I'd once had in the Caribbean. In today's world, this is priceless. But I hadn't really known what I'd got back then. If I had my time all over again.....

.....I would not change a single thing.

For Ronnie and Sharyn, this is their spot, their place in the world from where they seek answers to their own turmoil. Seems to me that his boat, and a front garden called the big blue sea that teems with fish, will provide them with all they'll ever need. And I say as much.

"There is a slight problem" says Sharyn, sipping white wine. "We've got a committee that calls itself the Turkey Beach Progress Association. Ray is one of its members, if that tells you anything?"

I think so. "You mean it's an anti-progress association?"

"Yeah, my bloody oath" Ronnie cuts in. "It's the non-members who want to see progress. This community is divided between those who want to see measured progress and those who don't want any progress at all".

"The association is doomed to fail" says I, meaning it. "Were I to come back in a few years time, I doubt I'd recognise the place. There'll be hotels, car parks, beach bars, you name it".

My arrogance is breathtaking. I've been here no more than a few hours and already I'm telling them about a place they know like the backs of their hands. Then again, how well do we know the backs of our hands? What I can see is that Turkey Beach has all the ingredients of a future tourist centre simply because it is where it is, and has got what it's got. Not so long ago, Port Douglas would have been like this.

The next day Whiskers Ray is up and storming. The 21st Century is coming down on him hard. Cops are down the road, he snaps, stopping all vehicles because there's been another robbery during the night. This time the thieves stole someone's boat; simply hitched it up to a 4x4 and drove away. The place has had it, rooted, he says again, and talks of setting up a Neighbourhood Watch.

Later, Ronnie drives me into Gladstone to pick up a money transfer. The local Western Union outlet is in a busy but soulless shopping mall. It could be downtown Denver or mid-city Manchester, swarming with humanity. I notice a few drops of sweat run down Ronnie's face. He is in the first stages of a panic attack and wisely hurries back outside to the ute.

"Christ, all those bloody people" he says on the way back. "Can't handle it, matey. I really can't take it".

Ronnie stops on the dirt track and fishes out a couple of beers. The robbery squad has long gone, but the campers have grown in number. Before long there are vehicles behind us and in front of us. "Jesus" Ronnie mutters, "Can't ever remember this much traffic before".

The secret is out. Turkey Beach is on the map.

At home, Sharyn puts on a silent black & white video taken off an old Cine-8 film. It shows the beach as it had been just after World War II, a collection of wooden huts and clapboard houses, outbuildings, old boats, grandmas in rocking chairs doing needlework, weather-beaten men out catching fish. It is another age, a long while ago; almost another place entirely.

Whiskers Ray comes by again and walks me over to Ian Simmons' house. Ian is a beefy man, 60 or thereabouts, a retired engineer who emigrated from Kent in the 1960s. He is totally Ozzified, and loves his adopted home. England is little more than a distant memory.

He is, I soon discover, head honcho of the Turkey Beach Progress Association.

He has a large brick house with sweeping views of the bay. There is a sudden thump on the big panoramic window. A small bird has flown straight into the glass, snapping its own neck. Ian gets up and goes outside.

"A dove" he says, unzipping his flies, pulling his appendage out, and positioning the dead bird in front of it. "*Just off for a quick root. Back in a minute*". Okay, pretty tasteless, but not without humour.

Ian Simons is an opinionated man with strong views on the environment and most other matters. His successful battle against the siting of a rocket base nearby is an interesting story, though not *Up All Night* material. Ian, who has made a decent pile for himself and his missus over the years, tends to hold court rather than conversation. He is the nearest thing Turkey Beach has to an unofficial self-elected mayor. Ray is sitting next to him and I can't help but think that if circumstances allowed, these two would make an ideal combination as bombastic small town mayor and his bong-toting sheriff.

Tomorrow I'll be moving on once more. In a very short space of time I've come to fall for this strange little place and its few people. Ronnie and Sharyn are mostly to do with this. I am so at ease in their company, in their house, and in their chaotic lives.

Ronnie is cooking up the steaks by the time that me and Whiskers Ray return. It is gone dark, time for a drink, and in Ray's case, a bong. He keeps it here at Ronnie's house. His wife isn't happy with the ritual, though I really do not know why. Since time began, mankind has always found a way to get high. If you think that Stone Age cavemen went without something to take the edge off the day, think again.

We've got beer and wine and puffing clouds. We've got the laughter of the night. Tomorrow's farewells are still far from mind.

Walla Station

ELEVEN
Sad Memories

Ronnie does not make primetime viewing this morning. At some stage during the night he's had a booze-fuelled battle with Sharyn. He dabs cigarette papers onto the claw marks running down both sides of his face, mopping up the seepage. I had heard nothing from my downstairs room. As soon as my head hits the pillow I'm gone someplace else anyway.

I hope he's done her no damage.

He hasn't. She emerges from their bedroom, neither eye black, both sparkling. It's just they way they are, these two. She has dished out his punishment, and he's taken it like a stoic Vietnam Rambo.

Ronnie seems troubled all the same. He's biting his lower lip. "Hate to see you go" he mutters, meaning it.

"Ronnie, I hate to leave, but.....".

"Yeah, I know. We'll take you to the highway". Which they do. Goodbyes are not easy. You make wonderful passing acquaintances on a trip like this, though few actual friendships. Ronnie and Sharyn are an exception to the rule.

A couple of lazy days out of the saddle takes its toll, but today, I have only got to make 30km to the next stop, Miriam Vale. Tomorrow though, will be a hard push – 80km to the town of Gin Gin, plus a further 18km beyond that to my next story.

I make Miriam Vale in leisurely fashion and check into a small motel. The main street runs parallel to the highway. It's got a Post Office, hotel, general store, cafe, and not much else. In fact, they only take up one side of the street. The other side is rough parkland. Later, I eat dinner in the hotel and watch a chap lose a pile on the poker machines. The player is being harrangued by a very young girl with wavy dark hair who cannot be older than four or five. The flashing lights and jangling bells have got her into a great state of excitement, and she barks instructions at him from high up on a stool behind. When he's lost all his money and loudly expresses his disgust, the girl scrambles off her stool and quickly abandons him. This one is a fast learner.

She looks towards her parents having dinner with another couple. Too boring for words. Then she spots me, alone at my table. She skip-dances over, her arms flapping like batwings and starts a conversation that babbles with nonsense. She has an electric charisma, and already I feel for the guy that destiny has earmarked for her in years to come. Her parents eye me warily, to the point where I begin to feel really quite uncomfortable. But I cannot blame them. With this one for a daughter, they'd be on a non-stop 24-hour alert.

When morning comes, so do the hills; not big climbs by any means, though strenuous undulations aplenty. The road is quiet and empty, cutting through heavy woodland. For once, there is some shade on offer.

I roll into the small town of Gin Gin towards late afternoon and call in at a pavement cafe for a sandwich. The waitress is a young lass of about 20 and seems eager to talk. She is learning the catering trade, she tells me. Working for peanuts, but no matter. Soon she'll be gone from here, heading for the big smoke and a glittering career as a society chef.

"Sydney, I assume?"

A look of horror fills her face. "Heavens no, Nowhere *that* big. I was thinking of Surfers Paradise or Brizzie".

Brizzie. Brisbane. Still another 400km south of here. This State of Queensland is one gargantuan piece of real estate. It makes Texas seem like a matchbox; England like a postage stamp. I wish her well and reluctantly swing back into the saddle, leaving her to dream of bright lights and culinary glory. I hope she makes it. The cheese sandwich seemed okay.

The last 18km feel more like 18 miles. About 12km outside town I turn off down a bush road that will lead me to my overnight destination. Not a single vehicle interrupts these last few klicks. Finally I arrive at a large, incongruous signpost that says: *WALLA STATION. Bed & Breakfast*. There is, I'm told, a story of some pedigree attached to this unlikely guest house so far out in the wilds, and I'm here to listen to it.

I walk the bike one last kilometre up a stoney dirt track that takes me alongside disused cattle pens and fruit-bearing mango trees, and eventually to the isolated homestead. It is a single-storey building with high ceilings and polished wood floors. In varying states of repair, it has been standing there for almost 100 years.

My hosts are Bentley Briggs and his English girlfriend Natalie Butcher. Bentley is a tall, broad, beefy, dark haired, mid-30s Aussie with the mildest of Down Under accents – the result of living for a few years overseas. Natalie, late 20s, is pure West Sussex English Rose, with a manifest passion for this house, this land, this man, and for their hoofy outdoor life rearing colts and mustangs for future employment on the big cattle stations of the interior.

"Some things never die out" Bentley asserts as we sit out on the broad rear veranda, sipping fruit juice and looking down across a sloping garden that sheers down to a small river below. "Choppers and motorbikes, they're utilised quite a lot for mustering and the like. But the horse is the foundation of the cattle station, and always will be".

They show me to my room – a large neo-classical chamber with a bed that would accompany Henry Vlll and all six wives. And the bathroom is just that – a room with a bath. I think it is the first bath I've encountered all the way down from Port Douglas and I luxuriate in the thought of a deep warm wallow.

"This room was always reserved for the Duke of Gloucester – a long line of them" Bentley states proudly. "And for the Governor-Generals of the day. The irony is that Walla was a working cattle station back then, 20,000 acres, not the small horse stud and guest house it now is". He shakes his head – an action somehow tinged with sadness. "It's a recent development, and some of it pretty personal. I'll tell you later".

We pile into a 4x4 along with an over-eager Collie and drive to a big paddock where about 40 horses are roaming freely. The stock is inspected every other day, so they pay us scant attention as we wander among them. There are two or three new foals stumbling clumsily after their mothers, who seem a little more suspicious.

I have this natural instinct to stroke and pat a neck or two, but am deterred by Bentley. He is in a pair of shorts, heavy boots, and wearing a wide-brimmed hat, as indeed is Natalie: the uniform of station authority that I recognise from a long time ago. I heed his words.

"I understand animal lovers" he says. "But there is one rule about the raising of stock horses – which is that you don't pamper them in any way at all. Their work on the stations is going to be hard, demanding stuff. They are not pets. Affection doesn't figure in the equation".

And suddenly I remember something about the station in Cootamundra. Twelve dogs chained up 24 hours a day, living inside a line of chopped, hollowed-out tree trunks. Every morning and evening they were given some form of nourishment in the form of skimmed milk from the station dairy; but hard, edible food they only got from the twice-weekly ritual of sheep or cattle slaughter. The dogs chomped with gusto at raw guts, cut up and shared out between them. They expected nothing more, got nothing more, yet remained keen and energetic workers at each round-up time.

A poodle parlour it was not.

Before returning to the homestead, they take me on a tour of a tiny graveyard where a couple of family members and a few lifelong loyal station hands are buried. It is overgrown and headstones are in disrepair. There is emotion in Bentley's voice as he leans over each grave, explaining who had been whom. I had not known until now that Walla Station was the boyhood home he had grown up in.

I dive into a deep bath while my hosts get the barbecue going. Later, we sit out in the still night, slapping at the occasional mosquito and gently drinking beer while Bentley delves into a little history.

His great-grandfather had bought the place in 1904, ten years before the start of World War 1. Between and beyond the two wars, the property had passed down to grandfather, then father. As a boy, Bentley had played in the stockyards, helped with the mustering, learned about the land, swung in the mango trees, swam in the river below, and did all the happy things which kids do who are born and raised to the bush. It had been home, a real home, with tight traditions.

Back in the days when England still had clout here, before telephones and long before television, agriculture was the country's primary industry and Britain its prime customer. Wool, mutton, beef, crops and other products from the land found their way to the Old Country on every cargo ship toing and froing across the oceans. Politically-minded members of Australia's tough ranching dynasties had influential contacts with the decision makers and the hoi-polloi of both countries. They ran their properties along the same hierarchical lines as wealthy British landowners, hence the Duke of Gloucester paid a visit to this particular station in 1920, returning time and again – as have his descendants over the years. The Briggs family knew the meaning of prosperity, falling into the nearest category that Australia has to an aristocracy.

Years pass and things happen, not all of them for the good. Primary industry became secondary industry; factories opened and people moved to the cities. Britain joined up with Europe, turning its commercial back on long time allies. Television arrived, the Beatles and Rolling Stones arrived, Japan re-emerged as an economic force, and for a long while the ranchers lost their way.

Piece by piece, Walla Station was sold off to make ends meet. Family pressures resulted in Bentley's father giving way to his brother – who then turned it into a cannabis plantation in search of fast profits and a way out of debt. By the time Bentley's uncle went to jail, the property was down to 300 small-time acres.

Bentley Briggs was working in England at the time. Pacing back and forth in a London flat, agitated, he suddenly decided to return to Walla Station for good.

But by now it belonged to a stranger, nobody in the family. His parents and other relatives were sceptical. The past is the past, they told him. No going back. Bentley didn't see it that way. He would do whatever was necessary to buy his boyhood back.

The homestead was in tatters, the stockyards derelict, the little graveyard neglected; but all of Bentley's powerful memories were fully intact – along with his sheer bloody-mindedness to carry this thing through. It was a brave thing to do. Natalie has been both a rock and a spur in the process.

Tonight there are just the three of us. The homestead has four polished guest rooms, three of them empty. Natalie and Bentley live in another house across the garden, once reserved for senior station personnel. They do not, they thank God, have to live in the original 19th Century homestead – a semi-derelict shack riddled with bullet holes from some dispute during the pioneering days. They would both dearly love to move back into the mansion, but.....

".....Got to make the repayments somehow" Natalie sighs.

We say goodnight around eleven. I lie awake in the huge comfortable bed and think about what it must be like to go back to a childhood home long after the family have moved out and on. I myself have this occasionally recurring dream that I'm back living in my own boyhood home in the West Midlands. My father is always around, though never my mother or two sisters. A few years ago, when the dream had been particularly powerful, I actually *did* go back, arriving unannounced and asking the owner if he'd mind that I take a look around. He was very obliging. Little had changed over all the years, except that everything seemed much smaller than I remembered. I still have the dream from time to time, though I'll not go back again, ever.

Unusually for me, sleep does not come easily. Outside, the silent night is anything but silent. Insects and wildife are out and about. There is running, rustling, scuttling, scattering, slithering, pouncing, and shrieking right outside my window and into the bush beyond. It is the nocturnal sound of stealthy attacks, sudden death, and nature in the raw.

"Carpet snakes" says Bentley the next morning. "This whole area is littered with them". For carpet snakes read pythons. "They're normally harmless to humans. I trod on one the other day. It looked up at me for a few doleful moments to say '*Hey, what did you do that for?*' They come out at night looking for rats and rabbits and likely prey".

Time will tell if Bentley makes something of his venture into the past. I get the feeling that he's unsure about a decision made on emotional motives rather than hard business savvy. The family fortune withered long ago. Now he and Natalie find themselves akin to, say,

Lord & Lady Bumbleton-Tweak on an aristocratic Skid Row, forced through circumstance to open the family home to the public. Bentley is a cultured man of the bush, a horseman, and a traditionalist through and through. The soul-bruising stuff of commerce and marketing is not his strongest point.

There are more memories to cover today – really painful memories for 15 families in various parts of the world. I am due to broadcast this afternoon from the town of Childers 40km away, and I need to get moving.

It takes three hours to pedal the distance, and I head straight to what was once called the Palace Backpackers Hostel. Colourful rows of trees and shrubs line the centre of a sloping main street. Childers is a typical Oz country town: small, clean, pleasant, quiet – and a popular stopover for young travellers who come to earn a few dollars during the fruit-picking seasons. Not at all the sort of place where murder lingers in the air.

In June 2000, Robert Paul Long, a disgruntled Aussie drifter, put a torch to the hostel building – resulting in the untimely, terrible deaths of 15 young backpackers from around the world. The hostel was destroyed inside out, totally gutted. Yet somehow they have managed to restore it as if nothing had ever happened. Well, that's how it looks from the outside – a two-storey brick building, with the upper level guarded by a broad veranda of wood and wrought iron. The ground level is now a tourist information centre, but upstairs, a long empty room with gleaming wood flooring devoid of all furniture, stands as a quiet tribute to those who lost their lives. In the far left corner hangs an oil painting of the 15 victims. They are smiling, happy, attractive, in their early 20s, and together again. A sunny meadow is in the background, as if to say that all is well and Heaven is a really cool place to be.

It was painted by a Sydney artist from photographs sent in by the youngsters' families – and an extremely moving piece of work it is too. I won't say I have tears in my eyes because I don't. But I can feel a lump in the throat.

What is it that make people like Robert Paul Long commit these awful deeds? Why do such people open fire in classrooms, shopping malls, or parking lots? Or set alight to discos and places like this backpackers hostel in peaceful Childers? All I know is that he was a 38 year old loner, a guest at the hostel amid much younger people of differing nationalities. And that he left no fewer than six suicide notes lying around the place, telling everyone that he had contracted lung cancer, had just two months to live, and was going to kill himself anyway.

Trouble was, he killed almost everyone else instead. And the cancer has yet to get him. Breathing still, Robert Paul Long is now serving life in prison.

Rhod Sharpe, the *Up All Night* presenter deals with my Childers piece the way only an old pro like him can. His soft voice softens further, his words are solemn and spoken with exact punctuation and brevity. No listener is left in any doubt as to the tragedy of this insane act.

But life goes on. Where next, he asks? To a tiny trawler port called Tin Can Bay, I reply.

"*What Can Bay?*"

Tin Can Bay. Another end-of-the-line place to which an open prison would compare favourably. For me, this is a memory lane job. In 1963, after leaving the stations down south, I hitched a ride north to spend eight dangerous months working on the prawn boats in that bay of misfits, rogues, and drifters. To a man, they were bail jumpers, ship jumpers, absconding husbands and army deserters; jailbreakers, tax dodgers, tricksters and cardsharps; hardened thieves, failed night-club bouncers and out-of-work debt collectors – all living aboard trawlers based in a settlement that had just the one pub, one bakery, one store, one cop, and one police cell. Oh, and one local lady who was always ready to meet the baser requirements of some 200 rough-and-tumble trawler hands with false names, off-by-heart alibis, and extemely dubious credentials.

It was a period of my life that I'll not forget easily. You'll soon see why.

TWELVE
Don't Come the Raw Prawn with Me, Mate

I spend a night at the Engineers Arms in the city of Maryborough before making for the bay. It is a funny place, this city of the walking wounded. Every other person seems to walk with a limp.

There is a radio piece I'm looking into here. A local man is building a riverside home, but the authorities suspect him of trying to avoid property taxes by passing it off as a boat. It is, they say, abundantly clear that this is a house, on dry land, with foundations, and without planning permission. The owner argues that he doesn't need planning permission to build a boat – and if you don't believe it's a boat, then nip around the back and you'll see a pair of outboard motors attached to the structure.

He gets 10/10 for originality.

I feel a little weird seeing the signs for Tin Can Bay along a newly-paved road, and weirder still when I wheel towards town. What's this coming up on my left? *A country club and golf course?* My own memory is of a few clapboard houses and a couple of hundred disconsolate trawler ruffians. I pass a small, tidy business precinct that accommodates doctors, lawyers, real estate agents, a newsagent, a hairdresser and a supermarket. Across the road, a fish & chip shop nestles between yet another estate agent and a car rental business. I cannot recognise a thing.

I pedal slowly down to the boats, passing along streets lined with palm trees and cool new villas. The streets, all additions since my day, are named after various species of fish. Cod St, Whiting St, Bream St, Oyster Parade, Coral Trout Rd. There's a marina stuffed with houseboats for hire. Ever so slowly, it begins to come back. This marina had once been a mangrove mudbank.

Tin Can Bay stands up a tidal channel known as the Great Sandy Straits, sheltered from the offshore winds by the eco-resort of Fraser Island. Had it been possible in some bygone era to pick this place up and dump it say, in Cornwall or the Caribbean, it would have unquestionably earned itself a reputation to rival anything in piracy and freebooting legend. But as things are now, the town seems to be doing its very best to erase any local history that came from its boomtime era of prawn fishing. Tin Can Bay has been discovered in a way that will doubtless happen to Turkey Beach at some time in the future. Property prices are doubling, tripling, quadrupling.

Okay guys, lets paper over the cracks and get superficial here. Lets have members of the Big Money Club only, please. Trawler hands, what few of you remain these days, kindly keep to your end of town.

I check into some waterside place called Cozy Cabins, which are precisely the opposite, but they'll do. Across the road, what is left of the prawning fleet – maybe 25 boats, where once it was closer to 100 – lies idle at the wharf. To my right is a cluster of trees under which I spent my first night here 40 years ago while looking for a boat to live and work on. Suddenly the memories come flooding. There is an abandoned bus shelter near the trees, next to which had once been the trawlermens' communal loo – the most evil-smelling thing this side of the Mississippi.

I get a flash panic attack and think about riding the hell out of Tin Can Bay. I can clearly recall a period during those eight months here when I'd fretted that I'd never get out of the place. For one nasty moment, the sentiment returns with a vengeance. Some things haunt the psyche for a lifetime. I should know. Skeletons rattle in every third cupboard I open.

I am going to hear that rattle right here in Tin Can Bay. Four decades may have passed, but I can already hear those bones getting ready to tango. This particular situation you will understand, and I hope forgive, because we do crazy things when we're 18 years old. For now however, that can wait. The panic attack has passed, freeing me up to go out and wander among the trawlers and re-live old times.

The boats are pretty much the same now as they were then. Wheelhouse, galley, and sleeping accommodation forward, with large afterdecks to take care of the business end of things. Each boat is equipped with mast and boom, twin trawl winches, a heavy pair of otter boards to spread the net, a large fixed tabletop called the sorting tray, onto which each haul is dumped; and underneath the tray, a massive icebox in which the prawns are stored and chilled.

It is a tough, dangerous business, performed between the hours of dusk and dawn. Out at sea, 30 miles or so offshore, the net is dropped and three hours of uninterrupted trawling begins. When it is time to haul in, the catch will be tucked into the Cod End, a kind of tailpiece. This is then winched up above the sorting tray, swinging and swaying with the ocean swell. But before opening the Cod End, you first get hold of a pair of heavy wooden mallets and crush the heads of the inevitable half-dozen or more sea snakes hanging partly out of the net in an effort to break free.

These things are lethal. It may take several hours to die from an ordinary snake bite, whereas it'll take only a few minutes if delivered by a serpent of the sea. If you're lucky, you'll be unconscious within 90 seconds.

Once the catch is on the sorting tray, and the net is back down in the deep again, you sort the prawns out from all the rest of the rubbish, working underneath a powerful decklight. By this time, 30 or 40 sharks will be tailing the boat, snapping up whatever is tossed back into the water. You must also keep a wary eye for the stonefish. It has several poisonous spines, enough to kill a man. I was stung by three of its spines and spent the next few hours completely dizzied out, while my right arm swelled to double its normal size.

Sometimes the net will bring in more than you bargain for; sunken hulls, outboard motors, crashed airplane wings, and every once in a while, the bloated remains of a human corpse. They are usually the unfortunate souls who've fallen overboard sometime previously. In my time here, four hands died in that manner. A couple of others were chewed up by sharks, and one went from a sea snake bite.

Taking 12% from an average nightly catch of some 250kg of king and tiger prawns, each one of them as long as your hand, we could make fair money. But it was easy to lose. Whenever a northeaster blew in, you could forget fishing for up to six weeks at a time. It was during these periods that Tin Can Bay became a hellhole. To borrow a menacing book title from novelist Jack Higgins, it would turn into *The Last Place God Made*.

Binge boozing and rowdy poker sessions formed the pattern. Fights broke out on the hour. Poker players, gambling for high stakes, thought nothing of stealing from fellow shipmates. An atmosphere settled in over the bay, like a deadly coil ready to spring. One guy got hoisted high up a trawler boom on one leg, and was left to dangle upside down all night. Others got tossed into the inlet or had their heads immersed into buckets of diesel. The sudden shout of "*Don't you come the raw bloody prawn with me, mate!*" meant that yet another dispute was coming to the boil. It was every man for himself.

There was a bloke who went by the name of Lanky Mac. He was very tall and as thin as a pencil, with a mean, humourless mouth, burning freckles, and a shock of red hair. Lanky Mac was on a wanted list down in New South Wales for his part in a warehouse robbery, and for a few other offences I daresay. One evening during a hellhole period I saw him emerge from his trawler attired in a crumpled suit, a dirty white shirt, and a torn pair of sneakers.

"Dressed to kill, Lanky" I called out. "Where are you going?"

"None of your fucking business, you Pommie bastard. But if you must know, I've got meself a lift into Gympie. Gonna get the four effs".

Gympie is the nearest town, some 50km away. "The four effs?" I called back. I hadn't heard this one before.

"Yeah. A feed, a flagon, a fight, and a fuck".

I watched him stride off, a long stringbean of a man leaning forward into the wind. When I saw him again the next day, he was still in the suit, Except now it was torn and shredded; both his eyes were black and bloodshot; there were bloodstains on his dirty white shirt, and his breath reeked of stale beer.

"How did you get on?", as if I didn't know.

"Yeah, did okay" he said, looking unusually thoughtful. "I got the feed, the flagon, and I got the fight. Didn't get the fuck; but fair-do's now, three out of four ain't bad is it?"

I suppose not, mathematically speaking. I said consolingly, "Well, there's always Big Bad Barbara".

Lanky Mac gave me a long unfriendly stare. Big Bad Barbara was the wayward twentysomething daughter of a local couple. She had buck teeth and a massive frame. The prawn fleet was her nightly escape from the monotony of this tight, tiny, cut off port. She would simply board a boat, any boat, and ask brazenly, "*Which one of you blokes wants it first?*"

Three, four, five guys a night; several nights a week when the boats were in port.

For a very brief time there had been a woman of about 30 engaged on a boat – by virtue of her knowing the owner, who had ordered his reluctant skipper to give her a go. She had a sharp, haughty manner. Those few men who did try it on received some unpleasant vitriol for their efforts. It reached a point during her short tenure where bets were taken as to who would be first to crack this feisty nut. It was Mission Impossible.

Until, one night.....

It was gone dark. The boats were tied up alongside each other in rows of four or five. Her boat was nearest to the wharf, but the tide was straining the vessel away from it, leaving a one-and-a-half metre gap between boat and dock. The woman – I forget her name – leaned over to grab a rope from a wharf post, somehow slipping in the process. This positioned her with both hands clinging to the dock, and with her backside bent sharply over the boat's gunwales. Put another way, this lady was going nowhere.

From some other boat back in the shadows, emerged a deckhand. He sized up the situation and, unable to believe his luck, stealthily came up from the rear. He pulled down her shorts and knickers, and then unzipped his flies. Throughout her loud shouts of "*What the...Oh God, no...I'll get you for this, you bastard!*", the deckhand pumped away rythmically, secure in knowledge that she could not turn her head around and identify him. It was said that all the way through this opportunist exercise, he kept a firm hold of the beer can in his right hand.

Later, once the culprit had made his escape and she had managed to scramble onto the wharf, she made an official complaint to the bay's one and only cop. As she related the details, a slow smile crossed his face. By the time she signed her statement, he was doubled up in belly-roaring laughter.

There is a town in the U.S. state of New Mexico with the rather odd name of *Truth or Consequence*. If ever they rename Tin Can Bay, they should call it *Insult and Injury* because that just about sums up its lawless past. The aggrieved woman left town the very next day, humiliated. I doubt that such an incident would occur today, precisely because this is *today*. But back then, back in so different an age, Tin Can Bay was somewhere that no lone woman should have been. Indeed, she had been advised by many to get out fast – a wisdom so aptly demonstrated by the laughing cop who considered her complaint hilarious enough to screw up and toss into the bin. You see, in that kind of a society, the deckhand's action was not seen as rape or any form of violation. Far from it. It was thought of as a highly amusing conquest that had just been waiting to happen. Besides, there was money riding on it.

Some say that Tin Can Bay derived its name from the aboriginal word *tuncunbar*, meaning big fish. Others claim it is a bastardisation of Toucan Bay, so called because of the area's prolific bird life – 137 species if I'm not mistaken. Either way, it ended up with the most appropriate of the three names. The other two possibilities are far too sophisticated for this place. All the changes over the years can only be for the better because Tin Can Bay could not possibly be a worse place than it once was.

I still feel weird being here again. Really weird.

I pedal another kilometre or so, to where the road runs out and saltwater takes over, calling in at a seafood processing plant on the way and buying a kilo of fresh king prawns. I can taste the memories as much as I can taste the sea. I have no idea what's happened to all those thieves and misfits of yesteryear; those men who scraped through life using names like Lanky Mac; or my own shipmate, Peewee ("that's all you need to know about me"). The one other thing I knew about him was that he'd broken out from an Australian version of Borstal. What became, I wonder, of some weasel of a guy known as Trump the Card? Trump had been a master of card tricks and cardsharping but was in serious trouble with a group of bookies over a big unpaid debt. And where is Big Otto, the Swedish sailor who'd jumped ship in Brisbane after breaking someone's neck in a bar fracas? There had been 200 such stories in Tin Can Bay. These guys are but a wee sample of them.

Where road meets water stands the last building of the bay. The Tin Can Bay Yacht Club. It is a low, waterfront building – a sort of luxury lean-to with a small bar and restaurant, plus an outside deck area. Right now it is closed, but a sign says it'll be serving dinner tonight so this is where I'll come to eat.

I pedal back into town, remembering the *Sleepy Lagoon*, the bay's one and only pub. It is still there, a grey-blue building set out on its own atop a rise. It has been refurbished, but has changed very little and I get my bearings quickly. There is a tight-knit group of grizzled locals huddled around the bar, crab catchers by the look of them. I order a beer and at an appropriate moment throw a name into the ring.

"Yeah, that one's still around. Never got out of the place, just like the rest of us". He scribbles down an address which I put in my pocket, and then make the error of announcing that I'd once worked on the boats here. That's done it. To a man, they turn their backs on me. Suddenly I am another unwelcome face from the enemy camp. It had been that way back then as well. Locals versus Trawlermen. We're all human beings of course, just different tribes. Seems I really am re-living the past.

I go out on the veranda and roll a cigarette. Then I take out the slip of paper and stare at the address. Bones begin to vibrate from an imaginary cupboard and I quickly put it back again.

After dark I ride down to the yacht club. The gentle slapping of water is audible against the hulls moored alongside. Across the bay, lights twinkle. The restaurant is doing good business. I head for the bar where one lone customer is in idle chat with a young barmaid with long dark hair. He turns out to be a mild-mannered trawler captain called Lindsay George and we soon get into conversation.

"Tin Can is just a base these days" Lindsay informs me. "In your time, you would have been in and out of here night after night. Not any more. Now we have to go way up to the Torres Straits and the Gulf of Carpentaria to make a decent catch. Stay at sea for three months at a time".

That has got to be tough. The longest working stretch I recall was ten nights in a row – after which your hands are cut and blistered, you are caked in salt, you are perpetually damp, and your temper is short.

"We've got a little more comfort on board now" Lindsay says. "Hot showers, TVs and the like. But yeah, it's a long bloody haul. Ruined my marriage, I'll tell you that".

It is a strange man who puts Tin Can Bay and prawn fishing ahead of his marriage.

On second thoughts, maybe not.

When I think about it, the institution of marriage seems strange in itself. Why do two perfectly sane individuals, each with their own thoughts and dreams, deliberately opt for a situation that guarantees the rapid fading of passion, followed by the certain assassination of dreams – until death or divorce do them part? I have done it myself, twice, yet I cannot suitably answer the question. An acquaintance of mine with a disagreeable wife, two unruly kids, a second mortgage, and in-laws from Hades describes his marital state as something of an achievement – insofar, he says, that he has managed to accomplish "the full and absolute catastrophe".

Ah well, we are but mere mortals, programmed to the doing of insane things every day of our lives; like working for the corporate sewer, picking up the phone and speaking insincere words to someone equally insincere at the other end; and driving home in crush-hour traffic, trying to get to the same place, by the same route, by the same method, at the same time as everyone else. Seems to me that insanity is rife – as are all the side-effects: office politics, paranoia, stress, rage, deceit, spin, lies.

And I wonder if I'm the most insane of us all – arriving back in the Last Place God Made astride a bicycle.

The Last Place God Made. It is as if Lindsay George is tuning into my thoughts. He looks around, then says, "You know what they call this club? They call it *The Yacht Club at the End of the Universe*".

"Apt" I reply.

"Yeah" he nods. "Very apt".

I make for the loo but at first have some difficulty distinguishing between the Ladies and Gents. One door says *Inboards*, the other says *Outboards*. It clicks and I chuckle aloud, deciding that *Outboards* is the one for me. Good Aussie humour.

The food is excellent and the atmosphere friendly, all a big improvement on years gone by. Later, when the club shuts, Lindsay and the barmaid come back to Cozy Cabins where we guzzle more wine. The young lady is called Sally. She is working her way through a degree in media studies by waitressing in the day and tending bar by night. Sally, brought up here, is desperate to get out of the bay, travel a bit, go to England maybe.

I encourage her to do that. Trouble is, she says, there's this man in her life.....

Suddenly I'm glad to be the age I am. Been there, lady; know all the dilemmas, the uncertainties, the pain. She asks if I'll go back to the yacht club tomorrow night, and I say sure, why not, I can't think of anything I'd rather do than spend another night in Tin Can Bay. She is not sure if I'm joking, and neither am I. It still feels weird.

The next morning I know that I'll be stopping over. The palm tree outside my window is bent over double, its fronds straining at righ-tangles to the trunk. This is no ordinary blow; this is the howling fallout from the edges of Cyclone Beni, a nasty piece of weather that's been raging out in the Pacific. Rain is attacking the window like an angry carwash, thundering on the tin roof, and bouncing high off the tarmac. I am not leaving in this.

I walk out onto the sheltered porch. The rain seems to be getting heavier and is all but obliterating a forlorn, sorry vista of prawn boats. A car drives by slowly, its wipers in frantic-mode and head-lights on full beam. Nothing else moves. I feel another panic attack in the making. I'll never get out of here.

A very wise man once told me that there is no such thing as a bad day. "What is a bad day for one activity" he stressed, "Is a good day for another. If you can't play cricket because it's raining, then you can catch up on all the other stuff you've been putting off; paying bills, writing letters, things like that. Boring I know, but you'll feel the better for doing them".

He was right, of course. So when there is a let-up from this rain, I shall go and visit the address on that slip of paper in my pocket. This is something I have to do, rather than want to do. Judging by the weather, it seems a good, bleak day for that.

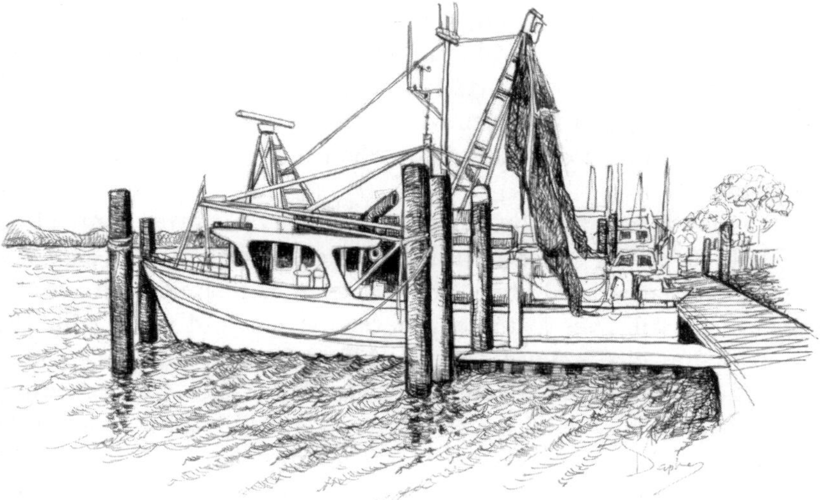

THIRTEEN
Borderlines

This is difficult. It is an uncomfortable thing I am going to do, and equally uncomfortable to talk about.

Let me put it this way. We are all supposed to remember exactly where we were on certain memorable or calamitous occasions – September 11, 2001 being an obvious date. The news of Princess Diana's demise was another very poignant moment, as was John Lennon's murder. Older hands like me won't ever forget where we were on the day that President Kennedy was gunned down in Dallas, Texas.

I remember all of the above, and precisely where I was at the time of each event. Just for the record, at the time of Kennedy's shooting, I was two days out of Tin Can Bay, holed up in a cheap Brisbane hotel awaiting the (then) once-weekly flight to Auckland, New Zealand.

I think too, that we all remember the first time we did it, if you see what I mean. If you don't, I'm talking sex.

At 18, I was a late starter by today's standards. There had been no real opportunity in England (the one time I got close, my mother stormed into the room and banished the girl from the house). I can tell you there was zero opportunity on the sheep and cattle stations – and frankly, Tin Can Bay seemed to offer the same amount of hope given to the inmate on Death Row when they finally come to strap him down.

We also remember the person, right? So I've got to come clean and talk about Big Bad Barbara, the fallen woman of Tin Can Bay.

Big Bad Barbara is not her name or even nickname. I call her that because she still lives in the bay, never got out, and never will. The business she runs is not a cafe, but I'll pretend it is anyway. Today, when the rain eases, I am going to call in on her. She won't recognise me, no chance of that, and I've no idea if I'll say anything or not. All I know is that this is some awfully strange thing that I have to do. It is part of my personal Ozzy Odyssey – and definitely not for airing on the radio; nor in my weekly tongue-in-cheek column for the *Western Morning News*. This is strictly personal.

Let's compare notes. Think back to when and where you were on the day – or most probably night – when your nervous virginity suddenly turned into a direful query, roughly along the lines of *Is That It?* Think, remember, then compare it with this.

One night I returned to the *Toni Christine,* the boat I lived and worked on with Peewee, the Borstal absconder. Assorted gasps, moans, and grunts were coming from below, and I hesitated to enter the wheelhouse, from which an open companionway led to our two bunks down in the foc'sle, the sharp end of the boat. Well after a while, I did. Peewee's small, wiry body was heaving away on top of this gigantic girl with buck teeth and a dress piled up around her shoulders. She did not appear to mind my sudden presence, and neither did he.

Peewee simply gasped, "*Nearly.....on......the......vinegar stroke..... She'll be gone......after.....that*".

"Christ, you must be desperate" I said, lying there in the dark after Big Bad Barbara had moved on.

"Ah, you're just jealous". I may have been too. I said nothing for a while, which was a giveaway. Peewee, who was the same age as me, said slowly, "*You've never done it, have you Pom?*"

'Pom' was my given alias in a place where *nobody* went by real names.

"I've been close" I muttered.

"Crap" he snorted. "The closest you've been was five minutes ago".

Not quite right, but as near as dammit. Then he said, "I'll fix you up with Barbara. She's not a bad root considering she's eight months gone".

"What?"

"You didn't notice? Are you blind as well as dumb? She's gonna drop a brat anytime now". Of course, I knew of her reputation and had obviously seen her around; but she'd never approached me, and no, I hadn't noticed. I had thought she was just.....*big*.

A few nights later, while Peewee and others were up drinking at the *Sleepy Lagoon*, Big Bad Barbara came back on board. Conversation was limited because that came with the territory. What there was of it went something like this. "*Peewee told me to give you a working over"..... "Oh, did he? Er, how long before you, um,"..... "Two weeks"..... "Oh, not long then"..... "No, so let's get on with it*".

So I did. On a hard bunk inside a 60ft prawn trawler, tied up to a wharf in The Last Place God Made; slipping and sliding across a huge firm belly; no foreplay, nothing like that. The lesson I learned from that night was that from there on in, sex could only get better. Poor Barbara. I actually felt sorry for her. She had not a clue who the father was, only that it's "*One of you bloody lot*".

Christ, what a pedigree.

Back to the present. Sometime in the afternoon, and between downpours, I pluck up the courage to enter Barbara's cafe. And I am instantly shaken.

My first thought is that she hasn't aged too much. The same big frame, same goofy teeth – and then it hits me. This woman is not Big Bad Barbara at all. She's her *daughter*. The one who had been inside her mother's womb that night 40 years ago, getting ready to pop into the world.

If I could have ordered a double scotch, I would have. Neat.

There are a few other customers, so it's not appropriate to strike up a conversation – not that I'm inclined to anyhow. Then, a few moments later, Barbara herself emerges from a rear door – and I know that we'll be doing no talking because she renders me speechless.

The years have been savage to her. She is obese, enormous, titanic.

Her hair is grey and straggly; her broad face worn and haglike; and her eyes are as dull as two brown envelopes. She wears a black wrap-around garment of some sort, pinned at strategic points around a shapeless body. Every waddling step she takes is an effort. She shoots me a disinterested glance, then busies herself at the till, counting the money.

My pulse is racing. I cannot believe that we did that thing, her and me.

I turn for the exit. There is no point, none at all, in bringing up the past. Truth be told, I cannot even bear to look at her. And I'm no oil painting either.

Truth hurts when it slams you between the eyes. God, I've got to get out of this town. Cyclone Beni, please, please bugger off. If I could ride away right now, it would be at twice the normal speed and without any effort on my part. That rattling skeleton would pedal me down to Brisbane all on its own.

There is no real let up in the wind and the rain, only an occasional lull. It makes the bay an uninviting place. With the wrong sort of memories, I'm finding it downright depressing. I sink into a mood that even the cheerful banter in the yacht club cannot shift. I do not enjoy moodiness, not in me or others. Mood is an anagram of Doom.

Next day, things are a little better – though not for everyone. It's overcast, but the wind has abated, and for now, the rain has gone. To the disgust of the inland community however, Cyclone Beni has veered out to sea again, dumping its watery load onto an ocean that wants none of it – but not onto a land that needs every last drop of it. *If the cyclone blows a few roofs off in the process, so what? We need that rain, matey.*

I speed out of Tin Can Bay without farewells or backward glances.

It takes three days to make Brisbane, via Gympie, Nambour, and Caboolture. Small town Australia gradually transforms into an impersonal mixture of motorways, heavy traffic, sprawling suburbs, and finally the concrete and glass and neon of the big smoke.

As cities go, Brisbane is pleasant, relaxed, almost continental – though not without the downsides which afflict every large metropolis. Blue lights flash, sirens wail, traffic is thick and slow, hotel rates are abnormally high. When I query the price with the desk clerk at the Goodearth Hotel on Wickham Terrace, he gives me a look that says I'm lucky to get a room at all. Didn't I know that people from across the state have been flooding into town all day? Cliff Richard is on stage tonight; one performance only.

Wow. Now I see.

The next morning I meander into the city centre to meet with a woman called Tracey Farr. She is the media co-ordinator for *Tourism Queensland* and has been instrumental in assisting with accomodation and my story ideas during the ride through this vast state of hers. I owe her a very large Thank You.

Not far to the New South Wales border now; some 2000km have been pedalled, another 2000 to go. There is a small psychological boost from knowing that I'm half way done. The bleak mood from Tin Can Bay has evaporated; ahead lies a 90km hike to the Gold Coast and my next stop at Broadbeach, part of the Surfers Paradise conurbation.

Getting there, through this well-populated area, turns into one of the most infuriating days of the odyssey. The rain begins as I cross a busy bridge taking me out of the city. It stops and starts all morning. Signposts are confusing. More than once I find myself wheeling down nondescript suburban streets leading to nowhere. When I finally make the southbound motorway, there's a big sign saying *NO BICYCLES. Use the Service Road.* Heading into Brisbane from the north, I'd come along a similar freeway, but do not recollect any such banning order.

These service roads are supposed to run alongside the motorway, from exit to exit. Trouble is, they swerve away, far from sight and earshot of the motorway, and I find myself heading towards places that aren't even listed on the road map. At one stage, the signs point me to Logan – a town that I have already passed through – yet what little light there is in the grey sky tells me I'm heading in the right direction, due south. None of this confusion is made any easier by the rain. It has set in for the day and is coming down steadily. There are many definitions of misery. I can promise you that long distance cycling through constant rain is one of them.

At some point, far from the motorway, I'm riding along a lonely, twisting rural road, not a house in sight. This doesn't seem right; can't be right. I'll keep going until I find a house, or someone to tell me where I've gone wrong. I spot a parked Land Rover by a paddock. There's a man with his back to me, urinating against a fence post. In his free hand is a can of beer.

"Excuse me" I call out, once he's got his zipper up.

I catch him off-guard. "Uh? Yeah? Wodder yer want?"

"Directions. And I wouldn't mind buying a can off you either".

He strolls over, emitting a loud belch. "Yer can have the directions, no bloody worries. But yer not getting the tinnie. Only got two left for meself. The missus don't like me drinking at home, see. So I stop off on the way back from work and sink a few on me own. Right here, 'cause there's never any bloody cops on this road".

I've taken a wrong turning somewhere. He draws me a complicated map that will get me back onto a service road. Darkness is beginning to fall and there's still about 35km to pedal through this weather. I thank him and ride away.

.....Six kilometres down the road, turn right. Go another four or five to a roundabout and take the third exit; then the first turning left after crossing a railway barrier. Follow the road until you see the sign for.....

It has been that kind of a day.

About 20km further on, in the wet and the dark, that kind of a day strikes again. I hear the explosion from the rear tyre as a six-inch nail rips through it, bending itself around the wheelrim and grinding Oggy Boy to a sudden slithering halt. I let rip with an explosion of my own, take a frustrated punch into thin air, and begin pushing the laden machine towards I know not where. With each revolution, the bike hiccups as the nail touches ground again. I ponder angrily on life's trivia. I mean, why was a perfectly good six-inch nail lying on the roadside anyway? What sequence of events removed that item of thin, pointed metal from a toolbox or whatever, to a random point on the highway? I get to think like this every now and then. It's an art form. The knowing of more and more about less and less.

Lights in the distance, a town of some sort. It is called Harbour City, I soon discover. The first group of buildings is a shopping precinct, amid which is an expensive restaurant doing heavy business. I park the bike against the wall and mooch over to the reception desk. The woman takes one startled look at this sodden, unshaven man with filthy hands and black fingernails, then says hastily "Sorry, we're overbooked". When I ask her to call me a taxi, a big one that'll carry the bike too, she cannot be more obliging. Broadbeach, she says, is only 12km away.

The blown tyre is a blessing in disguise. Now the rain is coming down as if Cyclone Beni has changed its mind about the ocean, and has elected to follow me instead. The water sluicing down the stormdrains is serious stuff. When the cab drives slowly through a flooding Surfers Paradise, all the colours of this neon-lit beachside city – every shade of blue, green, yellow, purple – seem to shimmer like images from a psychotic kaleidoscope. There is nobody out on the streets.

A slightly worried receptionist checks me into the hi-rise Beach Haven Club in Broadbeach. Tracey Farr, she of *Tourism Queensland*, has done it for me again. I'm on the 31st floor, looking down over what I think will be a spectacular view in daylight. The suite is luxurious, with two bedrooms and two bathrooms all to myself. A grand reward for a bad day on the road. Best of all, there's a kitchen. Now, for the very first time since Cairns, I have the opportunity to cook for myself. So for the next day or two, fast food and takeaways can go to hell and back.

In the morning, I see why it is called Broadbeach. The sun is out again, shining down on an expanse of white sand and blue ocean. Behind, tiers of hi-rise hotels and apartment blocks dominate the skyline, giving the Gold Coast the appearance of Miami Beach or Atlantic City. Surfers and sun lovers gather on the shore. Every 500 metres stand the yellow lookout towers of the lifeguards. I think there may be a story with those guys.

First things first. Get the bike fixed. The tyre has completely had it and the six-inch nail, wrapped firmly around the wheel, seems snug and cosy and claiming squatter's rights. I walk it to the lift and receive some odd looks from other passengers. There's a cycle dealer nearby who tells me to leave it with him, come back later.

Pavement cafes are brimming. Broadbeach is vibrant with colour. I had reckoned to probably loathe the place, but I don't. It's got atmosphere and there is hope in the air. This is a holiday town, man. Get down and boogie. Enjoy life.

The lifeguards certainly do. They don't make much money, but the procession of females walking in and out of their lives is endless. In reality though, it is not that glamorous a job; hour upon hour spent inside a lookout tower or down in a 4x4 parked on the beach. When a callout comes, it can be for any number of reasons, not just for a swimmer in difficulties.

"Some people think we're just here to prevent shark attacks" senior lifeguard Brett Paull tells me. "The fact is that we're working ever more closely with the Queensland Police. Thieves and hustlers can be a problem on Gold Coast beaches. They pester women, steal handbags, stuff like that".

"You mean you're a kind of Beach Police?"

"Yeah, sorta, though it isn't like *Baywatch*". Many lifeguards are trained paramedics, able to cope with near-drownings, cramp, heart attacks and the like. I ask about shark incidents but he says that the sharks are behaving themselves, been no trouble for a long time – partly because the lifeguards use their jetskis to round up the swimmers and surfers and shoo them out of the water every evening at 5.30.

Unfortunately, Brett Paull speaks a little too soon. The news filters through of a shark attack in neighbouring Burleigh Heads. An 84 year old man has died after his leg was ripped off by a marauding bull-shark inside the inlet. The authorities have put out to a call to catch the shark and do it in. By the end of the day, three bullsharks have been netted and killed; the offender among them, they say.

Looking south from my balcony, I make out the twin cities of Coolangatta and Tweed Heads in the far distance. The former is in Queensland, the other in New South Wales. An odd thing is the one-hour time difference between the two. This apparently came about following a disagreement involving dairy cattle. Queensland farmers rallied against daylight-saving, claiming it would alter milking times and cause discomfort to the cows. New South Wales did not buy this assessment and went ahead. It is the only time difference I know of to be governed by political latitude rather than geographical longitude.

It's an easy 40km pedal to the border, along cyclepaths aplenty. I stop for a sandwich in Burleigh Heads where the talk is of yesterday's shark action. Not too many people are in the water today. By early afternoon, I'm beside a magnificent Coolangatta beach, staring back at the distant skyline of Broadbeach and Surfers Paradise. In a few minutes, Queensland will be behind me.

An unremarkble sign welcomes me to New South Wales and the city of Tweed Heads. I cannot quite put my finger on it, but there is an immediate difference in ambience as well as in time. It seems a sulkier place than its twin; friendly enough, though not especially optimistic. Automatically, I wheel down the long main street towards the port area.

It has changed, but not out of recognition.

See, when I first came north to work on the prawn fleet, Tweed Heads had been my first stopover. The truckie I'd got a lift with from

Sydney pulled up his refrigerated vehicle beside a waterfront seafood plant in the middle of the night, loaded it with prawns, and turned back south again. I spent the night huddled in a small office with the plant's nightwatchman – which was infinitely preferable to what was to come.

The next day I was offered a live-aboard job on a dirty, battered old fishing boat, owned and operated by a crumpled, chronic alcoholic called Reg. The nightwatchman told me that Reg could never hang onto his crew for more than a few days, and that I'd soon find out why. Still, he added, it would be an experience. Teach me the rudiments of trawling.

In the three weeks I spent at Tweed Heads, I think we went to sea just three times. Reg only worked when the bottles and the money ran dry. One good haul of prawns would keep him and his wife in a boozy stupor all week.

Living aboard became intolerable. Foul, oily water sloshed around in the foc'sle bilge, out of reach of the pumps. My bunk was barely one foot above this revolting liquid. It had no mattress, so I slept on bare strips of damp wood, wrapped up in a damp blanket. The boat's interior lighting was out of order, unserviceable, forcing me to spend my evenings squatting in a cramped wheelhouse, reading paperbacks by torchlight. When the offer of a lift up to Tin Can Bay came my way, I was gone.

I check into a sleazy motel opposite the port. There are weeds coming through the concrete. A disillusioned manager mutters that the place is coming down to make way for a warehouse, and he'll soon be out of a job. So don't ask for any favours, 'cause you won't be getting any.

Just for old times sake, I take a wander around the port, actually almost a marina now. There are far more pleasure craft than fishing boats, and day-chartering to tourists appears to be the new thing: two-hour cruises up the Tweed River; half or full-day sportfishing out at sea, tackle included; or catch-your-own crab expeditions beside the mudbanks. Whoever named the boat for this venture came straight to the point. It's called *Catch-a-Crab*.

I've got no feelings, one way or the other, for this place; not like I had about Tin Can Bay. This particular memory is only that; a memory with no edge to it. Tomorrow, I'll get out of here early and make for Byron Bay, 70km down the coast.

There, I am told, I'll find the true definition of 'Alternative Living".

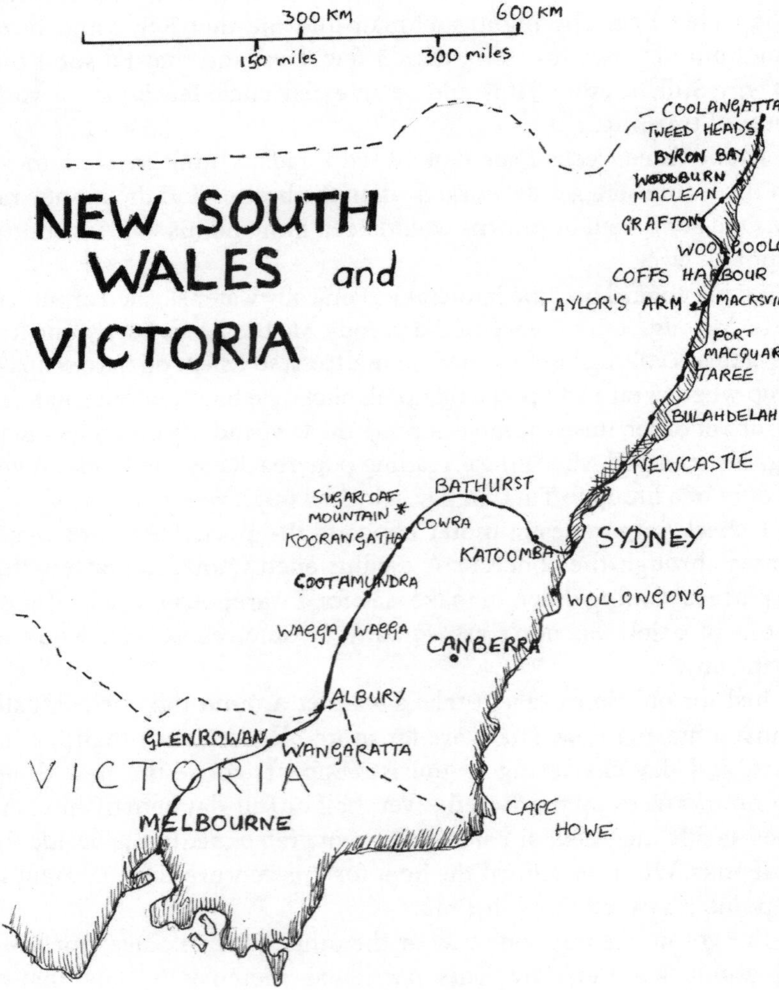
300 KM
600 KM
150 miles
300 miles
NEW SOUTH WALES and VICTORIA
COOLANGATTA
TWEED HEADS
BYRON BAY
WOODBURN
MACLEAN
GRAFTON
WOOLGOOLGA
COFFS HARBOUR
TAYLOR'S ARM
MACKSVILLE
PORT MACQUARIE
TAREE
BULAHDELAH
NEWCASTLE
BATHURST
SUGARLOAF MOUNTAIN
COWRA
KOORANGATHA
KATOOMBA
SYDNEY
COOTAMUNDRA
WOLLONGONG
WAGGA WAGGA
CANBERRA
ALBURY
GLENROWAN
WANGARATTA
VICTORIA
MELBOURNE
CAPE HOWE

Byron Bay

FOURTEEN
Spilt Milk

A bright sunny morning becomes gradually overcast as I push along the coast road to Brunswick Heads and finally into Byron Bay. It is Sunday and the traffic is dense. Most of it is heading for the bay, the easternmost point in Australia.

Quick instinct tells me I'm not going to enjoy it here. The overcast of late afternoon is dull and heavy. The town centre swarms with backpackers and tourists, all wandering around in circles. The beach itself is disappointing if compared to Coolangatta or Broadbeach. A sign outside the police station says, *Warning. High Theft Area.*

What the hell is the big attraction? And where is this alternative living? From first impressions, all I see is an expensive, crowded resort.

A sortie around the motels confirms these fears. Byron Bay rates are twice those of anywhere else, and I'm lucky to pay only $100 for a room at the Byron Motor Lodge. The same syndrome will apply in restaurants and bars.

Alternative living? I don't think so. But the motel manageress orders me to open my eyes, look around me.

"Well, I haven't seen even a single solar panel yet" I argue.

"What? Oh no, it's not *that* kind of alternative. It's more.....it's to do with the attitude. Hippyish. Arty crafty. Free love and things".

I feel my blood run cold. "You mean it's a throwback from the sixties? An Ozzified Goa?"

She thinks for a moment. "Yeah, that's about right".

And here's me hoping to collect an environmental tale or two for the BBC. Instead, I'm bidding in a twice-the-price sale amid hippies and deadbeats. How do they afford this place, I wonder.

Later, I wander downtown, which basically comprises of four short, busy streets. They teem with an average age of around 25. Backpackers fill the bars and takeaways. Wealthier types pack the restaurants. Music floats from every third or fourth establishment. There's a busker over in the shadows, finger-picking an electric ukelele, and he's good. The best thing in town, I'd say. As for the rest of it...

I would probably have enjoyed it once. But I've had the teeshirt a long time, and I see through all the bullshit. The police notice is wholly correct. It is a high theft area, and the villains are the traders. For reasons beyond my understanding, Byron Bay is on the 'must see' map. *So hike up the prices, mate; never give a sucker an even break; and look smart now, here comes another lot.*

Not everyone is on the make. I hear that a 750-strong group of local women did something extraordinary today. Like Bush and Blair, Aussie prime minister John Howard is hellbent on going to war with Iraq. These Byron Bay women are hellbent on stopping him. So this afternoon they gathered in a big open space, stripped bare naked, lay on the ground, and formed themselves into a shape that, from the air, reads *NO WAR*. Tomorrow, the pictures taken from a chartered chopper will splash the front pages all across the land.

I buy a takeaway and stumble back to the motel, irked that I've made the detour here. There's a fat bloke with a big round face and thick dark hair sitting out on the porch adjoining mine. He's swigging down a cold beer from an icebox by his feet, and he tosses one my way.

"Name's Phil" he offers. "From Sydney". We shake hands. Says he's only recently been laid off by the national airline, Qantas, after 30 years service as a catering manager. "Dunno about anything anymore" he mutters bitterly. "The wife doesn't want me at home all day. I'm too young to retire, and too old to get another job". After a short pause, he adds, "Lost, that's what I am, mate. Completely bloody lost".

We all lose direction from time to time, I tell him. It'll come right sooner or later. Phil isn't sure about that, and nods towards the small campervan he's travelling around in. "I don't even know which way to point that thing tomorrow. There's no going back to my old lady for a while. Now that I'm out of work, the bitch said she'd rather not have me around at all".

Phil says he'll be turning 52 next month, and is clearly upset about the state of his life. There is not a lot I can do except utter sympathetic noises. When I rise the next morning, he's already gone. Where to, I've no idea, and I don't think he has either – not until he gets there.

He comes in and out of my thoughts as I sip coffee and load up Oggy Boy. Once you start drifting from town to town, it is often easier to carry on doing that than it is to go back. Up to a point, I'm doing it myself. But at least I've got a reason, a daily destination, an end in sight, a plan of sorts.

Phil needs a plan. Hell, we all need a plan. If it doesn't work out, modify the details to suit.

Today's plan is to make 60km to the small inland town of Woodburn. It is en-route to the city of Maclean where I'm pretty sure a decent radio piece awaits. I pedal away from here with as many regrets at leaving this bay as for that other one further north.

I take the coast road to Ballina, where it joins up with the main road south. What began as the Captain Cook Highway at Port Douglas, then became the Great Green Way from Cairns to Townsville, then the Bruce Highway to the border, is now the Pacific Highway. On the way out of Ballina, I pass a large indoor market that advertises souvenirs, gems, and fresh seafood. On the roof is a gigantic, neon-lit plastic prawn about five metres long by two across. I stop and take a snap for the website and for my weekly column in the *Western Morning News*. What, I ask myself, would council officials and the like make of giant cornish pasties lighting up the westcountry sky? The thought amuses me. It's a nice little angle for the paper and good for my Oggy Oggy sponsors.

The countryside undulates through sugarcane and banana plantations. The wind, which has been relatively kind of late, switches back to a southeast blow. The day is hot, the going not easy, and I stop for a breather at the top of a brow.

"*Herro!!, Herro!!, Herro!!*".

I jump out of my skin. *What the.....*

"*Herro!!*", the voice yells again, drawing up from behind. He is mid-20s with sharp oriental features, a bright red shirt, and a flashing smile. His bike is laden to the gunwales with camping gear.

"You nearly gave me a heart attack" I snap, patting at my chest.

"I am Japanese Army Captain!" he declares with short, punchy breaths. "I ride bicycle from Cairns to Melbourne!".

"Really? And I Englishman who ride bicycle from Port Douglas to Melbourne". I'm one up already. We talk for a few minutes, and I ask him how he got along down the Alley of Menace.

The smile vanishes. "Very hard. Very hot. Sometimes no water. And very lonely".

It was, too.

He breaks into another big smile. "*Now we ride together!*" he shouts.

Oh no we don't. I explain that I'm not camping and that I've got a job to do. That I need to be alone and a free agent.

He says, "Okay, unnerstan'". He sticks a hand out and I pump it. Then he's gone, flying off ahead of me, pedalling with the furious resolve of a kamikaze pilot. I wonder if we'll meet again somewhere down the line and think probably not. If he keeps up that speed, he'll be in Melbourne next week. I've already nicknamed him *Boy Banzai*.

I cruise into the small town of Woodburn late in the afternoon and check into the Rod n' Reel Hotel – one of those places for down-at-heel travellers, commission-only salesmen, and truckies in need of a good scrubbing. Next door is a 24-hour cafe for 18-wheelers and other passing traffic. This is unusual. With the exception of larger stopovers like Rockhampton, I've had difficulty in finding anywhere to eat after 8pm. Small town Oz seems to shut down with the sunset.

Cleaned up, and ensconsed in a room that will only just fit the bike as well, I follow routine by drifting into the bar. It is large, with a cheerless atmosphere. Four customers sit around a U-shaped counter.

Now we are five. The man on my left reaches for the bartop payphone, making sure that everyone hears the call. For ten tedious minutes we get to learn about a fishing trip on the Richmond River. In keeping with his sport, he's telling whoppers.

In walks an off-duty cop, who is greeted politely. He orders a 12-pack of takeaway beers because he and his station mates are celebrating. Two teenage car thieves who've been plaguing the area have today been given 12 months each. The bar goes up in loud cheers.

"Tell yer what" says the loud fisherman. "If the jail's too bloody soft, have 'em transferred to my dog kennel. They can share it with my doberman".

"We'll keep it in mind" replies the cop, picking up his 12-pack.

"Yeah, you do that. In any case, I'm gonna put my next door neighbour in there if he gives me any more shit".

The officer raises an eyebrow.

"Coupla nights ago he threatened to blow me to pieces with a shotgun. Said I was playing my music too fucking loud".

There is something about this man that makes me uncomfortable. He is about 30, with thick black stubble and dark, angry eyes. He seems to crave attention. The cop says he'll drop by soon; meantime keep the music low. The man makes some grumbling reply and orders another beer. The barmaid shoots him a cold look, but pulls him a schooner anyway.

I do not stay long. The atmosphere, what there is of it, is all wrong. I go over to the cafe, order some grub and buy a carton of milk. As I walk back to my room, the man with the angry eyes and angry neighbour is having an altercation with another bloke out on the forecourt. He is told in no uncertain manner that he's not getting another drink. There's some swearing and threatening, but he finally takes the hint and lurches off down the street, swaying.

Next morning, I accidentally spill the remains of the milk. I buy another carton from the cafe.

"Just spilt half a carton on the hotel forecourt" I tell the woman at the counter.

"Is that right?" She taps her wristwatch. "In which case, I'll be hearing about that. Sometime between now and ten o'clock is my guess".

I can imagine. In places like Woodburn, the term 'small talk' takes on a new meaning. Best get out while the going's good. Soon I'm back in the saddle, heading for Maclean, 50km away.

While straining up a long incline, I see thick black smoke and a police car parked further up the hill. I pull up alongside, naturally curious and always on the hunt for another story.

My heart truly goes out to her.

She is blond, 30 or so, dressed in a black top and blue jeans. Sunglasses hide her eyes, and a gold necklace hangs around a slim neck. Her life is now smouldering in the charred ruins of a burned-out trailer attached to her car. The cop is leaning over the bonnet, filling out a report. He is sympathetic in a businesslike way.

She says to me, "You missed the show. Sorry. Half an hour ago there were three-metre flames jumping out of that thing". She pauses, looking at the wreckage and somehow manages a sad smile. "It's all gone now. Nothing left".

She's driven from the Gold Coast, also on her way to Maclean where she hopes – had hoped – to start up as an independent curtain maker. There are customers and premesis awaiting her arrival today. But all her materials and machinery, several thousand dollars worth, are – were – in the smoking trailer. How the fire started, she doesn't know. But what she is adamant about is that at one point, she had the blaze well under control with minimal damage... until along came a series of thundering 18-wheelers, eight or ten of them in a row. Their mighty backdrafts caught the dying embers, fanning the heat. That did it. In no time the trailer became a raging, unstoppable furnace. She is putting a very brave face on all this. My guess is that the tears will come later; when they do, they'll be hard and they'll be wet. "I've lost it all before now" she shrugs. "I'll just have to pick up the pieces and start again".

"Insurance?" I suggest hopefully.

She gives a sour, ironic chuckle. "Stopped at the Gold Coast and starts again in Maclean".

"Jesus" I breathe. "I'm really sorry". And I mean it, because I too know what it's like to lose the lot.

"What'll you do now?"

She shrugs again. "I'll think of something". Fate has dealt her a foul blow. This is spilt milk on a grander scale and I admire her magnanimosity when she wishes me well for the remainder of the journey to Melbourne. I wish her the same, only doubly so, and ride away.

Pedalling through the day, I think of her and Wandering Lost Phil;

and of losing it all. Sometimes, losing everything is no bad thing. Oh, it hurts at the time alright; but then other, usually better things gradually trickle in as replacements – the lessons of life among them. These days, I own nothing and live simply. It is how I very happily choose to be. All I hanker for is knowledge and truth. These you can take with you when you go; the rest you cannot.

Landowners, particularly in England, both amuse and annoy me. Blank stares greet my argument that it is not possible for anyone to actually *own* land. At best, they can only be mere custodians. What are we made up of – 75% water? How can such a fragile, temporary entity consisting of 25% bones, meat, fat, and 75% water ever own hard, solid, everlasting earth. It cannot. In fact, if anything, it's the other way around.

Here's a truth if ever there was. *The one and only thing that any of us truly owns is our own individual soul.*

The body is a kind of overcoat that we walk around in. The brain is an engine, a computer, powering our activities and putting thought into deed. But the soul, well, that is our very essence; the thing that makes each one of us unique from anyone else on Earth.

Somewhere out there in the big ether lies a Master Plan of which we are all a part. Its substance and dictum will eventually put Wandering Lost Phil back on course, and determine the next stage of that ballsy young blond's earthly existence. Because ultimately, I'm certain, the Master Plan shapes and dictates everything.

FIFTEEN
Bottom, Middle, and Top

Maclean stands on the broad Clarence River, about 15km from the coast. Much further inland is a town called Glen Innes. The common denominator is that they both lay vigorous claim to being the most Scottish town in Oz. I have not been to Glen Innes, but riding through Maclean's clean, tidy streets I see why it is odds-on favourite.

Every telegraph pole, and there are hundreds of them, is adorned in the tartans of the clans. Mackenzies, MacDougals, MacMillans, Macs this and Macs that; red and yellow; blue and white; blue, green, and purple. They make a striking addition to these otherwise dullish features of the landscape. They tell you that this town is going to be different.

I pull a dog-eared card from my pocket. On the way to Byron Bay I had stopped at some weeny town for a pub lunch and fallen into chat with a local named Bret. When Maclean cropped up, he scribbled down the name of a pal of his. Said he was known to one and all as

Beanz, that he owns a pub in Maclean, and would be good crack for a night at the bar. The card reads like an email address. Bret has simply written *Beanz@Bottom Pub*.

"*DotCom all ye faithful*" I mutter to myself, and set off in search of Bottom Pub.

Maclean has this long riverside drive that becomes a curving, sloping main street leading away from the water. By the time I'm at the other end, I've counted three pubs, not one of them with the name of Bottom Pub. I stop and ask a man who seems certain to know. He's got that reddish-blue nose and protruding veins of a clockwork boozer.

"You'll be needing the Clarence Hotel" he grunts.

I'm puzzled. "The Clarence Hotel is Bottom Pub?"

"Yeah. We got three pubs in town. Take no notice of the names on the door, they're horseshit. We call 'em Top Pub, Middle Pub, an' Bottom Pub".

Well, that clears that up. He points me back down the main street. "Bottom Pub's down by the river".

The Clarence Hotel is an unpretentious Ocker's bar, and a popular one. It is late afternoon and filling up with men on their way back from work, outdoor labour from the look of it. I ask the bartender for a beer, and for some bloke called Beanz who owns the place.

The barman – tall, slim, bespectacled, around 40 – chews on this for a few moments, then says "Did Beanz tell you that?"

"He hasn't told me anything. I've never met him".

"Then who did tell you?"

"Tell me what?"

"That Beanz owns this hotel".

"Some mate of his near Byron Bay. Bret someone or other".

He nods solemnly. "Okay. Beanz is not the owner. He's hired help, and he'll be in later. If you're looking for the owner, that's me. And here is your beer".

His manner is mild, not at all unfriendly, but he's put me straight and there's a definite *oops* in there.

I sit at the corner of the bar, getting my bearings. In strides this white haired guy who throws me a deep scowl, then plonks himself on the next stool, clearly agitated. After a few minutes, he turns and says, "Look, no offence mate. I come in here every evening – and you're sitting in my corner".

Another *oops*. We swap seats, and his attitude alters in a flash. He starts talking to me as if I'm an old pal. In fact, he talks a blue streak.

We're an odd lot, the human race.

The owner comes over and I introduce myself properly. As soon as he learns of my mission here in Oz, he becomes super-friendly, sticking his hand across the bar. "Bob Freebody" he announces. "If it's a bed you're after, you've got it. You're staying here".

It is an order I'm happy to obey. Until, that is, he takes me up to a dormitory-style room with seven beds, four of them unmade. "Bloody maid went home early" he grumbles. "Had a work gang in here last night. Said they might be coming back. Probably drinking up at Top or Middle. Best you pick one of the made-up beds".

As if I'd do anything else. I do not especially relish the notion of spending my sleeping hours among a snoring construction crew, but what the hell; it's all a part of the odyssey.

By now, Bob Freebody has taken me firmly under his wing. He introduces the regulars. They are all men, most of them with one eye trained on a sports channel highlighting the day's racing. Conversation is easy, friendly, and punctuated by delighted whoops or low moans, depending on which horse finishes in what place. There's an ageing, grey-bearded Ocker sitting alone. He wears a broad-rimmed bush hat, dirty blue shirt, baggy shorts, and a pair of flip-flops. Around his left wrist is an untidy white bandage. A whisping home-rolled cigarette hangs limply between two stubby fingers. In his right hand is a schooner of beer, frozen in time and space somewhere between the bartop and his mouth. His eyes are fixed on the racing. When the result comes, he lets rip with a long, painful, gargling groan and gulps down the beer in one hit. Beanz, who is now behind the bar, pumps him another without asking.

This hotel is way off the tourist map.

You may think I'm a bit over-eager on pub tales, but travelling the way I am – in and out of new stopovers almost every day – the pub is the only place I know where you can get the feel of things, meet people, hear stories, and build up a picture in so short a space of time. Looking around me now, I figure that Bob and Debbie Freebody must have a few treasured yarns of their own. When I nudge him on this, he grins wickedly, pulls out a folded card, and tells me to start reading.

The heading is in upper case. THE PERFECT PUBLICAN. Then come the details.

A publican must be a democrat, an autocrat, an acrobat, and a doormat. He must be able to entertain prime ministers, philanthropists, pickpockets, and pirates. And the police. He must also be on both sides of the political fence, as well as being a footballer, golfer, bowler, tennis player, darts champion, and pigeon fancier.

As he settles arguments and fights, he must be a qualified boxer, wrestler, weightlifter, sprinter, and peacemaker.

He must always look immaculate when drinking with bankers, swankers, commercial travellers, and company representatives – even though he has just stopped a 'beer throwing' contest in the public bar.

To be successful, he must keep the punters full, the house full, the tanks and storeroom full, but not get full himself.

He must have barmen who are clean, honest, quick workers and thinkers, non-drinkers, mathematicians, technicians, and at all times, be on the boss's side, the customer's side, and stay on his own side of the bar.

It is said that he home-wrecks, takes weekly wage cheques; in other words he saturates, confiscates, deteriorates, and propogates.

To sum up, he must be outside, inside, offside, glorified, sanctified, crucified, stupefied, cross-eyed – and if he's not the strong, silent type, there is always suicide.....

With the compliments of one of the above. Bob Freebody, Clarence Hotel.

Hmm. Sounds like an ideal future stunt for that illusionist chap, David Blaine. Or if you believe in reincarnation, the perfect calling for Houdini on his next time around.

A bloke with an orange shirt streaked with dust and diesel comes in. He's a logging contractor by the name of Arnie Boon and we hit it off instantly. Arnie is a Maclean native, but left town for a long time after going bust. Then he summoned up the will to come back, start again, pay off all the debts. Now everything is grand again. The straightforward, no-bullshit talk of these people, and the way they have accepted a complete stranger into their lives tonight, is just delightful.

The rounds flow until gone midnight. If the construction gang is still in town, then they're locked out for the night. Too bad. I've got the dormitory to myself, and I sleep like one of Arnie's logs.

Bob won't take a single cent off me for last night's food and revelries. He tells me to keep off the main highway and take a back road to Grafton, today's destination, 45km away. It means crossing the river by ferry at some point, but the road is flat, quiet, and free from heavy traffic. Suits me.

There is a slightly worrying aspect to the Grafton stopover, but I'll cross that bridge later. Right now, I feel great. I can plug Maclean's Scottish angle on the BBC, and I can make a good, quirky piece out of Top, Middle, and Bottom Pubs. And I can.....*hello, what's this coming the other way? Another story?* Yep, I think it is.

He wears a red cycling helmet, green shirt, black shorts. His bike looks like a packhorse, covered with long-distance bags and panniers. We pull up simultaneously and say hi. What's more, he's English. His name is Phil Dostal, 22, a biology graduate from Cheshire, out here on a year's break. And he has ridden his machine all the way from Perth, way over on the west coast, the other side of this vast continent.

"You pedalled across the Nullarbor?" I ask admiringly.

"Well, it wasn't too difficult" he replies modestly. "Water was a bit of a problem, but other than that.....".

The Nullarbor Plain stretches across half of Western Australia and through most of South Australia – about 1,400km of zilch. The Alley of Menace multiplied by four and a bit. There are roadhouses and motels every one or two hundred kilometres, but other than that it is one big empty desert where even the sight of a 36-wheeler charging down on you makes for a welcome change of scenery.

More than that, Phil is *circumnavigating* Australia by bike. He began in Perth in October 2002, and will end in Perth October 2003, from where his flight home to England is booked and unchangeable. Along the way, he's been taking up casual jobs to bring in a few bucks. He must have ridden about 5000km to date, with only another 5000 more to do all over again. It is a wonderful little radio piece, and the least I can do is to direct him to Bottom Pub where maybe Beanz can train him up as a barman, or Arnie will toss him a chainsaw.

I allow myself a wry smile as I write the directions, wondering what Bob Freebody is going to make of another pedalling pom calling in on him in less than 24 hours. Oh, it's a grand day and anything can happen.

Like Maclean, the city of Grafton stands on the Clarence River, and it really is a most pleasant town. There's a clocktower in the city centre from where four main roads head off to all four compass points, leading to quiet suburbs awash with colourful jacaranda trees. I check into the Civic Motel, close to the city centre, for a two night stay. Tomorrow is a BBC day.

Then I look up a local phone number and punch the buttons. This matter bothers me just a tad.

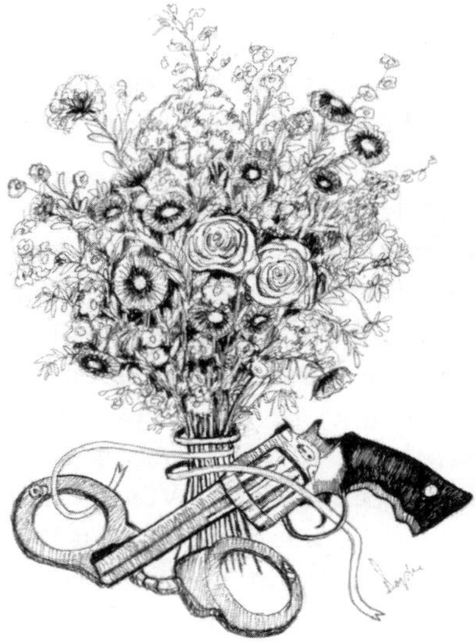

SIXTEEN
Marriage, Murder, Massacre

I am a lucky man. I have friends, real friends, many of whom go way back when.

I first met Selwyn in Wellington, New Zealand in early 1964. He is a year older than me, an Australian originally from Woolongong, south of Sydney. It is useful to say a few words about him because in some unsure way, he links to Grafton and to this odyssey.

Selwyn has travelled extensively since those early days in New Zealand. He is an adventurer with a taste for danger and the unusual. He worked the Mekong Delta during the Vietnam War on a hydrographic survey boat. He laid oil pipes across Africa. He came to live in London for a few years and we shared a flat for a time. Then he moved to Marbella, living aboard a motoryacht that he'd bought. Selwyn had a few ups and downs during this period, and he eventually moved back to Oz where he acquired a racehorse stud near Townsville. But it wasn't long before the taxman caused him quite some irritation, so he moved on once more, this time up to the Philippines where he bought a 60ft schooner. He has done this and that in his time – all Selwyn's schemes are grandiose – and he either makes a huge pile, or he crashes with a mighty bang. On a clear day, you can hear the echoes.

In the city of Angeles, some distance from Manila, he met a local girl named Merley. They married – he was in his 40s by then, but had not been down the wedding route before – and they produced two fabulous girls. At this point in his chequered career, he and a syndicate of pioneering Aussie expatriates decided to invest a few million into the building of a hotel in Vung Tau, Vietnam (the same town where Ronnie Jensen, he of Turkey Beach, began to get a little wonky in the head). It was 1991, and this was Vietnam's first major project by overseas investors since the war had ended in 1975.

At this time, my own life in England was at a crossroads. The Master Plan in the big ether bundled me aboard a Manila-bound airplane, where I stayed with Selwyn and Merley while sorting things out in my mind. I guess it was inevitable that, in a roundabout sort of way, I became loosley involved with his Vung Tau project. I'll go into more detail a bit later on in the ride. Right now, it's enough to say that the Aussie syndicate gradually split into two camps, arguing bitterly among themselves until the whole thing finally imploded – leaving Selwyn and a few others with short straws and empty wallets.

He decamped his family back to Oz, buying a house right here in Grafton.

Something has happened in the period between then and now, I'm not sure what, but it would be accurate to say that Merley and the girls are happy where they are, while Selwyn – unsettled and unfulfilled still – is back in the Philippines chasing another fortune; something to do with the missing millions of former President Marcos. Even though he phones religiously every evening, the family have not seen him in more than a year.

Merley answers my own phone call, pleased to hear from me, and suggests meeting for dinner. She'll bring the girls too.

They pick me up about eight, and we drive to the Bowls Club down by the river. At first it seems an odd choice, but it has an excellent menu and a good bar, between which is a somewhat incongruous dimly-lit room stacked with poker machines.

Merley is now in her early 40s. She is small and slim, with dark hair and dark oriental eyes. Her daughters have some of her looks, though very little in the way of Filipina features. They are western through and through, Australian all the way, both lovely girls.

I had called their father in Manila just prior to leaving for Oz, to see if one of my oldest friends would be in town on the day I passed through astride a mountain bike. If nothing else, his reply was forthright. "I'm *never* going back" he replied adamantly. "Because I don't like Australia, and I don't like Australians". I still find that remark rather odd, particularly since he's one himself.

My closest circle of friends had all thought that Selwyn and Merley had the perfect marriage – if such a thing exists. They had seemed inseparable from Day One. But now they are at an impasse that carries all the hallmarks of a slightly ironic and terminal fade out.

He steadfastly declines to leave *her* country, or to live in his own land; Merley downright refuses to leave *his* country, or to return to her homeland.

Tricky. The marriage has very clearly reached a stage where differing individual desires are taking precedence. Merley, I'm sure, is perfectly willing to sacrifice the union if it means holding on to the house in Grafton and staying put in Oz. Selwyn, for his part, seems to have more of an eye on the Marcos stash than on his own family. The one thing that flimsily holds it together is the nightly phone call.

But what happens when the phone goes click?

I had asked Merley to tell him that I'm taking her for dinner – and here we are now, sitting in the Grafton Bowls Club sipping white wine. It's all above board and straightforward, but that's not necessarily how an old friend will see things from far across the South China Sea. *Where are they? What is being said about me? What are they up to?* Time and distance, a pair of adversaries I know well, can play nasty tricks with the mind. I like Merley very much, but do not harbour any other thoughts about her, and vice-versa. Nonetheless, I try and imagine myself in Selwyn's shoes, and wonder how I'd feel about such an old friend were the situation reversed. I do believe that I might be a little uncomfortable with it. And the thought is making me uncomfortable now.

I resolve not to linger in Grafton a moment longer than necessary. The only people who can sort this one out are those two.

Later, back at the Civic Motel, I see a police car parked among the guest bays and it is still there in the morning. A plainclothes man carrying a soft leather briefcase gets in and drives away. He returns late afternoon, well after the BBC broadcast, and something sets my journo juices stirring. As he walks past my room, I call out with the offer of a beer.

"Yeah, could do with one" he says genially. "I'm Bill, by the way".

Bill is the regional Police Prosecutor. He is extremely pale for an Aussie, but then I notice a lot of loose skin flaking from his arms. I do not know the medical term, but I suspect he has that particular skin disorder that prevents the tanning process.

Today he's been in court over a nasty little matter concerning a jilted woman and her three brothers. They had been out to get her ex-lover, who took shelter inside the house of another lady friend. But they found him there, smashed up both their cars with baseball bats, then smashed every window in the house as the terrified duo cowered inside. Bill expects a guilty verdict tomorrow. One brother he thinks will go to jail, the other three culprits to receive hefty fines.

All along the ride I've been reading or hearing about increasing levels of violence afflicting this easy going, laid-back society. Bill agrees with zeal, and launches into a recent case of his involving a truly senseless murder.

There is this young hitchhiker out on the road somewhere along this part of New South Wales. Along comes another hitchhiker, a young girl, and they join forces. A car with two men in it draws up and offers a lift. What the two hitchers don't know is that these guys have recently broken out from Yass Prison, about 250km southwest of Sydney. The two cons take a shine to the girl and hatch a plot to get rid of her male companion.

The plot involves 'robbing' a mobile fast-food business, a big van that passes through the area every week, loaded down with the week's takings. Today's the day, but it's going to take three people to pull it off, they tell the pair. The male hitchhiker goes for it, hoping it'll make him look big in his new companion's eyes. They leave the girl in a motel room and head out to a remote spot just off the highway, to 'lay in wait for the van'.

There is no van of course. In this out-of-the-way place, the cons set about the youngster, knocking him senseless until, quite literally, he is beaten to death. They pull out a pick and shovel from the car boot, and finally dump the victim into a shallow grave.

Back at the motel, the girl wants to know where her companion is. Three men had left this place a couple of hours ago, only two have returned. The explanation she's given is simply incredulous. They tell her that when they managed to stop the van, the driver had pulled out a gun, declaring that he himself had heisted the vehicle half an hour earlier; that the cops would know by now, and he needed a hostage. The hitchhiker boy, they said, was abducted at gunpoint.

Whether she bought this implausible story, Bill doubts. In fact, she goes along with the two hoods on a spree of robberies along the coast: small isolated hotels, quiet petrol stations, vulnerable takeaway joints; two or three hundred dollars at a time. When things begin to get too warm for them, they turn the car around and head back to Yass. The guys know a few people there. For a while they remain on the loose, but then a chance remark made by the girl to a suspicious acquaintance gets back to the cops. They interview her subtly. Bit by bit, they trace the shallow grave and the hitchhiker's decomposing body. What had been a casual hunt for a couple of jailbreakers, now turns into a full-on manhunt for two violent killers.

They are caught, charged, convicted, and given life inside.

"Bring back hanging" Bill asserts. "They belong at the end of a rope".

Well Bill, perhaps that could wait for a day or two. Tomorrow, it won't be murderers hanging in the air. It'll be love. February 14, St Valentine's Day.

I'm afraid that I rather take the Al Capone view of Valentine's Day. A great day for a massacre. Certainly, a billion flowers are massacred for it; good champagne is slaughtered by the tankerload, tossed down unworthy throats before being thrown up again in the loo; lies, millions of lies, are told through Valentine Day cards, candlelit canoodling, and sweet-nothing whispers down the phone. The whole silly ritual is utterly cringe-making.

Interflora, I will use you on any day of the year except this one.

So the most heed I shall pay to this farcical time will be the blowing of a kiss to my partner – the bike – when it yet again brings me to my chosen destination. Tomorrow, this will be the seaside resort of Woolgoolga, 50km southeast of Grafton – where I shall sit and observe Australians in love. Or going through the motions, at least.

SEVENTEEN
Ruminations

There is not a lot of love in the air as I cross the river into South Grafton and merge back onto the Pacific Highway, where the southeast headwind scores a direct, blasting hit. Even the scenery seems uninteresting – as is often the case once it's been carved up to make way for a major highway. The concrete, the whooshing metal, the roaring diesels, the shredded truck tyres and broken glass on the roadside, all combine to colour one's view of the view, if you see what I mean.

But it's all worth the effort. Woolgoolga offers a welcome contrast to a tiring day of freeways and headwinds. It has that real seaside atmosphere that makes you want to rummage for a bucket & spade; and there's not a hi-rise in sight. The colourful main street, lined with beachwear stores and postcard racks, leads to a sweeping golden shore where the surf is up, and where a few experts are showing how it is done: crouching, balancing, sliding and swerving their multi-coloured boards skillfully along the foaming morass.

Others – not so skilled – stay up for a few moments, wobble like twanging rubber bands, then disappear in a mighty splash as their boards catapult into the air and come down again, like a series of disastrous rocket launches.

It is about 4pm. I watch the surfers for a while longer then think about finding somewhere to bed down for the night. Walking the bike along the main street, a man carrying two heavy bagfuls of booze stops me on the pavement.

"Nice bike" he says. "Looks like you've been travelling for a time". He is about 35, a bit on the scruffy side, unshaven with curly windblown hair. Behind him, maybe ten metres away, I notice a blond woman of roughly the same age in a pink jumpsuit. She turns her back on us, but doesn't move anywhere. Instead, she hangs her head and crosses her arms in what appears to be a deep sulk.

The guy pays her no heed. He wants to know about the ride from Port Douglas, so far away now. I edit it down to ten seconds. Then he casts his eyes towards the woman in pink.

"Christ, would yer just *look* at it" he says loudly. In response, she turns to glare at him, revealing a sharply downturned mouth.

"Christ" he repeats, "*Would yer look at the face on that!* Some Valentine's night we're gonna have".

This is more like it.

"Oy!" he shouts out, "Come off it, cow! Or I'll drink the bloody lot meself!"

This seems to have impact. Slowly she walks over, turning her head aside in residual defiance. The cheeks are puffed outwards and the lips pursed in a full-on pout.

"She's me woman" he grins. "On and off". The grin vanishes as he jabs her arm with a sharp elbow. "Aincha?"

She nods, says nothing, and rubs her arm. I've met one or two couples like this over the years; drink, fight, make up briefly, drink more, fight again. This pair do not seem like holidaymakers; not the type.

"Pure Woolgoolgan" he says. "Lived here all me life. But there ain't much work around and I might have to pitch camp. This dole money is shit". I stare at his two bulging shopping bags. There is something quite catching about his crooked grin. "Yeah, well, it's a special day, ain't it?"

"If you say so" I reply, glancing at the woman. The pout is now so deep, her eyes are almost coming out of their sockets. He grunts a goodbye, and I watch them move off. He is striding far ahead of her;

she follows in a sullen trudge. There goes one Valentine couple who'll be telling no lies tonight.

I park myself at a motel called the Balcony View, except I've no balcony and a concrete forecourt for a view. I'm sitting outside, rolling a cigarette, when a shining black and chrome Harley Davidson pulls up. A tall, leather clad man with dyed blond hair casually swings out of the monster's saddle.

We nod at one another, always a cue for conversation. He has a thick teutonic accent, penetrating blue eyes, and I'm beginning to think that those aryan blond locks may be for real. Says his name is Manfred, that he's ridden from Melbourne where he now lives, and is bound for Port Douglas, touring the country for the first time since he emigrated from Germany eight years ago. I explain that I'm doing roughly the same thing on a reverse route.

"You haff a bike?"

"Yes. But it's hardly a Harley".

"Ver is it?" he asks, looking around the forecourt.

I jerk a thumb. "Inside my room".

"In ze room? Show me please". This is very close to an order.

I can only say that when he sees a pushbike, not a motorbike, he freezes in mid-step and his blazing blue eyes begin to bulge like exploding ballshot.

"You are making fun of me, ja?" he says stiffly.

"Oh no I'm not".

"You haff come all ze way from Port Douglas on.... *on zat?*"

"I have".

Manfred shakes his head. The accent is getting thicker, assertive, sterner. "No, I do not think so" he decides. "No man could be so stupid".

He is getting annoyed. I don't know why, but pushbikes definitely have this affect on certain people. Pedalling across America, I was once told by an extremely angry woman that I was mad, quite insane to be doing such a thing, and that I ought to be locked up. There's been one or two along this ride with equal sentiments. The German seems to be joining the ranks.

His voice is as brittle as recycled cardboard. "I vill not tell you vot it is I am thinking".

"No need" I reply icily. "I already know".

As he leaves the room, I say pointedly, "Hey, Manfred. Have yourself a happy Valentine's Day, won't you".

He waves an aggressive, dismissive arm. "*Aggh! All zat is bullshit!*"

Seems we agree on something.

Darkness falls and the streets fill up. Pubs and restaurants overflow with custom. The atmosphere is easy, happy; could be that a little love is no bad thing – it's just lost on an old cycnic like me for whom there is none on offer. Flowers are everywhere I look. Vows and kisses are exchanged, along with lovers' gifts; necklaces, rings, earrings, wristwatches. The men receive ties, shirts, socks, anything that is the woman's idea of how their man should look.

I meander comfortably among hand-in-hand couples, strolling through open air cafes and pavement bistros. Maybe the summertime has something to do with this relaxing air. Winter can make people meaner, colder, less forgiving. Then, coming the other way, I spot the tall, blond, disconsolate figure of Manfred, wearing the grimly forbidding look of a firing-squad commander. He is clearly not enjoying tonight's luvvy-luvvy spectacle. Not wishing to re-engage, I quickly duck into the shadows of a sidestreet until he passes.

I think back to this time last year. South Devon. Jane. On the wane for both of us. But what do you do? Use February 14 to kill it off, a good day for a massacre? Or do you follow a few half-hearted motions, get a little drunk, go with the tide? I do know that we took the easy route – each knowing that the other wasn't going to be around in 12 months time.

There is nobody special right now, and I am not unhappy with that.

Neither am I unhappy for all these couples in Woolgoolga tonight. A high percentage will be stretching the truth of their feelings for one another, meaning that another percentage will become the willing victims of mild deception. But I suppose it's a case of so what, who cares, I know I don't.

Yesterday is gone; tomorrow may never happen. All any of us have is the Here and Now.

If a few insincerities make the Here and Now a little better than the There and Gone, you might as well utter them. But Manfred is right about one thing. In the end, St Valentine's Day is 100% bullshit. Probably half of this evening's couples will be with somebody else this time next year.

The roar of Manfred's Harley so close to my window wakes me early in the morning. I peer through the curtain and watch him ride away. He had said something about covering 400km per day since leaving Melbourne, and that thought leaves me ever so slightly envious. Of late, I've only been averaging 40 or 50 per day, and am growing just a little weary of the coast, anxious to make Sydney where I'll turn inland to the Blue Mountains, Bathurst, and down through the Abercrombie Ranges towards *Buronga*, my former sheep & cattle station near Cootamundra. Back into the bush; back into the real Oz.

Pedalling out of Woolgoolga, I pass a large white Seikh temple. A sign says that everyone is welcome. They have integrated well, those people. My thoughts flash back to the Seikh fruitseller near Proserpine and I wonder if he's got his man yet. If he hasn't, he will.

I ride with ever-thickening traffic, through Emerald Beach, Sapphire Beach, and on into Coffs Harbour, an industrial seaport where I grab a snack before carrying on towards the small town of Urunga. This is major banana country, plantations abound. For a few luxurious kilometres I travel along a cyclepath which takes me down and along a sort of dell. A cricket match is under way so I stop and watch for a time. Good village green stuff, Aussie style. Several spectators sit around shaded areas of the ground; men in straw hats, women fussing around with sandwiches and flasks. The batsman receives a poor ball, giving it a well-deserved *thwack*. It rises high into the sky, coming my way, and drops down three metres ahead of me, a clattering six. I retrieve it from a grass mound and sling it to a puffing, wheezing fielder in tidy whites.

Love that game.

Back on the highway, there's a young man walking towards me on my side of the road. On the other side is a young woman, walking in the same direction. Both are peering intently into the roadside scrubland as they progress.

"Problem?" I ask, pulling up.

"Yeah. Gone an' lost me bloody surfboard. Musta flown off the roof rack. That's $600 down the tubes unless we can find it".

I promise to keep an eye out as I press on down the road. A few klicks on, there's a big hand-painted scrawl announcing *Lady Finger... Bananas for Sale*. Does this mean that some fading aristocrat called Lady Finger is down to selling bananas on an Australian roadside, or does it mean that the breed of banana is called Lady Finger? I tell you, it's all happening today.

The sign for Urunga comes up and I turn off the highway, doubling back on myself for about three kilometres. Where the hell is the town? Eventually it appears over the brow of a hill, another small end-of-the-line place with distant views of the sea. It is Saturday afternoon, the shops are shut, nobody is on the streets.

I check into the only hotel in town, the Ocean View. If that sounds rather splendid, in an odd kind of way it is: old, rambling, slightly musty, with an enormous veranda at the front. The room is small and sparse, but the bar is ample, the menu good, and better still, there's a day/night cricket match on the bar room TV, Australia versus England. I keep myself to myself tonight, watching the game, but when I go up to bed I am extremely cross. England have been given a well-deserved skewering after putting in a dismal show.

I get moving early on Sunday and ride 30km to a town called Macksville, where I stop to make a phone call. This is a story I really must chase up.

As a kid, there had been three major influences that decided me to try my luck in Oz. One was a movie, *The Sundowners*, with Robert Mitchum, Peter Ustinov, and Deborah Kerr. It carried a theme about the roaming life of the sheep drover – that now-extinct, legendary breed of outback Australian who made his living on horseback, shepherding large flocks from sheep station to market, and vice-versa. Drovers still just-about existed in the 1960s, and I found the character very romantic.

Another influence was a now long-forgotten TV series called *Whiplash*, and the stories supposedly based on a stagecoach company known as Cobb & Co – the Down Under equivalent to the Wild West's Well Fargo. Once more, romantic.

The third such influence was a song by Aussie balladeer Slim Dusty. *The Pub with No Beer* had made it high in the UK charts, and once heard, never forgotten.

The song is not entirely ficticious. It is based on actual events at an actual pub. So today, if I'm prepared to make a 30km detour into the bush, I shall apparently arrive at a place called Taylor's Arm, population 217, and home to the Pub with No Beer. This I cannot miss. I'll make the call and tell the owner that I'm on my way.

A woman with a European accent comes to the phone. She says there are only two hills between Macksville and Taylor's Arm – so it will make a nice pleasant ride, off the beaten track; a Sunday drive; a piece of cake.

EIGHTEEN
The Pub with No Beer

There is not a cloud in the sky as I set out for Taylor's Arm. For the first few kilometres the road is flat and empty. There's a river far off to my right, which may explain why the surrounding country is so green and lush.

And as silent as an empty mansion at midnight. Utopia.

The first of the two hills looms up, not too steep but it provides a decent uphill puff; the sweat is rolling, but I get solace from the downhill rush, a kind of freeze-drying process. Soon the next hill comes into sight, and I know that this one is going to be a son of a bitch. It has all the same curves and gradients of that three-kilometre crucifixion on the very first day of this odyssey, and I dare say it is just as long.

You develop a prescience for such things.

By now of course, I'm far more equipped to take on such a foe. Thighs really are like rock, arms and wrists are stronger than they've been in years, and a new mental strength dispels any occasional doubt. So I tackle this beast with fitness, experience, and resolve.

Anyway, there are no more climbs today, not after this one. The woman at the Pub with No Beer had said so.

But by God, the afternoon is hot. Blistering.

I don't know how long it takes to reach the apex; seems like a week. I struggle slowly towards it, knowing my reward will be a long, refreshing downhill whiz, down to where the land flattens out again.

What? Am I hallucinating?

This is suddenly like Nepal. I went there once, back in the late 1970s. Trekked 18,000 feet up to Everest Base Camp. This detour is reminding me of that. What I see ahead of me is one goddam hill after another. The day continues to boil, and the sweat becomes a rolling river.

This is purgatory. Someone is going to pay.

It might be the couple in a car just behind, which I didn't hear coming. A Land Rover is coming the other way, towing a wide load just as I'm panting up another rise. I stop in the middle of my side of the road and uncap the remaining water, warm-to-hot by now.

"*Geroorf the bloody road!*" screams a voice behind me.

I turn, startled. A woman with short dark hair has her angry, chiselled face poking out of the passenger window. Something inside me snaps. I yell – and I mean yell – back at her in a way that no man would normally get away with. The car zooms past as I deliver the abuse, then hauls up to make way for the oncoming Land Rover. The man at the wheel – all I can see is the back of a finely-shaven head – is having an exchange with his unpleasant companion. He suddenly screeches off, moments before I catch up with his car.

Whether it's a *phew* for me or for him, we'll never know. My guess is that he's thinking anyone who can shout louder and angrier than her is worth a miss. Or that anyone mad enough to cycle these hills may have psychotic leanings.

The outburst makes me feel better. Much better.

From a non-cycling angle, these hills of the Nambucca Valley are really quite lovely, and not unlike the Cotswolds. They are semi-forested, lush green, rolling like a calm, deep ocean swell captured on an artist's canvas. In the far distance, they colour into a shade of blue, darker than the clear blue sky that meets them.

Altogether I count not two hills but 22. But now that a few

houses are coming into view, my ire is disappearing and my thirst raging. And suddenly there it is, coming up on the left. A single-storey wood and brick building with an unpainted tin roof and a surrounding veranda, set amid a rough patch of uncut grass. Somewhat contrarily, a large green sign says, *The Pub with No Beer. Victoria Bitter on Tap.*

I wheel around to the back entrance, puzzled to find a small wooden church standing in what are obviously pub grounds. Deities and Demon Drink do not exactly see eye to eye. A couple of Sunday drinkers are out on the veranda, bemused by this strange new arrival. They utter a friendly G'day, but my throat is too damn parched to stop and chat right now. This afternoon's ride has been a real ball-buster.

Six men and one woman are drinking inside this near-legendary bar in the funny little outpost of Taylor's Arm. The decor is pure bush, themed around the song. A shovel hangs on a big hook next to a framed picture of Slim Dusty. Walls are adorned with related items; stirrups, branding irons, leather straps, saddles, ropes, posters, even a hand-drill.

The young barman pours me a schooner and I gulp its content. He pours me another, which accompanies me on a brief inspection tour. To the rear of the small bar is a larger room used for functions and parties. It is regaled with more artefacts hanging from brown wall panelling. Fading sepia photographs of the pub recall bygone times; the 1920s, the Depression, the wartime years. There is one picture, taken around 1915, where the patrons and townsfolk are gathered outside. A couple of women in bonnets and black dresses spreading down to their ankles supervise a group of children. There is a saddled horse tethered to a rail, two men beside it. And there's a chap in a horse-drawn buggy staring at the camera – which was obviously one of those instruments where the cameraman hid beneath a big black hood, and then produced a smoking explosion that told him his snap has been taken.

There are more pictures of Slim Dusty smiling from beneath a trademark wide-brimmed hat. In one of them he is with Gordon Parsons, the man who originally penned the song as a flipside to a ballad called *Saddle Boy.* That song flopped, while the B-side rocketed up the charts.

I notice a poster containing the words to the song – a humorous ditty that nonetheless was so evocative of its time, and to the culture of the bush.

Oh, it's lonesome away from your kindred and all
Round a campfire at night, where the wild dingoes call
But there's nothing so lonesome, so drab, or so drear
As to stand at the bar of a pub with no beer.

The publican's anxious for the quota to come
And there's a faraway look on the face of the bum
The maid's gone all cranky and the cook's acting queer
What a terrible place is a pub with no beer.

The stockman rides up with his dry dusty throat
Goes up to the bar and pulls a wad from his coat
But the smile on his face quickly turns to a sneer
When the barman has to tell him the pub's got no beer

There's a dog on the veranda, for his master he waits
The boss is inside drinking wine with his mates
He hurries for cover, and cringes in fear
It's no place for a dog, is a pub with no beer

Then in comes the swagman, all covered in flies
He throws down his roll, wipes the sweat from his eyes
But when he is told, he says 'What's this I hear?
I've trudged fifty flamin' miles to a pub with no beer'

Oh, pity the blacksmith, for the first time in his life
He's gone home cold sober to his darlin' wife
He walks in the kitchen, she says 'You're early my dear'
Then he breaks down and tells her the pub's got no beer.

From this mini-museum, I gather that it started life as a pub back in 1903 – 100 years ago. Then known as the Commercial Hotel, it has been the local watering hole for banana planters, loggers and timbermen, stockmen and sheep shearers ever since. At odd intervals – the Depression, the war, and post-war years – rationing came into force, which included beer quotas. Whenever a fresh quota arrived, the loggers (in particular) would hurry down to the hotel and sink as much ale in as short a time as humanly possible, each one of them worried that someone might consume more than himself. Within days, sometimes hours, the quota would be gone.

It was this little item of local history that gave Gordon Parsons the idea and the title for the song.

I go back into the bar. A bespectacled bloke wearing a blue baseball cap atop a mischievous-looking face is needling his drinking buddy over a political debate. Next to them, two Ockers, one with a ferocious beard and the other with heavily-tattooed arms, are swapping jokes. Two younger men and a young lass are talking over in a corner. I overhear one of the jokes, and laugh.

> *There's this bloke walking along a busy Sydney street with an obedient crocodile on a leash. A cop car pulls up and the horrified officer tells the man to take the reptile down to the zoo; now, straight away, pronto.*
>
> *The man yields to the cop's demand. Next day, the same cop spots the same man, with the same crocodile, on the same street. 'I thought I told you to take that thing to the zoo!' he snaps irritably.*
>
> *And the man replies, 'Oh, I did, Officer. It was a good idea of yours. Thanks. We had a great time! So today we're off to Bondi Beach'*

It takes no time to get into conversation. I discover that the man with the fearsome beard is, among other callings, an accomplished banjo player. He is known as Banjo Bob Randall, lives here in Taylor's Arm, jams with other local musicians in the pub sometimes, has played with Slim Dusty and Gordon Parsons, and tells me that if I'm looking for a music story, go up the road and round the corner to talk with a guy called Frank Murphy. Frank, he says, is one of the last great musicians of the bush.

Bob rings him for me; *get yer arse down to the pub, Frank. There's some lunatic journalist in town, Pushbike Pom or something. He's buying.* But Frank's phone just keeps on ringing. We'll try again later.

The owner walks in and intoduces himself. Tony Brown is a stout man of about 50 with a big quiff at the front of an ample crop of greying hair. He's a bit harassed, problems he says with another pub he owns elsewhere. In the meantime, this one here is up for sale. He and his wife bought it 11 years ago for $450,000 and they're now asking $1.5 million.

The wife – her with the European accent and not much local knowledge – I have yet to lay eyes on. Tony asks me to hang around, stay the night, let's have a chat later on. He does not acknowledge the presence of Banjo Bob or his mate, both sitting next to me.

When he's gone, Bob says darkly, "You see that? Not a bloody word, not even a nod to us two".

It is spoken with something more than mild irritation.

"It's not a good idea to make enemies in Taylor's Arm" Bob mutters. "Too small a place".

He can say that again. "What's the problem?"

"Ah, he's trying to attract a different type of customer. Suppose we're not good enough for him".

Another local conflict. Somewhere a raw nerve has been hit. Enough for Banjo Bob and his pal to get up and leave. He scribbles down Frank Murphy's phone number and tells me to ask him about the Beatles.

"Why? Why them?". I am curious about this.

"He'll tell you himself". And with that he is gone, a big man with a big beard, dressed in a torn logging shirt. Seems to me that his face fits ideally in here.

I stay off this topic when the owner returns. I find Tony Brown congenial company, not the sort to deliberately spat with regulars. I guess it's simply the chemistry between the two men. You can't please everybody. I enquire why he's put such a famous place up for sale, why not the other pub?

"It's time for someone else to give it a crack. Eleven years is a long time to trade on a song, even one as famous and timeless as the *Pub with No Beer*. Eventually, you run out of ideas". He frowns and pauses. "The one new idea I do have is out of my control".

I raise an enquiring eyebrow.

"A re-make of the song. It's going on for half a century since the original Slim Dusty record. Definitely time for a re-make". And time to enhance the value of the property, no doubt. Tony and his wife are not from these parts and I strongly suspect they want out of Taylor's Arm. It's just too damn small.

"By the by, what's that church doing here?"

He grins. "One of my marketing ideas. Christenings, weddings, funerals, memorials, things like that. Occasions like those fill the bar before and after, you believe it. They come from far and wide".

While Tony goes off to organise me a bite to eat, the young bartender says "You can't blame him for selling up. It's all the undercurrents around here. A big drug problem, for instance".

"Really? Population 217?"

"Yeah, I hear you. But there's no work around, and nothing to do. People need alleviation".

I use the payphone to try Frank Murphy again. No answer. I'll try him in the morning. It is nudging towards eight o'clock and the pub has emptied out. I am its only customer and the sole overnight guest. Sunday night; quiet as a moonlit cemetery. I can hear my own breath.

Next morning I manage to get Frank Murphy on the phone. There is no time to meet up because Tony is giving me and Oggy Boy a lift back to Macksville where he's already running late for a meeting. But from our brief chat, I learn that Frank, now in his 60s, was born in Ireland, caught the ferry to Liverpool as a teenager, got to know John Lennon and joined his pre-Beatles group, *The Quarrymen*. But he turned down a place in the (then) unknown Beatles to join the RAF, and later opted to emigrate out here. In Sydney, he met a young lady who would later become his wife. She hailed from some place out in the sticks called Taylor's Arm.

His accent is pure Oz these days, and he tells me a story that is so in keeping with bush lore, that I wonder if he's written a song about it. Some years ago, while helping a friend to build a house just down the road, he suffered a very nasty accident. His pal, a powerfully built man, was hacking a log with an axe when the blade suddenly came loose from the handle. The sharp, heavy blade carried on through the air, all but embedding itself into Frank's skull. He was KO'd, blood everywhere, heavy stitching was required.

He was taken immediately to a medic in Macksville, only regaining consciousness on the last kilometre or two. But the doctor was out on his rounds. The nurse inspected the damage, telling him it will need at least 20 heavy-duty stitches, but he'd have to wait until the doctor returned in a couple of hours. Not wishing for this blood-stained roughneck to hang about the surgery, she said tersely, "*Haven't you got any shopping to do?*"

"Well" Frank concludes, "I passed the time away in a pub. And because the alcohol took some of the pain away, I guzzled it down. By the time I got to see the quack, I was so drunk he refused to give me an anaesthetic. So I just sat there while he stitched my head without any anaesthetic at all".

That's an *ouch*.

We never know what the Master Plan has in store for us, do we? Frank might so easily have become one of the Fab Four instead of living out his days in Taylor's Arm. But he's cheerfully philosophical about it, stating that he wouldn't change a thing, and that 35 years in the bush makes you an Australian, not a Liverpool rock star. His life story is a nice little extra for the radio.

I marvel at how effortlessly Tony's van climb's the 22 hills between his pub and the town of Macksville. In turn, he is gracious enough to marvel at how fit I seem to be for a man of my age; wishes he could trim down, lose a little weight himself.

The Master Plan strikes again. This is too good to be mere coincidence. As I haul the bike from the van, I notice a pair of cyclists, man and woman, wheeling into a servo forecourt. Furthermore, there's a small Union Jack stitched onto one of the pannier bags. Another story; it simply has to be.

And my goodness, it is.

Graham Barden and Mary Corbett are from Leicestershire. He is 63, she is 58. Both are retired from the Probation Service. And for charity, they are cycling around the world.

In June 2002, this intrepid couple pedalled off a cross-channel ferry at Calais, carried on through France, Switzerland, Italy, Greece, and Turkey. Avoiding the Middle East, they flew on to Bangkok, cycling through Thailand, Malaysia and Singapore. From there they flew to Melbourne where this part of the global marathon began. It will end in Brisbane, when they fly on to New Zealand, riding north to south through both islands. Following that, it's across the Pacific Ocean to Vancouver, and a west-east ride across Canada and finally down to Boston where the pedalling ends – all 17,000km of it.

I feel like a pipsqueak.

They give me a phone number in Port Macquarie, 85km from here. It belongs to a couple they met along the way who insisted, *insisted*, that the cyclists stay at their splendid house with splendid sea views "Because they simply like to collect people. The odder the better".

Seems that I'll suit fine.

In return, and with a broad grin, I give them Bob Freebody's address at Bottom Pub for when they pass through Maclean. This is going to freak the guy out. First, there's me on a bike, riding north-south. Next, there's young Phil Dostal, riding all the way around Australia; and in two, no more than three days time, into his hotel will pedal another two Poms, one of them over 60 years of age, cycling around the *world*. This, in the space of a week. The strangest invasion of the aliens that Maclean has seen since the Scots marched in.

Riding now towards the city of Kempsey, I honestly do wonder what the Master Plan has in store for me next.

NINETEEN
The Eager Undertaker

Days come, days go. This one does not have the heat and blue skies of yesterday. It is overcast and slightly ominous.

Early afternoon, the rain starts in earnest; low, darkening clouds roll overhead. The first bang of thunder echoes from some distant point. You know the whole shebang is coming.

When the lightning cracks, it is like amplified bullwhips. Fiery bolts illuminate a severe black sky and streak towards earth with lethal precision. The rain falls so hard, it stings like rubber bullets. Even the truckies, safe and warm inside dry cabs, pull into lay-bys or roadside venues.

Pedalling through this is like shooting the rapids down a perilous river of chance, flowing through some wierd neo-apocalyptic danger zone. But someone up there is good to me. A large servo is in sight on the other side of the road. I ride into a theatre of grinning faces, amused by this spectacle of a drenched, dripping wretch. As if to greet the new arrival, the skies let rip simultaneously with a shattering thunderclap and a vicious streak of killer lightning. This one stays in full, blinding view for several seconds.

The weather produces a certain cameradarie among awed travellers. Truckies, coach drivers, tourists, motorcyclists, and the lowlife of the road – a cyclist – come together in some sort of truce and temporary harmony. Nobody is leaving this servo until the storm relents. It is a bad one, really bad. A worried looking couple publicly announce that the end of the world is nigh and prayers would not go amiss.

Two hours later, the storm abates, rain eases. The town of Kempsey will be as far as I'll get today, another 20km further on. Back on the road, trucks spray leftover rainwater as they growl on past. Behind the wheel, humanity hardens up again as it rejoins the frenzy of speeding metal.

The next day, in clear conditions, I head for Port Macquarie. Only 45km, but another 'must see' coastal city, which gives me rise for deep suspicion. But another BBC day is imminent so I need a couple of settled nights. I mooch around the town for a while, taking the place in. Another holiday resort, though without the atmosphere of somewhere like Woolgoolga. It is more like a magnified Byron Bay – a gauntlet of tourist shops leading down to a disappointing seafront.

I fish out the phone number of the couple who 'collect people'. No answer. Nor later. Finally I cruise back towards the edge of town, away from the sea and the business district, where overnight rates are more sensible. On the brow of a hill, there's a small motel next to a funeral parlour. I check in, taking instantly to the couple who own the place, Craig and Margaret.

"You want the quiet side or the not-quite so quiet side?" asks Craig.

"I'm sorry, what?"

A slow, wide smile spreads across a long, lean poker face. He jerks a thumb over his shoulder. "That side backs onto a funeral business. *Very* quiet at night".

This man has gallows humour. I daresay it's needed it in the motel trade.

He jumps on that. "Big fat women. That's when a sense of humour is called for. They, er, mess up the sheets, big time. Almost without exception. Dunno why, but it's a fact. Dirty bitches".

My instincts are honed. If he carries on like this, sooner or later Craig is going to come out with a gem or two. Could be worth pursuing. "Beer" I say. "Six o'clock, my place".

"Done deal".

We lounge out on the porch next to my room, cold tinnies in hand. Craig is a tall man, 40 or thereabouts, dark hair, and a face that so expertly alters expression to match whatever it is he's saying or hearing. He has it down to a pat.

When I mention that, he says "I was a bank mananger in Sydney before coming up here. Making the appropriate face at the right moment was part of the job".

"Turning down loans, you mean".

Now the face brightens. "Sometimes I enjoyed that. Particularly if I didn't like the customer". He leans forward in his seat, clasping both hands together. The expression transforms into the saddest of hangdogs as he talks into the face of an imaginary customer.

".....*We're so sorry, Mrs Jones. The bank searched this way and that to find a way to help. No can do, I'm afraid*".

Then the face lightens, radiating a positive message.

".....*Look at it this way, my dear. At least you will not be in debt to us*".

Next, at a precisely-timed moment, the expression swings 180 degrees to that of a cold-blooded repo man on a mission to collect.

".....*At least, no more than you already are. Which, Mrs Jones, brings me to the small matter of calling in the loan.....*".

I'll lay odds that Mrs Jones carries several rolls of fat.

A car pulls in, rolling into a parking bay. "Interesting bloke in that car" Craig says. "Danny's a real go-getter, an entrepreneur. In fact, he recently bought the funeral home next door. He lives in Sydney, but seems to be spending more and more time up here".

I watch him climb out of the car, a tubby middle-aged chap in a shirt and tie. He's got a round suntanned face and thick grey hair. He spots us, waves at Craig, says he'll be right over with a beer, and disappears into his unit.

"Maybe you should get a job with him" I opine airily. "I'm sure you do the most mournful face in town".

Craig frowns a tad. "Funny, that's what he said. Well actually, I have been helping out on certain occasions. Been more and more of them lately".

"Yeah? Doing what?"

The voice is resonant, the word stretched out. "*P-a-l-l-b-e-a-r-i-n-g*".

Now the expression becomes funereal and sombre. Maybe it's a trick of the fading light, but I swear his pallor is changing into a brilliant shade of embalming fluid.

Danny emerges from his room and comes on over, taking short, fast, strides. He's got a tinnie in his hand. "*G'day, owyergoin*" he says, gripping my hand eagerly. Charisma oozes from his pores. We chat in the getting-to-know-you mode, and I soon learn that he's spent most of his career doing deals in the pub trade, buying and selling hotels. Now is the time for a change of direction, he stresses.

He's done that alright. From noisy public bars to the silence of the dead.

I am suddenly becoming curious about the death business – not so much about it's daily workings, but more about the people that it attracts into its ranks. Seems odd to me that this personable, outgoing character, at the very prime of life, has opted to indulge his working hours among the departed; to endure procession after procession with the weeping bereaved, in and out of the cemetary or the crematorium.

Unless there's a wad in it.

"There's a buck to be made, sure" he replies openly. "I won't deny it. But it isn't only about money, it's about the challenge. I do things in a different way to other people. Like thinking *laterally*, if you know what I mean. Anyway, I mean to bring new ideas to this industry. Someone has to get rid of the taboo; to challenge all its morbid perceptions and traditions".

"You're going to bring it to life?" I laconically suggest.

He grins the grin of somebody not expecting to be measured up for a pine box anytime soon. "Take tonight, for instance. I'm off to the Rotary Club. It's holding a raffle in aid of the local Rugby League side. Could even be that the funeral home will be an official club sponsor by the time the night's out".

The way it works, he goes on, is that in a town the size of Port Macquarie, no single business concern can afford to support the club on its own. So the entire business community throws in equal, affordable amounts of money – and the first two company names to come out of the hat become the team's official sponsors for this year's Rugby League season. Good idea.

Well, will you credit it? Danny's funeral house gets second draw, which means the name will be adorned on the sleeves of each player. The first draw went to a private hospital group. Next morning, he still cannot believe his good fortune.

"This is just fantastic!" he enthuses, punching fist into hand. "Incredible! So now do yer see what I mean about lateral thinking?"

Maybe I was born dense. Danny's look certainly implies it.

"Listen, out of all the companies in Port Macquarie – building firms, bars and restaurants, opticians, lawyers, accountants, dry cleaners, garages and car dealerships and all the rest – the draw came out in favour of a hospital and a funeral service!". He raises his head towards the heavens and adds, "Thank you, Lord". Then turning back to me, "This is an actual Godsend, don't you see?"

"Danny" I say testily, "Put me out of my misery".

His face is alight with passion. "Rugby League, okay? Tough game, okay? So each time the team gets out onto the pitch this season, dressed in gear that's advertising a hospital and a funeral home, it's gonna perform a kind of *Haka* – yer know, that Maori war dance that the All Blacks do, trying to spook out their opponents just before the game starts. Only ours will sound something like this: '*We're gonna put you in HOSPITAL! We're gonna BURY you!*'".

Underneath all this razzmatazz, Danny is a kind, thoughtful man. I spend an hour with him doing his rounds, hand-delivering funeral charges to the next of kin. His bills are accompanied with bouquets of flowers. Like Craig, he's got just the right face for the right occasion; he knows all the stances, gestures, tones, utterances. I doubt he'll be needing to send his clients the red-coloured reminder. I add him to my list of stories for today's BBC slot.

Elsewhere in town, the meat and potatoes which keep the local newspaper going are in plentiful supply. According to the *Port Macquarie News*, a pair of teenage thugs are going inside for five years for robbing and beating up a taxi driver; a man has been charged with six counts of fraud after going on a $20,000 spending spree with someone else's chequebook. There has been an anti-war rally downtown, well attended by students; and a venomous snake has caused alarm by slithering through a crowded public car park and disappearing into a storage shed. Among the trade ads, an outfit known as Rusty Bolts Engineering offers an unrivalled welding service; a bloke who calls himself *Tree Fella* will prune your trees or cut 'em down; and Joe's Home Maintenance says that no job is too small, really it isn't, call now. In the personals, a sexy woman will talk to you about anything for $5; an agency called *Ring-a-Fling* claims to have local women aplenty on the hunt for casual affairs; and a bisexual transvestite with hot legs is up for anything.

I am not much more than 300km from Sydney now, and decide to make mighty strides towards it at 100 klicks a day or more. He doesn't know it yet, but there is a man there with whom I really want to have a talk. He has defied the critics and sceptics by producing something that in my view is really quite outstanding.

TWENTY
Saved for a Rainy Day

The Pacific Highway.

I suppose it sounds rather grand, as if running along a coastline with breathtaking ocean views. But for the most part, it is a two lane monotonous inland freeway. Perfect, if all you've got in mind is the fastest possible route from A to B, which is certainly the intent today. I pedal from Port Macquarie like a man possessed.

I pass through Taree and on to a little place called Nabia, pleased to have another 100km out of the way, and meaning to make another 100km to the city of Newcastle after a good, deep sleep.

.....If you want to make God laugh, tell Him you plans.

Next morning, I cover another 30km before it comes down again, a dark heavy cloud spreading from horizon to horizon, laden with what seems like a million tons of water. The sky's bladder can take it no more, and by the time I make another 10km to the settlement of Bulahdelah, neither can I.

The falling rain is here for the day, which means so am I; which also means the night. *Dammit*. Or some much less-polite expression.

Bulahdelah, population 1,100. A few buildings cluster together forming a sort of main street. An old hotel, a bakery, a cafe; a food-store, Post Office, real estate agency, a phone box. It looks dismal in the rain, but then I guess everywhere does.

I get a small room at the Plough Inn Hotel. It's got two bunkbeds, a small fridge, a TV, and a view of an unsurfaced car park, now a rusty-red patch of puddle-strewn mud at the edge of some grassy wasteland sloping down to a river. A group of campers are setting up tents beside a small fleet of outboard-powered skiffs. Something is going on down there in the gloom.

"Supposed to be the annual Bass Fishing Tournament" says a guy in a chef's hat, busily loading up a buffet table. "But it did this last year, rained for the entire two days. And the year before. There was no fishing then, and there'll be no fishing now unless the weather lifts. If it doesn't, most of them will gone by nightfall, and I doubt they'll be back for more next year".

Bass, that elusive prize-catch that Americans have turned into a big-bucks professional sport. Devotees in small, sleek, overpowered shallow-water boats, forever chasing the big one, in and out of narrow creeks, mudbanks, flats, and swamps. The American icons of this sport have got their own fan clubs and their own TV programmes, earning vast amounts from tournament purses and commercial endorsements. Those guys would not be seen dead in a riverside tent. And I suspect they might draw the line at Bulahdelah too.

"You coming to the bop tonight?" he asks.

That's a word I haven't heard in a long while. "What bop?"

"We party every year at tournament time, here in the hotel. What room are you in?"

I tell him and he nods. "You'd best join in then. Because after dinner this area becomes a dance floor". He points to a small landing about three metres from my door. "And that becomes a stage for the band. Your room will get it louder than will the boppers on the floor. Goes on 'till three in the morning".

So any which way I play it, electric guitars and thumping drums will pound my brains tonight. Maybe it's time for a bit of rock n'roll anyway. I wonder if they do requests.

Right now, I'm passing a wet afternoon lying on a bunkbed,

drifting in and out of assorted thoughts. Among them are Selwyn and Vietnam. Now seems a good moment to briefly revisit those times, saved for a day such as this. In fact, today Bulahdelah reminds me of that hard-bitten land. These lashing rains and bleak skies are not unlike Vietnam in the monsoon season.

If the story seems unrelated to the bike ride, bear with it. There's a link.

Having arrived at one of life's difficult little crossroads in late 1991 – the sort with no signposts – I flew to the Philippines to take a little time off with Selwyn and Merley. Most of it was spent aboard his 60ft schooner, the name of which I forget, where we idled away the days with a bit of sailing and a lot of relaxing at a deepwater anchorage amid the palm-fringed bay of Puerto Galata.

At this time, Selwyn was immersed in his hotel project. Construction of the *Seabreeze Hotel* was well under way in the Vietnamese oil port of Vung Tau. Western oilmen, increasingly sniffing around new offshore exploration blocks, were the principal target when it opened for business in a few months time.

Sitting out on the schooner's afterdeck, Selwyn rolled open a nautical chart of the Saigon and Vung Tau area. As the crow flies Vung Tau is just slightly to the north and about 35 miles to the east of Saigon, stuck out on it's own at the tip of a peninsular. But by road, he told me, it is double that distance because you first have to drive north to the town of Bien Hoa, then double-back down the long peninsular. The road, he insisted, was potholed and chaotic, desperately clogged and polluted by trundling old vehicles, many of them U.S. Army leftovers from the Vietnam War; backfiring trucks with bald tyres; ancient buses belching out black clouds of diesel; laden-down Ox carts; and thousands upon thousands of battered motorbikes and creaking old bicycles.

In other words, a guaranteed accursed nightmare. Oil companies with a presence in the region forbade employees to travel on that route after 6pm. Bandits were becoming a nocturnal hassle. But the nature of an oilman's business made toing and froing between the two centres unavoidable.

As he related this to me I stared at the chart, eyes affixed on a winding river running through Saigon and on down to the coast. About eight miles east of its estuary, across a stretch of sheltered saltwater, was the city of Vung Tau. Surely the answer to this disastrous road would be a fast boat?

A boat that could offer the oilmen and other Seabreeze guests a fast, scheduled service between the two points, operating under the wing of the hotel. I mean, why hadn't anyone thought of this before?

I felt – really felt – that stirring kick of excitement when a viable idea comes suddenly out of nowhere and clunks solidly into place. So did Selwyn. Not only that, over the following days the idea grew rather than faded as we trimmed it here, tweaked it there, until it became a reality waiting to happen. I was 46 at the time, divorced, and seeking fresh direction. I had come to the Philippines to think a few things through, and here I was staring at the answer to my own prayers as well as an oilman's.

I extended the trip. We flew from Manila to Saigon, took the nightmare trail over to Vung Tau, met the guys involved, all Aussies, and a deal was struck. I would return to London, set up a separate UK company to joint venture with the hotel's own Vietnamese partners, raise the necessary money, choose the boat, and ship it out in time for the hotel's opening ceremony.

You can change your life in a snap. All it takes is self-belief, tenacity, commitment, faith, balls, gusto, perseverance, persuasion, resolve, nerve, luck, blood, sweat, and a river of tears; plus a few other much tougher attributes, like the ability to find a lot of money. Dead simple. Try it sometime.

Anyhow, thus was born the *Jungle Jet Navigation Company*, a more sophisticated version of the Cayman Islands enterprise of 21 years before. But why such a name? Who was going to take that seriously? Well, if they didn't, then I'd make them. The Saigon River flows through miles of jungle and savanna, carrying so much surface debris that propeller damage would be inevitable. The answer to that worry was to skip over the river's flotsam in a boat pushed along by water jets.

I could hear the two J-words screaming in my head. A ready-made brand name that rolls off the tongue. "*If you're going to Vung Tau, then take the JUNGLE JET*". A clear winner.

Boats and Adventure. They go together like Sodom & Gomorrah. Despite the occasional effort, I've not got either out of my system.

For two years, I swept back and forth between the UK and Vietnam. There had been one period in the very early days when a ten-day trip turned into three hungry, penniless months. Key people gave me a wide berth. During this time, the wheels began to wobble on the hotel syndicate. It had split into two camps; bitter and acrimonious rivalry became the talk of the expatriate community.

I resolved to go it alone. Back in England, I re-grouped my thoughts and set about rousing up a few people. Vietnam was suddenly becoming a destination, getting onto the tourist map and onto the banker's map. By then, I probably knew as much as anyone about the place. Interested parties became actual investors. Small amounts trickled in, seed money they call it, which grew into much larger sums as the project developed.

The boat was scrapped in favour of a 14-seat hovercraft. Once-reticent oil bosses began inviting me for drinks. Shell Oil said it was ready to commit to permanent seats, as were others. The Standard Chartered Bank asked me to address a big lunchtime gathering of visiting British businessmen and delegates from the Department of Trade & Industry. I delivered the speech from the table of the British Ambassador. Channel 4 News asked for an interview. Princess Anne came on a three-day visit and we chatted for a while. A Greek shipping family talked of a $2.4 million investment, and would I kindly fly to New York to meet with its representatives.

It was a heady time.

Then one day, while negotiating a sizeable contract with a geophysical company, its boss took me up onto the big flat roof of his office block – and I suddenly realised I was standing on history. This building had once been the U.S. Embassy, and on the very spot where I stood, the last American helicopter had lifted off amid desperate scenes below as the tanks of Ho Chi Minh, only hours away, advanced mercilessly on Saigon.

Up there on that roof I could amost hear the pandemonium, the cries and wails of the terrified South Vietnamese as their last hope whirred high up into the sky and faded from sight. We've seen these distressing images on film, on TV, and in the press – and I saw them again then, right in front of my eyes, as if the director of some Vietnam War movie had just yelled "*Action*!" through a booming megaphone resting on my shoulder.

Standing on that infamous roof, I came to understand that I view life and all its events through the eyes and mind of a writer and traveller. I did not view it – not then, or now – through the eyes and mind of a hardened businessman, a salesman, a numbers man, a company man, a PR man, a beancounter, or a diplomat.

In creating Jungle Jet, I had turned some back-of-an-envelope vision into a reality – and the reality into a growing personal nightmare. This wasn't for me, negotiating passenger contracts and the like. I'd almost rather a noose around my neck than a tie: and talking of ties, this was fast becoming one.

Up there on that roof, with a willing and paying customer by my side, I suddenly wanted out, almost with the same urgency of all those poor souls screaming, trampling, and scrambling for the last helicopter.

Fortunately, the corporate minds now connected to the Jungle Jet project took the same view. *Times are a'changing in Vietnam.This man is too much of a maverick.* Shortly afterwards, while I was back in London for a couple of weeks, they grouped in a clandestine board meeting at the Seabreeze Hotel. When my phone rang it was to tell me I'd been fired, that they'd buy out my shares, good luck, and so long.

I put down the receiver – and punched the air with glee. Free again. Free as the sea breeze itself.

As we journey through the different stages of our lives, there come such defining moments; some inner voice demanding that we shut the door behind us, open the one in front, walk through it, don't hesitate, and do not look back.

It is, I think, an unwise man who ignores his inner commands.

This wisdom has been an unspoken part of this bike ride, occupying my thoughts on and off, ever since Turkey Beach, where Ronnie Jensen had elbowed my own memories of Vietnam. They are not as bad as his, but they could have been had I not heeded that shouting demand coming from somewhere inside as I stood transfixed on a roof of questionable fame.

I'll be hearing a lot more than the inner voice this evening, that's for certain. The rain keeps falling down. Several competitors have already decamped. Later on, I drift into the hotel bar which is slowly filling up with local revellers. They're going to party whatever the weather.

There's a foursome, late30s, sitting at a nearby table. One of the men is several kilos overweight and is dabbing sweat from his brow. The other man is thin and gaunt, all bones. He is with an exceedingly fat woman who wears a dark blue dress made of material that glistens and dazzles against the light. Next to her is a pencil of a woman in a white blouse and blue jeans. She's got short wavy hair, a small mouth, and a pair of wire glasses perched upon a beaky nose. This one is doing most of the talking and she doesn't mind who hears.

"What I like" she's saying, "Is for Ray to cook the tea when he gets home from work, so I can put my feet up and watch the telly. We've just bought a new one, all the channels. After he's done the washing up and put the kids to bed I let him go down to his shed –".

"The only place I can get some peace" the overweight man growls. The thin man next to him nods and takes a pull of beer.

"If Ray had his way, he'd be down here at the hotel every night. There's no way I'm allowing that".

"Too right" says the fat woman. "It's the same with my Ken". The thin man, Ken, stares into his beer and says nothing.

Ray swallows the last of his beer and gets up for another. The thin woman gives him a sharp, hawkish glare. "You just watch the amount you put away tonight" she snaps. "We'll be dancing later, you and me. I don't want you treading all over my feet like the last time".

"Right now I'd rather tread on your face" Ray calls back as he heads for the bar.

"See what I mean?" protests his missus. "When he's had a few, he gets a mouth on him, that one".

The sound of a band tuning up comes from the dining area, drowning out the rest of her complaint. Soon, everyone heads towards the music, provided by a duo called *No Control*, with a little help from a synthesizer. Tables and chairs have been moved around the edges to make way for a dance floor and there's no shortage of takers as the band belts out an old Jerry Lee Lewis number, *Great Balls of Fire*. But it's a very strange mixture of foot tapping going on out there. Two or three couples are jiving; others are doing some sort of old fashioned twist; and there's one couple waltzing around the floor.

At first the duo puts out some reasonable stuff, but as the evening wears on, it becomes clear that their well-rehearsed repetoire is pretty limited, and they begin to make mistakes. At this point, when the floor has emptied out, the thin woman with wire glasses and a beaked nose drags an unwilling Ray into the spotlight for all too see. *No Control* is making an attempt at the Ray Charles song, *I Can't Stop Loving You*. The woman is making a much harder attempt to lead her husband around the floor, look everybody, this is how you do it. But

Ray has clearly stuck to his guns tonight and tucked away a few. Before they complete the first circuit, he lurches forward. She tumbles backward. Next moment, they're both down on the floor, him on top. Her legs are kicking wildly in the air, and I can see the raw anger in her face as she tries to push him off. But Ray is going nowhere without help. The music grinds to a slow halt as his thin friend and another man heave him up and sit him down at a table where he promptly falls fast asleep. His wife's face is flushed and her mouth is tighter than Ebenezer Scrooge's wallet. Ray has made a big fool of her and he's going to live to regret it.

It all goes downhill from there. The duo begins to live up to its name. At one point, the singer forgets his words; their guitars trail off, leaving only the tap-tapping of the synthesizer to offer any form of salvage.

People begin moving back to the bar. This cannot go on. Mercifully, it doesn't. By midnight the band has very wisely packed it in. Outside, it's still coming down but I've made up my mind. I'm out of here first thing come rain or shine.

The Sydney Solar Sailor

TWENTY ONE
The Doctor

A grey and damp morning. Positive thought is required. Today is a great day for a long, concentrated bike ride.

Some 60km later, I reach the industrial city of Newcastle in the early afternoon. Like its Geordie namesake, this was once a serious coal port. These days it is dominated by the BHP steelworks, but seems like an OK place. Now that the sun is out again, I'm spurred on to another 40km and the town of Wyong.

I pass a large banner tied to a roadside fence. *Suzi Quatro. One Night Only. Donlayson & Wyee RSL.*

There are two ways of looking at this. Either the diminutive rocker is down to performing at a Returned Servicemen's League in a town that the rest of the world has never heard of; or these RSLs really do have something going for them. I've been hearing good things about the RSL all the way along the ride, but have yet to set foot inside one. I make a mental note.

Tiring, I make Wyong just before dark, glad to have another 100km out of the way. The main street is on a rise, upon which stands the suspiciously named Grand Hotel. The manager tells me I'm lucky to get the last room in town. There's some reunion going on and everywhere is full. He won't allow Oggy Boy into the room, says he'll lock it away in a back office. And oh, there's a $20 deposit on the key – a sure sign that that the downside of the big city – suspicion, mistrust – is only 95km away.

I go through a back door into a weed-strewn yard, clamber up the fire escape, proceed through what must be the dingiest corridor in Oz and, with a hefty shoulder to the reluctant door, come to rest in Room 7. It has got six beds inside, two of them with bare mattresses; a naked light bulb dangles from a high ceiling; the fading wallpaper is damp and peeling. I think tonight is a good night to go out, maybe take a look at the local RSL.

Returned Servicemen's League. It sounds like the British Legion or the Derby & Joan Club. Tea and biscuits, the vicar, blue-rinse hair, jumble sales.

It is a members-only thing, but the guy at the door waves me through into a large, well carpeted area with a bar, restaurant, stage and dance floor, and an acre of poker machines. It seems to be an all-ages, family kind of place, and what the connection is with returned servicemen is not at all clear.

Up on the stage, a duo called *Wilson & Lightfoot* make easy work of good old country songs. They are a class act, professionals. Compared to these two, Bulahdelah's *No Control* should rename itself *No Hope*.

Yes, I can see Suzi Quatro packing 'em in to a place like this. It concurs with all I've been hearing. The food is good, the prices low, the atmosphere congenial. Someone tells me that those evergreen rockers *Status Quo* are beginning an Oz tour shortly, and they're booked into a number of RSL venues. I'm glad I've come here tonight. It's very enjoyable.

I am not so glad about the Grand Hotel. Its management could learn a thing or two from the Wyong RSL. In the morning, 9am, I find all doors to the main building locked. Oggy Boy is inside, and I want to be gone. I hammer on the back door until a tired face eventually glares at me through a barred window.

"Go away!" he shouts. "We're closed!".

"Hey, I'm a guest here! I want to check out".

"We're closed!" he shouts again. "Come back at eleven".

I protest. Vigorously. He pulls out a bunch of jailer's keys and reluctantly lets me in. There's my bike and $20 key money to retrieve – and would a mug of coffee be completely out of the question? In the end, I get all three. But the palaver.....

Back on the road, I pass through Gosford and Hornsby amid dense traffic. Green open spaces are getting scarcer, swallowed up by the perceived needs of urban humanity; the screwy values of lives immersed in acres of brick.

"*Herro!! Herro!!*".

I look to my left. *Boy Banzai* is jumping and waving from inside a bus shelter. I had reckoned him to be much further ahead by now.

He's inside the shelter repairing a punctured tyre. There are scabs and bruises on his arms and neck. "Have bad accident. I think truck driver not like bicycles".

Captain Tsu Yo Shi, Japanese Army, was just this side of Taree when he got rubbed by a storming 18-wheeler. He was flung into the scrub. His bike got dragged along the highway, twisting the front wheel, buckling the pedals, tearing his pannier bags until somehow the mangled machine jumped free. The incident has cost him two or three days in repairs to bike and to some stinging oriental pride. Still, he's alive and riding, but I think he's had a very, very narrow escape.

I ride on towards the Sydney skyline, mindful of trucks once more. In the suburb of Strathfield I stop for a break, struck by the sheer number of South Koreans roaming its tight little streets. They seem to be running everything; foodstores, cafes, newsagents, taxi-cabs. I think I am going to find Sydney a very different city to the one I remember.

Once ensconced in the Capitol Square Hotel on the corner of Campbell and George Streets, I clean up and go for a stroll. Ah, George Street. If I follow you to the other end, you'll lead me down to Circular Quay on the harbour front. I've trodden this board before.

I am surprised to find it all very much as I remember. Tall grey buildings casting twilight shadows on a narrow downtown thoroughfare. It is quiet this evening. The loudest sounds are coming from a busker with a parrot perched on his left shoulder. He's simultaneously playing his guitar and blowing down an aboriginal didgeridoo. The parrot squawks, "*Money in the hat! Money in the hat!*".

Circular Quay has altered little over all the years. There's an increase in tourist boats doing the harbour rounds. A large cruise ship is tied up where once had been the wharf for immigrant ships. Behind, the Sydney Harbour Bridge spans the bay. Across the water are the unmistakeable white sails of the Sydney Opera House. From this angle, they look like mis-shapen wings from a gaggle of demented geese.

Close by is an area called The Rocks. I wander over, another small memory rising from the depths. This place *has* changed, and how. I remember a drab warehouse district, home to trucking outfits, freight depots, and tugboat operators. Now it is alive with people, music, bars, cafes, neon lights. Only the architecture remains the same, the old blending in with the new.

When I departed the sheep stations I made Sydney the first stop, just for a month or two. I rented a tiny flat in Bondi Junction and got myself a job down here in The Rocks. It was the kind of job that turns clock-watching into a job in itself. My boss, a Swiss-Jewish immigrant whom I only knew as Mr Lander, had a wholesale business trading in cheap Japanese trinkets. He was also the fussiest little man, five-foot-three if that, who ever walked this planet.

Each morning, Mr Lander would don on a dismal-brown duster coat, consult his clipboard, then bark out something like, "*Item number 4451!*" I would obediently reach for Item 4451, only to feel this whoosh of rushing air as he darted underneath my armpits and grabbed it first. And so it went like this, hour after hour, day after day. The point of my tedious job was completely lost on me.

I would spend lunch hours down at the harbour, gazing at the boats. It is where my curious addiction to all things nautical began, and I was looking for a way to get to sea. On the floor beneath Mr Lander's musty storeroom was a transport company working a regular seafood run between Sydney and Tweed Heads. Its boss had told me about the prawn fleet, offered me a lift in one of his refrigerated trucks, and the rest you know.

Funny how things work out. In an indirect way, I owe the experience of Tin Can Bay and Tweed Heads to my job with an obsessed little trinket salesman and his storeroom stuffed full of plastic earrings and worthless necklaces.

Later, returning along Pitt Street, a man suddenly springs out from a shop doorway and comes alongside. "S'cuse me, mate. Can I talk to yer for a second?"

I know what's coming. "Sorry, I'm in a hurry. Late for someone". I walk a little brisker.

He catches up again. "Look, it'll only take a moment".

I stop and hold his stare. He is about 35, part Aboriginal. "I don't have any money" I say, not straying too far from the truth.

"Have I asked yer for any?"

"Are you going to?"

"Yeah. Politely".

"I've just told you. I don't have any". I sound and feel impatient.

"Well I've asked yer politely! The least yer can do is be polite back!". There looks to be fire in his eyes now, as if angry at me; at his situation; at the world. His stare becomes a glare.

I don't know where this is going, except not into my pocket. "How many times do I have to say it? *I don't have ANY MONEY*".

Suddenly he winks and is grinning like a Cheshire cat. "It was worth a try" he says almost warmly. "No offence intended".

"None taken".

He offers a hand and I take it. Then he turns and slowly walks away. A few moments later, I'm calling after him. "*Alright, hold on!*" I pull out $10 and he comes speeding back, snatches it, and retreats sharply.

From a safe distance he calls back, "*Never fails, mate. It's the technique!*"

I had white-lied to him, and he knows that. This is what he does for a living, hearing that same denial 99 times out of 100. But he's sharp, clever even. He knows how to turn a negative into a positive. In some perverse way, I think he may be due those ten dollars.

Next morning I call the doctor. Not any old quack, this guy. He is a man with extraordinary vision who jacked in a secure medical practice to pursue an environmental project that is slap-bang in an area of keen interest to me. Besides, it will make a good radio piece, and he tells me to meet with him at Milson's Point, a small northshore marina, 2pm.

In this land of blazing sunshine, I've been disgusted by the lack of interest in all things solar. Every day the sun delivers to Earth 27 times more energy than the entire world population uses in a year. It is a staggering statistic, but true. It would be fair to say that Australia gets a decent chunk of this daily download, yet I'm scatching my memory to recall the last time I noticed a solar panel anywhere. I think it was at the *Forest Flying* centre up near Mackay. Yes, that's it. In fact, the *only* other place where I've seen utilisation of this natural resource was back at the very beginning, at the remote Heathlands Station in faraway Cape York.

In parts of Asia, Africa, and South America whole villages are powered by solar. In Switzerland, Germany, and Scandinavia eco-minded firms power entire office blocks with solar – even in winter. In other areas of endeavour, energy from the sun plays a vital role. The three-man crew of *Breitling Orbiter*, the first hot air balloon to successfully fly non-stop around the world, relied on solar for cabin lighting and navigation systems. Archeologists, mountaineeers, ocean sailors, and others of the big outdoors power their computers, phones, radios, and hot water systems through this gift from the Gods.

That there appears to be so little interest here in a hi-tech land awash with sunlight is near to unbelievable. Which makes my admiration for Dr Robert Dane near to boundless.

Milson's Point is not so much a marina as an untidy waterworld of ageing workboats tucked into an oily creek amid which the shiningly futuristic catamaran *Solar Sailor* stands out like a Maserati in the middle of shanty town. A sea of blue chrystalline solar panels run 21 metres from stem to stern and from beam to beam. She is a licensed passenger boat that plys her trade around Syney Harbour – using only the rays of the sun for propulsion.

If I'm a little too keen on boats, I'm actually far keener to see a world of diminishing power stations, oil refineries, ghastly supertankers. In creating this machine, the authoritive Dr Dane is significantly stirring an awareness of sustainable energy in a lucky nation that needs to take a good, long look at what nature has given it.

Robert Dane welcomes me aboard. He is early 40s, tall, slim, with a sharp nose and a mass of curly brown hair. He wears a blue teeshirt, casual khaki trousers, and carries a commanding air.

It is a beautiful afternoon, not a cloud anywhere. "All this sunshine!" he exclaims, spreading his arms as wide as they'll go. "All this free fuel! And nobody's using it. It is *crazy*".

The vessel earns its keep through charter work; tourist cruises within this celebrated harbour; parties and wedding receptions; floating conferences; and as a glamorous demonstration of natural power from the sun. This afternoon, he's got a group of 30 Singaporean businessmen turning up, all anxious to find out how it works.

He takes me on a guided tour. The engine room is probably cleaner than a hospital operating theatre. Two small 40kw electric motors are housed inside shining stainless steel casing. They are wired to a bank of batteries, in turn wired to a terminal that is itself wired to the panels. Energy in a flash; sunlight hits panel; panel converts to electricity; batteries store it. It is true what they say. The best things in life are free.

I'm no scientist, and to me this is all a miracle. Okay, so you're lying on a beach soaking up the warmth. Next to you is a blue-coloured panel doing exactly the same. You're getting brown, falling asleep – while the panel, wired in every sense of the word, is somehow producing instant voltage from a fiery planet millions of miles away.

Amazing, methinks.

The 30 Singaporeans come tumbling off a special bus and charge down the dock in an eager oriental crush. Just before I leave, the forthright Dr Dane takes me aside and offers an opinion about something. I stand and listen in respectful silence, neither shaken or stirred by his words.

The sun can give us electricity. It can also give us cancer.

The Doc had noticed a tiny bump in the corner of my left eye-socket. I do not know how it got there or what it is doing there. But apparently he does. I have come here to see his solar dream machine – and I'm leaving with a negative piece of news at a time of my life when I've never felt fitter.

"You'll have to get it cut out" he orders.

"Or?"

"Or it'll spread down to an optic nerve. You'll go blind. Slowly, it will kill you off. I'm going to refer you to someone".

I promise you, I'm as calm as a quiet leafy lane. There is a clarity in my head; some mental cleansing agent is wiping away any confusion. The Doc rummages through an address book in his briefcase, ignoring his party of monied businessmen from Singapore.

"Doc" I say, "Listen to me, please. Firstly I've got a bike ride to finish, stories to tell, including yours. I don't have time for this. Not now, or in the future".

He gives me a very cool stare. "Meaning what?"

"I've had a helluva life, really. All nine of them, plus an overdraft.

If your diagnosis is correct, then that's the way it is".

I am no hero, masochist, or hypochondriac. If my mind is clear, and it is, then I'm no madman either. We are all dying; some of us are further up the line than others. That's all.

No amount of surgical attention is going to prevent the final gasp.

TWENTY TWO
Whiplash

I do not allow the Doc's diagnosis to affect morale. No doubt when the trip is over I'll give it some thought; apply some positives; but for now I'm only concerned with moving out of the city and out towards the bush.

Disinclined to jostle with urban traffic today, I ride down to Circular Quay and board the RiverCat to Paramatta – once a West Sydney suburb, now almost a city in itself. From there I pick up the Great Western Highway and pedal an easy 40km to Penrith, where I bed down early in readiness for tomorrow's tough one – a 45km uphill hike into the thinning air of the Blue Mountains and the city of Katoomba.

The first few klicks are easy enough, but then the mountains loom and the climb starts in earnest. This is going to be hard, slow going, and I have to stop every 200 metres or so to give a short break to aching thighs. The little town of Blaxland – named after the explorer who blazed a trail through here in the early 1800s – comes and goes. Or rather, I do. Through Warimoo, Springwood, Faulconbridge, Linden, Woodford, Hazelbrook, Lawson, and Bullaburra. By the time I reach Wentworth Falls, only 6km from Katoomba, I simply do not have the will to stop and gaze in awe at a spectacular 270 metre drop. If I stop now, I won't be getting back in the saddle again.

Today is saving the best until last, Trying to find the way from downtown Katoomba to the Alpine Motor Inn, I take a wrong turn down a very steep incline. Which means I've got to somehow get up it again. But it is simply un-rideable, too damn steep. I walk the bike up, straining so far forward against gradient, weight, and gravity that my feet cannot get a decent grip. Slipping, tumbling, cursing, sweating, I do not want to see another hill in my life. A kid of about eight is sitting on top of a dustbin, kicking his heels, watching me with a big grin. Finally at the top, I feel more than happy to forget all about Dr Dane's assertion, sorely tempted to wheeze out my last gasp here and now, pleased to be gone.

Today's ride has been a bitch.

Later, still alive and sitting in an armchair perusing a tourist freesheet, *Blue Mountains Monthly*, I spot an extract from a newspaper item of nearly 200 years ago. It is dated May 11, 1813.

> *Mr Gregory Blaxland, Mr William Wentworth, and Lieutenant Lawson with four servants, five dogs, and four horses loaded with provisions and ammunition, crossed the Nepean River at four o'clock in the afternoon and proceeded, by their calculations, two miles through forest land and good grass. They encamped at five o'clock at the foot of the first ridge.*
>
> *On the second day they ascended the ridge, finding a large lagoon of good water, full of very coarse rushes.*
>
> *The explorers encamped that night at the head of a deep gully, coming across a kangaroo that had just been killed by an eagle.*

Whenever we think we've had it tough, like I do today, it's no bad thing to reflect on how much harder things had been in bygone times. I don't know how long Blaxland's expedition lasted, but they'd have been rough, tough days and nights, trying to find a route through these mountains – though I guess the servants would have been of some consolation.

My great-grandfather's two-year solo attempt to discover the North Pole between 1905–1907 comes to mind – a man who in England was used to the luxury of servants. Alfred Harrison survived two arctic winters, stayed with Eskimos, and at times had to survive by shooting Musk Rats. In his stiff-upper-lip diaries, he complains not once.

And here I am, warm and snug inside a motel room; TV, hot water, coffee, the lot. I don't know whether to laugh or sneer at my own pathetic-self.

There is one sight in Katoomba I cannot miss. The breathtaking spectacle of the *Three Sisters* rock formation at Echo Point: three giant, rough-edged sandstone penises standing high in the still silence of the sweeping Jamieson Valley, itself a panorama of forests, plateaux, ridges, and rock. Completing the canvas is a deep blue haze hanging over the distance, apparently created by a constant vapour emitted from acre upon acre of eucalyptus trees below. It could easily be one of the world's Seven Wonders, but I suppose whoever decides these things figured that with Ayers Rock and the Great Barrier Reef, Oz has more than its fair share. Politically, too awkward; might tip the tourism balance, upset a few nations.

There's a noisy busload of Japanese tourists milling around Echo Point. The spectacle has become such an attraction that its viewing area is in some demand as an outdoor wedding venue. Less publicised are the grim statistics which make this spot Australia's equivalent to Beachy Head. Here is where the depressed and downhearted come to leap away from it all.

I've a contact in Katoomba, a Pom, who is capable of wearing as mournful a face as any which the Port Macquarie pallbearer can express. He is doing so today, as if contemplating one last visit to Echo Point himself.

I first met Robin in New Zealand, 1964. He is the elder brother of a friend and we still run into each other from time to time; in England, in Spain where he has a villa, and now here in Oz. He is out here for a few months, staying with his second ex-wife now that the dust has settled between them. She put down roots in Katoomba after Robin jumped ship from the marriage but he is as footloose and rootless as ever. He threatens to move, here, there, anywhere except where he actually is at the time.

Robin has a dysfunctional family situation. There's an Englishwoman on the Costa Blanca with whom he shares some sort of life, but the poor woman has Parkinson's Disease and is in and out of nursing homes. There is an ex-wife and a son here in Australia, but for some reason the son won't have anything to do with him. There's another ex-wife and son across the Tasman Sea in New Zealand; there is a brother who has long been settled in Cape Town; also another brother, my friend, living back in their native Winchester. Robin flits wearily between the lot.

So it does not surprise me when this man – who has done well for himself over the years – taps his glass in a Katoomba pub and says, "All I care about these days is this. The drink".

On that obvious note, I get up and buy another round. The barman, who cannot be more than 22, says, "Last one, mate. No more".

It is 6pm. We have been in there less than an hour.

"Excuse me?" I respond.

"Last round. I'm not serving you again after this".

In brittle voice, I ask why so.

"That's your third rum and coke in an hour".

"So? It's what you're open for, isn't it? I expect your boss would rather it be my tenth".

"Yeah, well fuck him. If you get loaded, cause some grief, it's me who the law holds responsible. It's me who gets fined and sacked. All that you get is a good laugh at my expense".

It must be a NSW state law, holding the bartender liable. I remember the troublesome bloke in Woodburn being refused another drink. All the same, Robin and me have been talking quietly, causing no bother to the barman or anyone else. His stiff, humourless attitude irks me.

"Do I look as if I'm going to give you grief?" I ask snappily.

"You do now. Distinctly".

"Well if I do, you're the reason".

He spreads his hands. "Hey, listen. Don't blame me. Blame the law!".

I can't win. Not without losing my rag. I must accept this; back off and leave. Robin agrees. Today he is a whingeing Pom, more than willing to be critical of his host country.

"Still got that inferiority complex; the convict mentality" he growls as we search for another bar. "Nothing's changed".

I am not inclined to agree. Some say that the difference between Poms and Aussies is in the blink of an eyelid, which is the view I hold. Others say it is in the gap of two oceans, America lying inbetween, with a stranglehold on both our countries. On the surface, Oz is going the way of America. But underneath there is something deeper. Like England, its humour and history will prevent it from total capsize into the cultural abyss that is the USA.

A particular aspect of Australian history is much in mind as I push on towards the city of Bathurst, via Lithgow, enjoying some good downhill speeds and feeling happy again.

About 30km from Bathurst the rain comes down, a bleak Manchester drizzle. There is a distinct shift in temperature. For the first time, I am feeling cold. My fingers, poking out from a pair of cut-off cycling gloves, have gone numb. It has switched from summer to winter in an afternoon.

I pass a curious sign on the side of the road. It reads: *8 out of 10 Speeding Deaths*. That's all it says. If it's trying to say that eight out of ten motoring deaths are caused by speeding, it's with an extremely poor use of English. I carry on around a sweeping bend, worrying about the education of those in authority. Then another sign looms up: *Occur on Bends. SLOW DOWN.*

Ah, yes, clever. They are educated to high standards.

I check into the Coachman's Inn Motel, this side of downtown Bathurst. The motel is clearly trading on the local folklore surrounding Cobb & Co, the legendary stagecoach company. It has certainly drawn me to this city, influenced as I was by the *Whiplash* TV series of so long ago.

Bathurst is a lovely place; Australia's first inland settlement where the colonial architecture, apparent everywhere, screams history from its heady days as a goldrush town in the 1860s. It would have been a rougher place back then, when 50 pubs thrived in a population of just 4,000. I can almost feel speckles of gold dust blowing down the main drag, William Street.

Next morning I go down to the Visitor Information Centre, to be greeted by the pleasing sight of a fully-restored Cobb & Co stagecoach. Bright, shining red coachwork on four large wooden yellow wheels. Royal Mail is signwritten across the top of the bodywork. But inside the coach, it is stark and cramped, and I can only imagine the discomfort endured by travellers of yesteryear. The suspension system comes from a series of leather straps, raising the bodywork from the chassis – creating a swinging, rolling effect with every rock and bump in the road. It was common for passengers to complain of a type of seasickness.

The company was formed in 1852 by an American, Freeman Cobb, down in Victoria. But Cobb was a poor businessman, and persistent rumours that he'd fled from California dogged him all the way – even here in a country founded on convict labour. After ten years, Cobb sold out to a consortium led by another American, James Rutherford (portrayed in *Whiplash* by Robert Graves), who moved the HQ to Bathurst – the hub of goldfield activity. He arrived in 1862 with eight stagecoaches and 52 horses. Under Rutherford's guidance the company grew and grew, eventually travelling 20,000 scheduled miles each week, and with a total horse-count of 30,000. As many as 6000 horses would be harnessed every day, switching to fresh teams at every coaching inn set about 20 miles apart.

Teams of five or seven horses pulled the vehicles, usually at a trot, and at an average speed of 7mph – roughly half that of a bicycle. Despite the terrible roads of those days (and they frequently had to go off-road to avoid fallen trees or to cross shallow creeks), Cobb & Co gathered a solid reputation for punctuality.

As for the drivers, they were almost revered. To be a stagecoach driver for Cobb & Co was to be today's equivalent of a celebrated folk hero; maybe someone like Red Adair, the oilrig firefighter; or the yachtswoman Ellen MacArthur. Not only were they exceptionally skilled at controlling teams of horses – each horse had a separate set of reins – they became much in demand for their ability to spin a good yarn. Male passengers, not women, would be invited to pay a little extra to sit up top with the driver, ride shotgun and open gates, in return for a few well-embellished tales from these heroes of the bush. And they had names to match such talents; *Charlie Matthews, Mick Dougherty, Ned 'Cabbage Tree' Devine*. For these guys, their stages became quite literally the stage for a one-man show.

The *Whiplash* episodes had seized the imagination of a spotty 15 year old youth in England, his eyes glued to black & white images of distant adventure. And somewhere deep in his psyche, it had laid buried for 42 years. Gazing at this restored piece of very basic machinery, even the cynic in him still sees something romantic about Australia's answer to Wells Fargo.

In reality, a stagecoach ride would have been an ordeal. The 300km route from Sydney to Forbes, a town 150km west of here, took 53 hours. Two days, two nights, and five hours. You can cross America, coast to coast, in a Greyhound bus in almost the same time.

There would have been a deep longing among passengers for the rolling nightmare to end; for a bath, for a pee, for a break from some bore who cannot stop talking, and with whom they'd rub knees or jostle shoulders with every jarring bump. It would have been like riding some brutal ghost train at a funfair, only worse.

Now, as then, reality has a way of maiming and strangling all romantic notions. This one comes heavily down to earth when I search out what had once been Cobb & Co's headquarters on the corner of William and Howick Streets. Today it is.....

.....*Today it is the G&T Bar and Grill.*

Thud.

Modern Bathurst is known as much for motor sport as for Cobb & Co. From 7mph, let's go to 207mph. For one weekend every year, a different kind of horsepower screams along the track at Mount Panorama on the edge of town. The Bathurst 24-Hour race is the southern hemisphere's *Le Mans* and is starting to attract serious players from the sports car industry. BMW, Ferrari, Jaguar and others. Just for the hell of it, I pedal around the course. The only noise is of two bicycle tyres whirring along the smooth surface of the track. But you know, even in sunlight there is something spooky about empty racetracks. It is as if the pits, grandstands, and chicanes are somehow occupied by a silent throng of invisible ghouls.

Back in town, I pass a McDonalds franchise where a peculiar ritual is going on in the car park. A big posse of bikers, 40 or more, prepare to move out in orderly style. The pack leader, a fat guy with a big viking beard and a horned helmet, sits patiently astride his Harley. When everyone is ready he leads off, followed by two riders alongside each other. One by one, the pack becomes a roaring conga line of glinting metal and black leather. At the rearguard, two parallel bikes tie up the formation. It is like some disciplined cavalry exercise; the colonel up front, followed by captains, lieutenants, privates, and a couple of sergeant-majors at the rear. Maybe that's the intent. Nobody is going to argue with this bunch.

The following day, Sunday, I ride out myself, turning southwest for the town of Cowra 90km distant. The day is sunny and hot. When I stop for a few gulps of water, another trivial memory charges me in the face. Flies, millions of them, surround me from out of nowhere until I'm practically frantic with irritation. All the way down the coast, flies have barely been in evidence. Nor up in the heights of the Blue Mountains, or in the cold drizzle while pedalling to Bathurst. But today, far inland and moving ever deeper into the bush, it looks to be their day in court.

I had become used to them out on the stations. The common everyday sight was of 15 or 20 flies crawling around everyone's face. You learned to live with it, a petty fact of life in Australia's back country. But I've been a long time gone, and now even the sound of a fly makes me cross. If I ride casually, they ride with me, hovering infuriatingly just in front of my face and eager for a good helping of human sweat. I pedal with gusto.

About 15km out, I hear the popping noise of another puncture, rear tyre. But bloody hell, I've inadvertently left the vital repair kit in Katoomba during one of my regular clear-outs and tidy-ups. Meant to buy one in Bathurst. Forgot.

I walk the bike down a slight hill. At the bottom there's an entrance to a small cattle station. I try to roll a cigarette while swiping at the flies and thinking this through. I cannot push the bike 15km back to Bathurst, nor the 15km on to the next town, some place called Blaney. Hitchhiking isn't the answer, not with a loaded bike for company. And I can't just stand here all day.

I hadn't planned on visiting this particular cattle station, but.....

As I grind out the homerolled, a car comes bumping down the station track, leaving a cloud of dust in its wake. An elderly man is inside, his elbow poking out from the driver's door. He asks what's up.

"Puncture. I've forgotten my repair kit".

He sizes me up, then says helpfully "Go up to the homestead. Ask for my son, Michael. He'll find you something to fix it with. Never know your luck. Might feed you as well. There's a barbie going on".

I thank him, push the bike up to the homestead and tap on the flyscreened door. A tall, barefooted man with cropped dark hair answers. He's in his 30s, wearing a green shirt and a pair of work trousers.

"Are you Michael?"

He looks at me for a moment, slightly suspicious. "That's me".

I explain the problem. Michael barefoots it across to a shed, emerging with repair patches and glue intended for cars and trucks. They'll do fine. He points to an outdoor tap with a bucket beside it and leaves me to it, but says to come inside afterwards and clean up. Messy business, punctures.

Bubbles from the bucket tell me there's not one puncture but three. What the hell did I ride over?

Task completed, Michael invites me into a large living room where kids and grown ups are tucking into piled-high plates of barbecued meat. A family get-together, he says. Sons, daughters, nieces, nephews, aunts and uncles. I count eleven of them. Before long it is as if I'm one of the family, back in the bush again, where hospitality to strangers comes as naturally as breathing.

Someone asks what brought me to Bathurst. A strange fascination with Cobb & Co, I reply.

There is a silence. Suddenly everyone is looking at everyone else with smirks and smiles. Did I say something?

Michael is grinning hard. "You've come to the right homestead".

"I know that. The tyre's fixed, and I'm being fed. Thank you".

"No worries. And here's the bonus. All of us here are Rutherfords". He lets it sink in slowly, then says "James Rutherford, the head of Cobb & Co, was my great-great grandfather".

I am thunderstruck. There's no other word for it. It is as if what started with *Whiplash* is coming to the most coincidental of climaxes. It's almost like the unexpected twist-in-the-tale at the end of a good thriller. I mean, what a way to round off a 42 year fascination.

But there is something else in all this. I could so easily have had that puncture a mile before, or a mile further up the road. Or maybe not even had it at all. That it happened directly outside Michael Rutherford's cattle property sets me thinking. Somewhere in this, there is a great big *why?*

What food for thought. What a neat piece for the radio. Thank you, puncture.

I stay well into the afternoon, giving up all thoughts of making Cowra today. Instead, I pedal on 15km to the township of Blaney.

I all but sing my way there, happy with the day's events. And happier still of such clear reinforcement of what to me anyway, is another blaring truth.

There really is no such thing as coincidence. What happens to us in life, all of us, is meant to be – the Master Plan at work. It really is as simple as that.

TWENTY THREE
A Cafe in the Bush

Between Blaney and Cowra is the weeny township of Mandurama, so small it is not listed on my map. Even so, I'm glad it's there. Because this morning both tyres puncture within minutes of one another. I stop every ten minutes to pump them up, unable to fathom this sudden spate of hissing air. Both tyres had been harder than Schwarzeneggar's biceps when I set out today.

While I pump, flies swarm around my sweating face. Swiping them away is futile. They're back in microseconds.

One thing is certain. I'm not going to get a repair kit in Mandurama. It is a slighty shabby one-horse town with a store, a hotel, a small petrol station, a few residential streets, not much else. The Mid Western Highway cuts right through it.

Blink. Gone.

The woman at the petrol station points to some kind of ramshackle workshop across the road with a rusting heap of a car parked outside. She says the bloke who owns it is my best hope.

I walk a dejected Oggy Boy over to the workshed. Inside, a bald, craggy, cantankerous old man – wearing blue overalls with more holes than cloth – sits in a cramped little office, snapping at someone down an old telephone. His desktop is stacked high with spanners, screwdrivers, speedometers, carburettors, alternators, oilcans. He pays me no heed whatsoever as he listens to excuses on the other end of the line.

The workshop is a grander version of the old man's desk, littered with toolboxes, hosepipes, carjacks, engine blocks, grease pumps, oil drums, welding gear, old tyres, hubcaps, a generator. Somewhere in the background a radio is playing country music.

The old man puts down the phone. "Yeah?" he enquires, his head cocked slightly. A snarl crosses his face at the mention of bike punctures. "I hate bicycles. Hate the bloody things".

"Is that a yes or what?"

He sighs. "Yeah, okay. But first I gotta drive to Bathurst. See my lawyer. Yer'll have ter wait until after lunch. Say two o'clock".

Three hours can seem like three weeks in a place like Mandurama. I might as well hunt for a story, though I don't think I'm going to get one. A woman shopping in the General Store tells me there's a vineyard just out of town called Golden Gully Wines, Cabernet a speciality. No story there, I decide. But there's some wild conjecture that Prince Harry may be coming out here to spend part of his Gap Year on a neaby sheep station. If true, that would be a certain radio piece. But nobody's supposed to know anything, it's only a rumour, and she clams up.

With no transport, there's nothing for it but to wander into the Mandurama Hotel. Three men are sitting at one end of the bar, beers in hand, talking with a beefy bartender. Two of them seem willing to talk with me, but the man in the middle shows immediate signs of hostility, as if I'd broken up a card game. They know nothing of Prince Harry, they say; rumours, hell, around here they come and go every half-hour. We make small talk for a while, then I immerse myself into a crossword syndicated by the *Sydney Morning Herald*.

Sometime later, I walk past the three men towards the loo. While standing at the urinal, the unfriendly one of the trio comes in, parks himself right next to me, and stares dead ahead. I attempt some polite trivia, but he plain won't answer. Not a single word. Must be to do with his condition. I cannot think what else.

He is a dwarf, perhaps three feet tall. I say coldy, "*Okay, buddy. We'll play it your way*" and walk out – more philosophical than angry. I watch as his mates haul him back onto his barstool, upon which he looks to be quite normal.

There's chat of a local barn dance tonight. Everyone in town is turning up for the big event. The dwarf says he can't wait to show everyone how it's done; the twist, rock n'roll, Waltzing Matilda. For an insane moment I think about stopping over the night; check out a local knees-up; observe Shorty over there Walk the Talk.

For a tedious half-hour I wait outside the old man's locked-up workshed. It is 2.30pm and no sign of him. A middle aged woman with a hawkish face comes down the empty street towards me. I ask if she knows where this bloke lives. In a town this size, she couldn't not know. First right, next left, third house on the left.

The old man is back from Bathurst. His rustbucket car is outside. I knock on the door.

"Yeah?" he calls from somewhere inside.

"It's the Pom with the bike. Time's getting on a bit".

"What's yer bloody hurry?"

What's my bloody hurry? It is strangely difficult explaining to motorists what life is like on a long-distance bicycle. They think in terms of 100kph, not 15-20kph. They do not view steep hills as any form of obstacle. There is no problem driving in the rain or driving at night. But there is a problem pedalling at night – and I can see this is where today's ride is heading. Into the dark.

The old man shouts, "Go and wait by the shop! Lemme finish me lunch".

I'll have to be patient. No point in rattling him more than he already is. His lawyer must have delivered some bad news.

Finally he comes backfiring down the road and unlocks the workshop. I get the wheels off Oggy Boy, then the tyres. He takes one sneering look at the inner tubes, clucks his tongue and asks with that same cocked head, "*Yer been on the grass, mate?*"

I raise an eyebrow. Spliffs are okay, but not my scene.

"Yeah" he carries on, "Yer been on the grass alright. See this thing?" He extracts a tiny needlepoint seed from the tube. "Bindey eyes, that's what we call 'em. Sharp seeds from roadside grass. It's why people around here use reinforced kevlar tyres. These little bastards, they'll blow ten tyres a minute".

He inflates the tubes and puts them into a tank of foul-looking water. Five different sets of bubbles dance around the dark liquid. He inspects the outer tubes, his sharp eyes missing nothing. Dozens of spikey bindey eyes are lodged into the rubber, waiting their chance to pierce more holes and deflate the tubes again. One by one, he plucks them out.

"Trucks" I explain. "I tend to move over whenever an 18-wheeler comes by".

That is totally lost on him. He's an oil and engine man. "Yeah, well, either buy a set of kevlars or keep off the grass".

I shall heed his advice. Reinforced tyres it is. There are fewer trucks this far inland but the Mid Western Highway, grand as it sounds, is mostly a one-lane road. To keep off the grass is to occasionally invite decapitation. *Boy Banzai's* near-miss has been a sharp warning.

There is still 35km to make today. I worry about more bindey eyes, more punctures in the dark. The choice is stark. To overnight here, go to the barn dance; or press on down the highway to Cowra.

"Yer doing this for charity?" asks the old man.

I shake my head, feeling just a little mean. Perhaps I should have added a good cause to the ride. The *PedallingPom* internet site is booming.

"Good on yer" he drawls. "Most of the money those bastards collect goes straight into their own pockets. Just give me five bucks for the patches".

I give him ten, and he's happy. I doubt that he makes much of a living from his oily workshop, but by now I realise that he doesn't care. Not about money anyway. It has been a job well done in an old fashioned way. He has a certain pride, an eccentricity; the sort of man who you take for some grumbling, untidy old bachelor – but maybe with half a million stashed under his floorboards that nobody knows anything about, and he barely remembers himself.

There are still a couple of hours daylight left. I opt for the saddle; take a chance with the bindey eyes. If I pedal hard enough, I'll reach Cowra by dusk. I really do not want to stay in Mandurama; nor to lay further eyes on a dancing dwarf.

This is an area of rolling open rangeland. Station homesteads and their outbuildings dot the landscape here and there. I've a few small hills to deal with, but the traffic is light. The two or three times I pull over to let a truck roar by, is done so with extreme caution. The ratio of a pair of vulnerable patched-up bike tyres to the abundance of roadside bindey eyes is probably two million to one.

I wheel into Cowra at sundown and check into a Best Western. Later, I take a wander through this quiet agricultural town, built on all sides of a rise. There are none too many people around tonight, and I eventually walk into a large bar where there's just the one customer; a commercial traveller he tells me, eager for a little company. The barmaid, a dreary young woman of about 25, responds to my request for a glass of white wine by passing me some warm, off-colour liquid that tastes like nitro acid.

"This is corked!" I splutter.

"No it's not" she says, puzzled. "I pulled the cork out myself".

"No, I mean it's off. No good. Undrinkable".

She shrugs, unconcerned. "Wouldn't know. I'm a beer and vodka girl".

"Please open a chilled bottle. This is warm enough to wash the dishes with".

She shakes her head. "Can't do that. Not until this bottle's finished. Pub rule".

I've been having this sort of problem along the way. Small town Aussies working in the pub trade do not seem to be completely in tune with the finer points of their industry. They tend to view customer relations as something that borders on servility – an ingredient that simply is not in their genes. The barman in Katoomba is a good example; and that disgruntled night manager at the Grand Hotel in Wyong another.

I get up to leave. This is an encouraging sign for the barmaid. She says to the commercial traveller, "Drink up, please fella. Gonna close up now. No customers". It is just gone 8pm.

I grab a Pizza takeaway and head back to my motel room where a regional freesheet, *Southern Weekly*, gets me into the mood for the pending visit to the sheep & cattle station near Cootamundra, only a couple of days away. I am now in out-and-out ranching country.

The paper's front cover confirms as much. It is a full page colour picture of a young boy hand-milking a cow. Inside, are display-ads for Hereford and Angus breeding bulls; for Merino and Poll Dorset sheep; for kit-form shearing sheds, put 'em up in a day. A columnist called *Old Man Plains* claims that the present drought will kill more cattle than Australia's version of Mad Cow – Johne's Disease – will over the next five centuries.

He is full of statistics. From his column I glean that the federal government in Canberra has set the latest nationwide Kangaroo-cull a target of 6.55 million marsupials. The export of Australian livestock has hit an all-time high; over six million sheep, almost a million head of cattle, and 135,532 goats. In 2002, Aussie farmers bought 8,000 tractors and 1062 combine harvesters, worth $3.5 billion; and that last year was the seventh-driest on record with only 209mm of rainfall.

There are handful of stories on lightweight crime. Police are suspicious that two allegedly-stolen cars are insurance frauds. One has been found in flames by the Cowra golf course, and another's been completely gutted by fire. A 52 year old woman is fined $359 for spitting at a cop, apparently a serial offender in such deeds; and a five-times drink driver suffering from clinical depression has been disqualified for a year and fined $1,359. It's odd, that $59 figure in both fines. And lenient by UK standards.

I think of the old station with mounting anticipation and hope it's still there. It might be just some tiny farm by now, most of its 8,000 acres sold off, just like Bentley Briggs' horse stud back up near Gin Gin. No matter what, I'm going back anyway to look at the place that taught me the rules of the game. To jackaroo on an Australian station is to receive an education like no other. So be warned, there'll be some gruesome detail coming up. On these places, the living is hard; and the dying is harder still.

First I've got to get there. There's about 110km and a broadcast day between here and Cootamundra. In Cowra, I buy a new set of reinforced tyres and then pedal 60km through patchy-green drought affected ranges towards the city of Young, another agricultural centre.

Next afternoon, following another *Up All Night* broadcast, I pick up the phone book that includes the Cootamundra area. I delve into the Ws, looking for my former employer. But there is no Wally Ward listed. I suppose he must be dead by now. There is a Ken Ward, his cousin I seem to recall; a horseman from hat-to-heel, seldom seen without a pair of silver spurs wrapped around elastic-sided riding boots. And there's a number of other Wards whose names are ringing distant bells. The Ward clan was, maybe still is, a classic Australian ranching dynasty and Cootamundra bigshots.

I pick one at random, David Ward. He is a second cousin to Wally Ward's four daughters, all of whom I remember vaguely. He gives me the number of the eldest, Roslyn. She must be around, David says, because they waved at one another from across a Cootamundra street just this morning.

I really do not think that Roslyn will remember me, but she does – and thus begins an hour-long conversation, filling the gaps of time. Wally, whom I'll talk of later, died ten years ago. His brother Hope, is still going, just about; and cousin Ken is still up there in the saddle, spurs jangling. The station was sold off before her father died. Getting older, and with no sons to carry on the tradition, he had not been left with much choice. Devastating for everyone, Roslyn says. But *Buronga* is still there, and she's certain that whoever owns it now won't mind if I pedal up and say G'day.

Then she hits me with a thunderbolt. "Did you know that Dick Holland came back to live in Cootamundra?"

There are some people whom you never forget and often think of. Dick Holland is one of them, another Pom who somehow found his way out to jackaroo country. He too had worked at Buronga and we became the very best of mates. I've thought of him often through the years, wondering what became of him. Seems I'm likely to find out in person. Roslyn gives me his phone number, which I dial as soon as she's off the phone.

A very Australian accent answers. Is that Dick, I ask?

"This is *Deek*" he says pleasantly.

"And this, old buddy, is Quentin".

The briefest of pauses. "*Quentin van Marle?*" He hasn't forgotten either.

He wants to get into his car and drive over to Young there and then, but I put the brakes on that notion. I've still got newspaper and internet work to do; besides, I think it better that this unexpected event be given a little time to sink in. We've got four decades to bridge – which means that it will go one of two ways: we'll either pick up where we left off; or find that Father Time has done a hatchet job on what had once been the very firmest of friendships. Either way, it will make a great little human-interest story, and I'm thrilled at the prospect of seeing him again.

"I'll be with you tomorrow" I tell him. He gives me his address and says I'm staying at his house whether I want to or not.

It is a beautiful morning. The riding is easy, and my spirits are high as I consume the sunny colours of today's 45km trip through wooded bushland along a one-lane road that is now grandly called Olympic Way. The deep blue of the sky meeting the green of the trees, meeting the dried yellow of the land.

About 30km on, close to a one-horser called Wallendbeen, I see a curious sign hanging at the dusty entrance to a station of sorts. *Yandilla Mustard Oil Enterprise. Visitors Welcome.*

Curiosity gets the better of me. I pedal down a rough track leading to what might pass for a community hall. Nobody seems to be around. I press a bell and wait. Soon an elderly woman in a red-check shirt and dark trousers appears from a hedged-off homestead.

I offer the usual explanation, BBC and so on, and she invites me inside the hall. It is, in fact, a showroom for mustard seed oil – with an outdoor balcony cafe at the far end, from where I can swat the flies and gaze out across the grain silos into the rolling bush beyond. This has to be one of the oddest sites for a cafe anywhere. She brings me some coffee and a slice of homemade cake, and pulls up a chair.

Kaye Weatherall is a wonderfully well-preserved 73 year old with locks of striking silver hair, bright shining eyes, and an accent closer to Eton Square than the Australian back country. She had moved to England as a young woman, worked for the Foreign Office which transferred her to Nepal. There she met and married a British mountaineer who, as a teenager, had been an Everest Base Camp member of the ill-fated Mallory-Irvine expedition. Mickey Weatherall went on to receive an OBE. After many years in Asia, they finally settled right here on this 500 acre property called Yandilla, where they landed on the idea of producing oil from mustard seed.

Until now, I'd never heard of mustard seed oil, but it seems to have a history. Kaye and Mickey (now deceased) first came across it in India. But the Indian version contained too much erucic acid to be imported into Oz. However, Aussie scientists had developed a less-pungent seed suitable for home consumption and the government encouraged pioneering-minded crop growers to give it a shot. The end-result is bottled and sold as a replacement for the fattier cooking oils.

Wihout a trace of self-consciousness, Kaye says "It's also the perfect massage oil. Very nourishing and most invigorating, I can assure you".

Kaye produces 150,000 litres per annum – storing half, selling the rest. A determined woman carrying on with her late husband's work. She misses him badly, but has a noticeable independence of spirit. And she is cultured to a degree that puts her head and shoulders above the likes of me.

This is an unusual place to find someone of Kaye Weatherall's pedigree; but she's at home out here in the sticks, doing what she does. A marvellous little BBC piece.

An hour later I hit the ouskirts of Cootamundra. There's a sign at the city limits displaying a cricket bat, ball, and stumps that announces this to be the birthplace of Sir Donald Bradman. I had spent a year in this area without knowing that the most revered of all baggy cap batsmen had been born here.

I carry on into a town that is larger than I remember, but recognizeable all the same. The same long main street and low buildings; the same quiet hum as the town goes about its business; the same air of a prosperous, civilized ranching town.

I find Thomson Street and sniff out Number 83. It is a single-storey brick and wood affair with a small front garden and a narrow pathway leading to the back, from where I hear voices. I walk the bike down the path, coming face-to-face with a friend who I've not laid eyes on for 42 years.

TWENTY FOUR
Dick Holland

There is that critical moment, that flash in time that somehow breathes in all the passing years and then exhales them into the here and now. In his youth, Dick Holland had been a Robert Mitchum lookalike, a dead ringer for that much-lamented actor. The resemblance is still there, particularly in a pair of droopy eyes which correctly suggest his unflappable demeanour. Okay, so the hair is thinning, the body sagging a little; but in that instant I recognize the very same Dick Holland that I so looked up to as a greenhorn jackaroo a very long time ago.

He is four years older than me. Back then, the age difference created a different balance. He was 20, had been at Buronga for two years, knew all the ropes, and was far more competent than any of the hands who came and went. I was 16, wet behind the ears, not the first clue what I was doing. A clear hierarchical case of Pom Number One and Pom Number Two. Dick lived in cosy brick hut adjacent to the main homestead. I lived in an uncosy wooden shack 300 metres up a dirt track.

But when each working day was over, the friendship forged ever-deeper. After the evening meal, we'd go back to his brick hut and listen to music, talk, laugh, crack jokes until an enforced 9pm curfew had me stumbling back to my shack by torchlight.

All of this comes flashing back in the briefest of moments as our eyes meet and our hands grip in a firm, strong handshake. This is going to work. We are already taking up where we left off. The meaner side of Father Time has backed off from this one.

We sit in a shaded barbecue area at the back of the small, neat house he shares with his Australian wife, Denise. The tidy back garden leads down to a garage and workshop. A sign on the garage door reads *Steptoe & Son*. Dick will never completely lose his Englishness, despite an adoption of the Down Under accent.

Dick's life has not been plain sailing, not by any means. He stayed on at Buronga for several years after I left, then upped and quit after one clash too many with the dictatorial Wally Ward. Later, he married Denise and they moved up to Queensland where he tried his hand at an assortment of trades. Somewhere between then and now, he returned to England to visit his father on the Isle of Wight, only to find that the old man had died the day before. Eventually, they returned to Cootamundra and he went to work for another of the Ward clan, Stephen, a station owner and rising politician. Dick ended up running the whole show, but the two men could never agree on what constituted a living wage.

After that, they moved into town and he went to work for the council, digging graves at the city cemetery – until he suffered the first of two heart attacks which, to his great disgust, forced him into early retirement. There is still an 88 year old mother, a sister and half-sister, living in the northeast of England, but contact is spasmodic. He'd always been his father's son, opting to stay with the old man when his parents divorced in the 1950s.

Despite such close proximity, Dick has not been back to Buronga since his final altercation with the boss. So that makes two of us. Tomorrow we'll drive out there together and, for better or worse, revisit old times.

Denise Holland is a bespectacled fiftysomething woman with short brown hair, wearing a loose yellow shirt over a pair of long blue shorts. At first she seems a little sceptical of my presence, perhaps worrying that it'll put Dick into a state of excitement that does no good for the heart. She is a trained nurse and knows about such things. But we warm to one another and she soon becomes accepting. They have a son and two daughters, all married and flown the nest. But Molly, the yougest, lives locally. Molly and hubby Craig are dropping by for a drink this evening.

The drink turn into an impromptu barbecue and a late night. Steaks sizzle, beer and wine flows like a running stream. Molly, a bubbly young thing, talks of buying a ranch in Texas one day. Denise shakes her head, muttering something about rattlesnakes. Dick is smiling, looking happy.

Later, Denise pays me what I think is a compliment. "He hasn't smiled and laughed like that for ages".

TWENTY FIVE
Buronga

Twelve kilometres southwest of Cootamundra, Dick swings left off the Olympic Way, following a potholed road until we reach a large gate and a sign reading *Buronga*. It is difficult to describe how I'm feeling as we bump along the track towards the main homestead; a strange mixture of nostalgia, anticipation, and *deja-vu*. First impressions say that nothing has changed. Nothing at all.

The brick homestead, built in 1920, is exactly as I remember; as is Dick's brick hut where we whiled away the evenings. We park the car and walk along the same familiar track leading to the station yard. The outbuildings are all there, in various states of repair; meat room, storeroom, grain silos, water tanks, lean-to's, and the old dairy where twice a day, we'd hand-milk a few cows for station consumption.

In the yard, there's a cattle muster going on, heavy hoofs stirring up the dust as the creatures move restlessly around penned-in stockyards. Far out to my left and up a slight rise are the woolsheds and shearers' quarters. To my right, the same rough gallows – a structure of death standing like a pair of sawn-off rugby goalposts – where I spent many a twilight performing the grisly task of sheep slaughter. And 300 metres up another track, the second homestead where Wally Ward's brother and his family had lived, behind which, and out of view, I assume my old wooden shack still stands.

It's like I've never been gone. Any minute now, Wally Ward – short, stocky, snarling under a wide-brimmed hat – is going to stride out from somewhere around here, barking orders, the ever-present bullwhip coiled in his grasp.

There are a couple of hats milling amid the cattle. The brown wide-brim belongs to a man, the white floppy job to a female. The man, tall and lean, is wearing a green shirt and blue jeans. The woman is in a pink shirt, white shorts. Strands of blond hair appear from under the hat. She has a broad, attractive face and a dazzling smile.

They are David and Mary Booth, both in their 40s and the station's present owners. We explain what we're doing on their property. They are so friendly, so receptive, that for a wild moment I think about asking for my old job back.

It is mid-morning, *smoke-oh* time. That used to mean a tin mug of black tea poured from a flask, and a homerolled cigarette sitting under the shade of a tree. Today it means the homestead, Mary's homemade biscuits, cups of tea out on the terrace.

There is an ante-room leading from the homestead kitchen where Dick and I would eat breakfast and dinner. We were not permitted into the homestead-proper, and this is my first peep inside. There's a long corridor, several bedrooms to the right; a huge, much lived-in sitting room to the left. And this porch-type terrace, looking out over the rolling contours of the range.

David says that they bought the place from a guy called Chris Murphy, known in rock music circles as the manager of that ill-fated group INXS – whose lead singer, Michael Hutchence, had been found hanged in a Sydney hotel room while embroiled in a very public spat with Bob Geldof. Murphy had attempted to turn Buronga into an organic farm, but it didn't work out. The land was sold off in sections. David and Mary have got the bulk of it, 4000 acres, and nowadays he says, it's business as usual: 700 sheep, 200 cattle, 100 goats.

"Meat" he says bluntly. "That's what Buronga is about".

Yes, I remember. Meat. Let's weigh on this for a moment.

Your local butcher doubtless does a good job in displaying his fare from underneath polished glass counters; supermarket freezers go one better with razzmatazz packaging that deliberately avoids even the slightest hint of animal slaughter. But death is what it takes before you can get your teeth into a barbecued sausage or a cheeseburger. Abattoirs have their own mechanised systems of slaughter to keep the masses fed. But sheep and cattle stations, well, they do it their way when it comes to feeding the family and the hired help.

There had been three separate Ward families to support, plus a couple of hungry jackaroos. A sheep was killed twice a week, a steer maybe once every six weeks. When I ask David how he goes about the business of death these days, he draws an ominous finger across his throat and says, "The same time-honoured way. Nothing's changed".

Dick and me would take it in turns. The first time I did this deed, I wanted to throw up; but it was part of the job and I had to get used to it. A sheep was selected for killing sometime in the afternoon, then locked into a holding pen, a condemned cell of sorts. At sundown, when the flies had gone elsewhere, the execution took place in the following manner.

First, grab the sheep – which can always be relied upon to attempt a fast getaway; next, nestle its back between bent knees, forcing the back of its head across a thigh. Then, with half a dozen swift, savage, swipes of a finely-honed knife, cut it's throat. The procedure ends with a hard and rapid snap of the neck.

The animal is dead, but for two or three minutes afterwards, as the blood drains into the dusty soil, nerve ends will cause it to wriggle and writhe. It is not a pleasant act.

Then begins the skinning and gutting. The skin comes away easily from the body and will later be cured for sheepskin coats and the like. The guts are removed and, at Buronga anyway, cut up raw and divided between the dozen station dogs tied to kennels of hollowed-out tree stumps scattered around the yard. Nothing goes to waste. The carcass is then hung up on the gallows for a couple of hours to stiffen and dry.

At least a steer had the dignity of being shot first. Other than that, it was the same process, only longer and tougher. To extract the intestines meant first wrapping them with heavy duty chain and literally towing them from the carcass with a Land Rover.

For a while, Wally Ward had experimented with a quota of near-feral pigs. Killing a pig was a ghastly job, stabbing it through the heart and putting the body into a cauldron of boiling water to loosen the hair from the skin. I won't go any deeper into this topic, except to note that it was never a good idea to get in the way of the boar, the stud, when this exercise took place. He went berzerk every time, seriously trying to scrabble over the fence to get at you, snorting furiously, teeth baring in utter rage. One of the Ward clan had warned me about this. The boar will charge at you, bowl you over into the dirt, then sink his gnashing fangs into the jugular.

"*He won't even leave your boots, lad*", he said, walking away laughing.

I can believe it. One morning I came across a dead dog in a nearby creek. Not one of ours, a stray I guess. Wally told me to cut it up and throw it to the pigs. I wasn't going to do that; not to cut it up. That was asking too much. He mused on this disobedience for a moment, saw my point, and said, "Okay, chuck it to them wholemeal".

There was a mad, squealing scrabble for the dog. Within minutes it had been torn apart, devoured, nothing left. Curious to see what else they'd eat, I found some dirty old sacks and tossed them into the dry, dusty pen. They too got torn to shreds. There was a useless coil of thin-gauge wire that I threw in for good measure. The pigs drew the line at that, but only after giving it their best shot.

David offers us his ute to explore the station properly. First stop is 300 metres up the track to my hut. It is still there, though in some dilapidation. There's a red corrugated-iron roof and a brick chimney. The window is boarded up and the door looks ready to come off its hinges with the first good sneeze. Inside, it's a musty jumble of tired old furniture and assorted rubble. But it's enough for it all to come racing back as clearly as in a digital photograph. In one corner, there's my bed – or rather a mattress slung onto a piece of plyboard resting on four five-gallon drums. In another corner, the bookcase that had been stuffed full of cheap paperbacks; and the fireplace, where on winter nights I'd get a good blaze going. And in an ante-room, an old iron bathtub, no taps or running water. To fill the bath, I'd go 300 metres down to the dairy, boil water, and carry it back up in buckets. To have a bath took about two hours of water-boiling and a few kilometres of walking. A tough luxury.

Buronga has 50 large paddocks, all with evocative names. *Bronze Wing, Lightning Ridge, Kangaroo, Red Hill, Gardiner's Lookout, Horse Field, Green Springs* to name but a few. We bump slowly along their rough tracks, Dick driving, while I open and shut the many gates. Poms One and Two, the old hierarchy back in play.

There were no full days off at Buronga – the cows had to be milked twice a day, including Sundays. In the period between the Sunday milkings, we'd walk up into these paddocks, armed with .22 calibre rifles and shoot rabbits. Even at 16, I could stroll into a Cootamundra gunstore and buy boxes of bullets, no license or ID required. Not any more. Gun laws have tightened up considerably since a mass shooting in Tasmania a few years ago.

We struggle up to *Gardiner's Lookout*, a high, boulder-strewn ridge that looks out across miles and miles of rangeland. It also directly overlooks the road that is now called Olympic Way, but was once little more than a track used by the Cobb & Co stagecoaches, horsedrawn buggies, and lone riders. The ridge and the paddock are named after Frank Gardiner, the only Australian bushranger ever to have been granted a pardon. Up on this rocky ridge, he would spot likely prey trotting along the track towards Junee, the next town along. Then he'd ride down a steeply wooded slope to a bend in the road where he could take his victims by surprise. Gardiner was one of many so-called Gentlemen Outlaws. There was one guy who called himself Captain Starlight – almost a folk hero because of his extreme courtesy to women while relieving them of their valuables. Ned Kelly, the most infamous bushranger of all, was not of these parts. He was a Victoria man, and I'll be crossing into his territory shortly.

Back at the station yard, we meander up to the old shearing sheds, now in a visible state of disrepair since the INXS manager cleared the land of livestock in favour of organic agriculture. Rather than renovate the sheds, the new owner uses a neighbouring station's facilities when shearing time comes around.

Shearing time. Hard, tough, sweaty, greasy, backbreaking work for all concerned. I do not remember how many sheep we had at Buronga, but at least four times that of the present 700. A typical shearing day would go like this.

Rise earlier than usual and muster the day's bleating flock up into the woolshed's stockyards. The shearers, six of them as a rule, are ready for a 6.30am start. They are paid per sheep shorn and want to get on with it. Tempers fray as the day wears on. We jackaroos take on a new term – *roustabouts* – the shearer's glorified name for a dogsbody. A roustabout's routine was thus: drag a sheep out from a pen and hand it to the sweating, cursing shearer. Gather up his last fleece and dump it onto a large table they call the grading tray. Pull out all the mess that these animals automatically accrue in their wool – thorns, burrs, dried shit – and stuff the cleared, greasy fleece into a sack-lined woolpress, just in time to grab the shearer his next sheep and begin the process all over again. Inbetween, sweep the decks, press the wool into tightly-bound bales, and make a tally of sheep shorn. A shearer's count must match the roustabout's tally. It can become a hot tempered contest, cooling off during two 15-minute smoke-ohs and the half-hour lunch break. As the day heads towards knock-off time, the tiring shearers begin to make mistakes, resulting in many cut and bleeding sheep.

Theirs is a tough life; as much now as it was then.

Camaraderie would return at the close of play. Chilled beers came out, removing the day's tensions. At Buronga, these men had their own quarters and their own cook. The disused shearer's quarters are still there. A rusting tin roof and faded yellow paint peeling off wooden walls. It is in the same sad state as my own shack up the hill.

There was never a shortage of routine tasks. In its most literal sense, fence-mending took up a lot of time. As did chopping wood, painting the sheds, cutting a nuisance-weed called burrs, milking cows, feeding pigs and dogs, and saddling up *Old Smokey*, the station horse, for mustering or boundary riding, or just to give the reluctant old nag a bit of exercise.

At various times of the year, there'd be other work to do. Round up the sheep and get them into the sheep dip – an arsenic-laced canal that helps prevent infection from lice and other unwanted insects. Then there was the lambing season – after which came the castration process for would-be rams. This ritual is performed by placing tight 'elastic bands' around the testicle cords which has the eventual effect of numbing the organs and severing the links.

Not so with the young bullocks. They came in for the real thing. Ropes around their legs, they'd tumble into the dirt, held down by Poms One and Two – there is a knack to this – while a third person sliced out their testicles with a knife. On releasing each new steer, we didn't hang around. Get over the fence quick while they bucked, kicked and snorted, hoofing up the dust and charging around the stockyard in one great big maddened display of lost manliness.

The same rope *'em and hold 'em* procedure applied at branding time; hot metal hissing into tough, hairy hides, identifying the station to which the stock belonged. We performed the same rapid leap over the stockyard fence while the freed steer arose from the dust and went about another enraged one-man stampede.

To be a jackaoo was to be a seven-day-week Jack of all Trades, and truly a master of none; a dairyman, a butcher, a lumberjack, a fencing contractor, a horseman, a 4x4 driver, a sheep and cattle drover, a roustabout, a cowboy, and more. The pay, Australian £6 per week, plus grub and shack.

The memories, all of them, are just so goddam clear that while walking back from the woolsheds, I get this sudden panic attack. *It's two o'clock. Time I was back at work. Wally Ward will crucify me, idling like this.*

True.

True that for a flashing moment I had thought exactly that. And true, Mr Ward would have been very much less than pleased.

Wally Ward was born to this place called Buronga. He had a slim, nervy wife and four young daughters aged 16, 14, 12, and 6. Roslyn, Jennifer, Pamela, Evelyn. Now, four decades on, I can understand why he had such a short fuse and eternally-worried frown, with three familes to support from just the one property – through all the lean times, the bushfires, the droughts, the collapsing wool and cattle prices. Everyone on his back, day in, day out; including his cantankerous old dad, Cecil, who'd done things differently in his time and never lost an opportunity to say so.

Small wonder that Wally took on a tyrannical manner. Even an old hand like Dick chose his words of protest carefully. I was overwhelmed by the man's barking authority; 16 years old, already taller than him and growing; Wally, 45, going nowhere high – yet a man with a presence, a force to be respected and reckoned with. With the benefit of hindsight, I can see where he was coming from.

If Charles Dickens had been an Australian, Wally would have been one of his characters.

From talking with his daughters, I now know there was another side to him – a side that he did an excellent job in disguising out on the station. I now know that despite his daily troubles and tortures, he

The gallows at Buronga

was always ready to help out a good number of folk in the Cootamundra area: people with a multiplicity of afflictions – nervous breakdowns, gambling, unemployment, alcohol and all the rest of it – and was awarded the Order of the Australian Medal before he died in 1992.

This afternoon, I feel him around. Very strongly. So does Dick. "Eerie, isn't it?" he says.

I owe Buronga. It toughened me up, living at the sharp end of things. It taught me how and why everything we require for survival as a species comes from the land: wood, water, fruit, vegetables, crops, dairy produce, meat; a bottle of beer, wine, whisky, all start with the land; even clothing. Above all – and bearing in mind that vegetarianism was but a distant vision in those days – it showed me that if the human race wants to eat, then blood has to be spilled.

It is clear to me that the obese and the ignorant, stuffing their faces inside McDonalds, do not have such thoughts. Their Big Macs will appear, presto, because there's some acne-faced youth in a baseball cap and headphones who says that they will.

Mmmm.....great, gimme another. What's on the telly tonight?

Such first-hand knowledge was good grounding for the very

outset of a working life. Worth a bit more than an algebra lesson. The thread running through my own life began with this place far out in the bush. In its way, Buronga developed my taste for all of life's possibilities. Without it, no way would I have coped with the rough and tumble of Tin Can Bay. If I hadn't come out here to do this sort of work, experience this sort of life, then.....I don't know.

Well actually, I think that I do. There are no ifs. This sheep & cattle station and subsequent episodes of my life must surely have all been part of the Master Plan. For sure, were it not for Buronga, I would not be here on this bike ride, enjoying a strong, re-forged friendship in the very same place where it began. Buronga is full-circle for me, like the return flight of a whirring boomerang. On a personal level, it is the highlight of the whole odyssey.

Back at Dick's house, we mull over what has been an extraordinary day. Dick has spent so much of his life working for the Ward clan; if they are not in his blood, they are certainly under his skin. When Wally died – at the time when Dick was working at the city cemetery – he even found himself digging the man's grave. Some people are impossible to escape.

Dick reminds me that his working days are over. He's free at last.....

"Dick" I taunt. "You're forgetting something".

"What?"

"The next life. The big sheep station in the sky. Guess who is going to be waiting for you, whip in hand?"

"Oh God" he groans, rubbing an arm across his brow. "I never thought of that".

Ned Kelly's statue at Glenrowan

TWENTY SIX
Ned's Last Stand

It is not easy saying farewell. But in the end, what else can you do but turn your back and ride away?

I load up Oggy Boy preparing to do just that – all too aware that me and my re-found mate might not be seeing one another again, not in this life anyhow. This unavoidable thought hangs tacitly in the air.

Today's destination is the city of Wagga Wagga, 85km along the Olympic Way. It is level riding for the most part except for one almighty hill in Junee – a town that abounds with classic colonial architecture. But I carry the excess baggage of sadness as I move through the day's sunshine. It is lodged somewhere within and refuses to budge.

Wagga Wagga is the unofficial capital of the Riverina region, an area of NSW that starts south of Junee, and carries on down to the Victoria border at Albury on the banks of the Murray River. From there it spreads about 150km west to Deniliquin and beyond, turning 120km north again into remote horizon-to-horizon flatlands around the ranching town of Hay. The Riverina, lush and irrigated in the south, becomes a harsher and sparser treeless plain in the north. Hay is a town on the edge of the outback, as against merely out in the bush. There's a mighty big difference.

How do I know? Because Buronga had not been the only station that I'd worked on; just the biggest and for the longest period. The two others, for three or four months each, are in the Hay and Deniliquin regions.

But this is my first visit to Wagga. It is a spread out city of about 60,000 with a downtown area of long streets and low buildings. It is late afternoon. The streets are quiet, almost empty, and then I remember it is Saturday. The stores closed up at lunchtime – not a bad tradition either.

I check in at a Best Western and take a stroll while daylight lasts. The long main thoroughfare is called Baylis Street. At one end is a railway station, obviously built in times gone by and probably a listed building. At the other, maybe 1,500 metres along a broad commercial boulevard lined with all the usual trading houses – stores and banks, offices, burger and pizza takeaways – is a small bridge that takes me into Fitzmaurice Street, where everything changes. This is the old town, the Wagga Wagga of yesterday; old red brick buildings with wrought-iron balconies, and an ambience of another era. The Civic Centre, set amid streams and gardens, cleverly divides the two.

It has a playhouse, aptly named the Civic Theatre. A poster advertises a recent production called X-STACY. The play is based upon true stories of Wagga's modern youth – and the poster is wonderfully honest in stating that the production has been largely funded by the city's Community Drug Action Team. It has lifted a couple of reviews from regional newspapers.

One takes the form of a grandparent's letter published in the *Northside Chronicle*. "*I watched their faces. My heart ached.....Every school student, every parent and grandparent, in fact everyone everwhere should see this play*".

The *Courier Mail*: "*The play is agony to watch but also a joy, because it is such a powerful theatrical experience without any false notes.....The play will strike at your gut and your heart. And your soul.....if you think you've got one*".

Yes, I think I've got one. We all do.

Wandering back down Baylis Street, I pass a second-hand clothing store called *On the Rebound*. I'm feeling a bit like that myself right now, though not over a jilting by some lover. That's been a while. Dick Holland and such strong memories of Buronga have affected me far more than I thought. I cannot properly explain this feeling of inner sadness – but it's there, trapped inside my psyche, ricochetting off mental walls.

I think I'll grab and pizza and go to bed. And hope that sleep drags me into no dark realms tonight.

Feeling much better the next day, I take a ride around quiet Sunday morning streets. I follow a signpost pointing to Wagga Beach, thinking it may be a watersports lake that I've heard of around here. I'm wrong. It is a small patch of dark sand on the edge of the Murrumbidgee River that is overlooked by a rather mediocre caravan park. There's a few fixed tables atop a grassy bank, and an ugly public lavatory beside which a tramp is fast asleep.

There are beaches. And there are, um, beaches.

Back in town, I pass two women setting up a pair of tables outside a hall. I'm riding on the sidewalk, so I stop and say hello. Both women are the wives of rival candidates in a pending local election; and both eagerly hand me ballot papers for which I am clearly not eligible.

The Liberal Party is fielding a candidate called Daryl Maguire. His name is in big bold upper-case letters next to a box into which he's placed the figure 1. The four other candidates are named in tiny lettering, alongside tiny boxes. The figure 1 implies that citizens may vote in order of personal preference, rather than for one person only. Maguire's main rival represents the Country Labor Party, a bloke called Col McPherson (Col is for Colin, not Colonel. His missus assures me that he's not trying to hoodwink anyone). He too has a large figure 1 ticked into his box, with the command that your second choice must be the chap from the Green Party, or The Greens as they're called here.

There is something almost innocent about these two women. They are on good terms, joking with each other, no bitchiness or snide remarks. I don't know if it's the same with their two men. On the surface maybe but not, I think, if it comes down to the wire. Politicians – I've met and argued with many – have one common denominator: a lust for power that knows no bounds at polling time; kick him hard, send him tumbling; another bootful as he staggers up; then watch him fall again with the KO delivery. And afterwards, in the victory speech, the usual laudation for the loser. "*I want to thank my opponent for the good, clean, tough fight he put up. What a guy. If it wasn't for the wishes of the electorate, I might have voted for him myself*".

The nature of the beast, you say; and beasts they are.

Today I'll head for the town of Culcairn, 65km away; overnight there, and tomorrow cross the border into Wodonga, Victoria. I know that it's all level riding, and so long as the wind holds, it should be a simple thrust through this greener, more populated part of the Riverina. From Wodonga, I'll do a further 50km to Wangaratta where it's broadcast and media time again. The penultimate pieces for radio, newspaper, and for an internet site with many more hits than it perhaps deserves. I am very grateful for so much interest. It has prompted this more detailed account you're reading now.

There have been days when the cycling's been all but secondary; short rides from here to there, with the stories taking precedence. And there have been those utterly-concentrated days of pedalling; for instance, the Alley of Menace when the only thing that mattered was getting to the other end. This is one of those, the 180km mission to Wangaratta; a heads-down time, get it over with; think of something else when the legs begin to ache.

A good time for some final reflection. There is just one more story from another time that I'd like to run by you now.

In 1994, on leaving the Vietnam project, I had to find some new way of making a living. Returning to day-to-day mainstream journalism was out of the question. After two years of living far away from the norm, I could no longer put up with crush hours, megalomaniac bosses, or the poison that is office politics. It was time to steer whatever talents I have towards another vision. Time to create a job for myself; use my head; discover how to earn my keep from doing what I really like to do.

Which is what I'm doing now; writing and travelling in the simplest possible manner.

So I looked back on the years, recalling previous escapades, mishaps, calamities, unexpected situations. Hell, there was an abundance to choose from – but the one with seemingly most potential was that eerie night on Dead Man's Chest in January 1969.

I thought about it; then thought some more. Until the plan formed and became another mental reality. I would go back, live on that awful place for 31 days, one day longer than Blackbeard's marooned pirates had to endure – and would thus set one of the most bizarre records ever.

There was method to this madness. Most everyone dreams of escaping the humdrum from time to time. Deserted islands and tropical sunshine feature high on the list. The link with Robert Louis Stevenson's *Treasure Island* could do no harm, and just the name of the island itself, Dead Man's Chest, was hellish enough to arouse interest. There would be people who'd want to read about a crackpot escapade like this.

The *Sunday Times* concurred. We made a deal. Then I went out into the marketplace and found a sponsor, a rum company. There was something ironic about doing that. To land oneself onto a desert isle, where money does not exist, is a strangely expensive and difficult thing to achieve.

I was 49 at the time. Like-minded friends were envious. Everyone else put it down to 50, next stop; middle aged madness, gone loopy, flipped. But I had discovered that December 4 of the same year would mark the 100th anniversary of Stevenson's death. And that's what did it.

The voice within screamed at me to get on with it.

It was a hard but rewarding month. November 3 to December 4; alone on a barren, rocky isle that measures 250 square metres by 100 metres high. I lost a great deal of weight, grew a beard, gradually leaned how to fish, and came to know how wonderfully liberating it is to be without human company. A few people came calling in private boats, but I was always glad to see the back of them.

Across the water, the now-inhabited Peter Island throbbed with wealth; a palm fringed playground for the rich, where after dark, lights twinkled and the music from steel bands drifted across the two mile channel. An island where money talks in low murmers. But there on my island, the currency lay in its rocky beaches, in the woods behind, in the rainwater, and in the sea itself. A tough, stubborn place that never gave anything up willingly; every stick of firewood, every fish, every drop of water had to be earned and paid for in some manner. And yet I felt inexplicably rich during that abnormal month, particularly at sundown when the sea would gradually alter colour from its varying shades of blue into a blazing sheen of golden copper. At moments like those, it was a downright privilege to be there.

The hardest part of all was on December 4, 100 years to the day that Robert Louis Stevenson slipped away on the south sea island of

West Samoa. The day that VISAR, the Virgin Islands Search & Rescue team came to take me off my hermit isle and deposit me back into society. The Peter Island resort threw a party, and for a couple of days I mingled awkwardly among the rich and famous, trying to rediscover some small appreciation for the values and bearings which I'd discarded during the past month.

It took time to settle back into urban ways. Never far from mind was the next adventure, the next means of escape, whatever that might be; like a mountaineer looking for another Everest. Which is why I'm here now, riding a bike down an Australian highway, obeying the demands of an inner voice or a low boredom threshold – which probably amount to the same thing anyway; and knowing that in a few days, this journey too will be over.

Afterwards, home to England; back to the proverbial drawing board to dream up another one. It's a bizarre way to live as the years advance.

Or is it? I cannot think of anything more tedious than the nine-to-five treadmill, grudgingly performed in return for a weekly or monthly salary – in order to do it all over again the following month, and the month after that. If the majority of wage slaves are living with only old age and a pension in mind, then I'd rather do it my way; take my chances, and take my retirement in chunks as I go along.

Someone else who did things his way, right until the bitter end (and a bitter end it had been) was the infamous Ned Kelly.

I've now crossed the border, carrying on through Victoria's flatlands, and closing in on Wangaratta. After a couple of nights in this moderate country town, it'll be on to Glenrowan where the bushranger famously made his last stand against the police.

Wangaratta, another agricultural centre, has just two claims to fame as far as I can tell: an aviation museum called *Airworld*, with a decent collection of old and vintage aircraft; and the interred remains of a bushranger known as Daniel 'Mad Dog' Morgan. The man has the unusual distinction of being buried without his head. It was severed by a surgeon after his death and sent to Melbourne in an effort to find out if the outlaw really was insane, or just a real bad boy. Going to those lengths, I guess there must have been some way to establish the difference.

I pedal out of Wangaratta and take the old road to Glenrowan, where barely a single car disturbs the 20km ride through quiet, woody bushland on another glorious Australian morning. This town could not be more different to Wangaratta; what few commercial buildings there are in Glenrowan, population 950, are set spaciously apart from one another. Most seem to be trading on the Ned Kelly legend.

The Glenrowan Hotel invites you to pop in and drink a toast to Mr Kelly; the greasy spoon next door wants you to try a delicious Nedburger. Then there's a souvenir store-cum-small musuem commemorating the man. And a little further down the broad main street, an enormous and exceptionally ugly statue of the bushranger himself, rigged out in all his homemade armour – a heavy ironclad bullet-proof vest and a rough iron helmet resembling an inverted bucket. He's wearing yellow trousers and a long brown coat, with a sawn-off shotgun in his hands. It is as if Ned Kelly is controlling Glenrowan from the ouija board.

The souvenir store is called Kate's Cottage, the name of Kelly's sister. Out back, there's a life-sized replica of the tiny shack-like cottage where the Kelly's had lived, somewhere nearby. It's got dirt floors and rough furniture; an old clock sits atop a mantelpiece and a rifle hangs from the wall. There's a kitchen table in the centre of the small room, a pair of benches alongside. There's an old iron stove, pots, pans, and oil lamps; and most remarkably, a writing desk. The two small bedrooms are especially pokey, where tacked-up sacking is used in lieu of curtains. This had not been a well off family.

In the museum is a photo of the real Ned Kelly. A large crop of sweeping dark hair, with the parting on the right; long bushy eyebrows, a large broad nose, wide mouth, and a wild, unkempt moustache and beard.

There is a young lad, all of 15, hanging around the place; a school dropout I quickly learn, whose only interest in life is the history of the Kelly gang. He makes a living by conducting walking tours around the Glenrowan area, to anywhere of Kelly significance. What young Mike Lawson doesn't know about his subject is probably not worth knowing anyway. I gladly let him fill in the blanks for me.

Ned Kelly, born in 1854, was the son of a transported Irish pig thief. He quickly followed his old man's footsteps by becoming first of all a horse thief; then a bushranger and bank robber; and then a cop killer. It was this last deed that spurred the Victoria police into a do-or-die search for the gang, culminating in the Siege of Glenrowan on June 28, 1880.

Cops everywhere come in for their fair share of abuse, always will – though few are likely to receive the verbal treatment that Kelly reserved for the Victoria police. The gang had just robbed a bank in the Riverina town of Jerilderie, and having locked the cops up in their own jail, it treated admiring locals to a drink in the hotel bar. Here, Ned Kelly delivered a speech in which he referred to the police as..... "*A parcel of big, ugly, fat necked, wombat headed, big bellied, magpie legged, narrow hipped, splaw footed, sons of Irish bailiffs and English landlords*".

So, not much love lost then. The police finally cornered the gang inside the Glenrowan Hotel, smoking them out by burning it down, killing all but Ned Kelly himself – who emerged from the smoke, guns blazing, looking like the creature from the black lagoon in all that ironware. The armour proved only partially effective. Altogether he took 28 bullets in the legs and body before stumbling to the ground, alive but defeated.

Young Mike says chillingly, "At ten o'clock, on the morning of November 11, 1880, they led him to the gallows inside the Old Melbourne Gaol and put the noose around his neck".

He tells me to visit the place when I reach Melbourne. The gallows are still there, and the prison is a goldmine of Australian penal history.

I shall, I reply. And I will.

The Kelly cottage

TWENTY SEVEN
The End of the Line

I press onwards, overnighting in the riverside city of Benalla. Which leaves just 160km between me and Melbourne; only two days pedalling remain.

Every long journey has its highs and lows; they go with the territory. Fortunately, the lows have been few and far between. The first day out of Port Douglas certainly had its moments, with menacing traffic and a good dose of sunburn. Tin Can Bay.....well, that was a manic combination of ups and downs, verging on the certifiable. There was that grim day riding through the rain from Brisbane to the Gold Coast. And in Bulahdelah, I experienced the deepest sense of futility watching relentless rain come down while listening to a dreadful duo called *No Contol.* And of course, saying adieu to Dick Holland was a very difficult moment for the pair of us.

The highs certainly outweigh the lows. It had been a wonderful day out with the bush pilots, flying from outpost to outpost, Cairns to

Cape York and back. *Forest Flying* turned into a great afternoon in the company of a pair of true originals. Getting through the Alley of Menace from Sarina to Rockhampton was an achievement in itself. The time spent with Ronnie and Sharyn at Turkey Beach was especially satisfying. Bottom Pub in Maclean.....well, I can only say to those terrific people '*Good on yer, mates*'. And the Pub with No Beer – even those 22 unexpected hills, climbed in searing heat, are not quite so pugnacious now as they seemed at the time.

The Port Macquarie undertaker, what a character; and in Sydney, the solar-sailing Dr Robert Dane, despite his medical assertions; Cobb & Co in Bathurst, along with the Rutherford family; and naturally, that return visit to Buronga with Dick Holland. And now, in some funny way, Ned Kelly is getting to me.

I doubt that he was as bad as the authorities made out. I think he was a product of the system, living in an era of intensely hostile relations, a 'them and us' situation, in which the Kelly's were continually persecuted by narrow minded authority. He had been a first-generation Australian of impoverished Irish convict stock, existing under an insensitive stiff-upper-lip British rule. Another case of the welding torch meeting with a bundle of dynamite.

Perhaps the Old Melbourne Gaol will throw more light on the man.

The wind is not going to allow a simple end to this odyssey. As I begin today's 85km push along the Hume Highway to a town called Seymour, it gets up and howls right into my face, declaring invisible warfare. The flat terrain becomes hilly, with a number of long, strenuous gradients. After all this time on the road, it should all be dead easy by now, another piece of cake, but it's not. Maybe psychology has gone to work on me, the way it does with marathon runners. The last miles are always the hardest and the longest.

Think positive. You're on the home stretch, boy. Every single turn of the pedals brings you that much closer to the chequered flag. Keep your head down; carry on pedalling; think of something to make you laugh.

Carry on Pedalling. That brings a smile. I dream up some lunatic scenario for another Carry On movie. Sid James, Hattie Jacques, Kenneth Williams, Barbara Windsor on a bike ride through Oz; saucey slapstick on wheels.

Halfway to Seymour, I call in at the small town of Euroa, thirsty for a cold beer. It is lunchtime. The pub has that no-hope atmosphere that goes with daytime drinking on a working day. A couple of young men are playing an idle game of pool. There's a woman sitting at the bar, chain smoking from two packs of cigarettes stacked beside her drink. Other regulars, few of them smiling, mutter quietly or stare into their glasses. The only person in here with a job is the barman.

I ride on into the stiffening wind, arriving at the uninspiring town of Seymour in the late afternoon. It is a spread-out cluster of truck-stops, tyre depots, and servos. I can think of better places to spend the last night of the tour.

The headwind is up again next morning, relentless in its velocity. Only 90km to the big smoke – and every metre of the way is going to be a battle. I keep telling myself that it's just a matter of resolve. The wind is doing its level best to blow me back to the border, but dammit, it won't succeed. I pass a place named Broadford, 70km to go. Then comes Wallan, 50km to go. Mid afternoon, Craigburn, and only 30km remain. The traffic densens, the usual urban sprawl begins, and finally the city skyline comes into sight. Face and arms are burning from the sun and the wind as I press on through a sea of brick and concrete – until I suddenly realise that I've actually arrived in downtown Melbourne.

"*Voila*" I whisper to myself. And that's all. There is no elation, no inner cheering or whooping; nothing but the feeling of relief that I'm off that highway and out of the wind. The long trek from North Queensland is over.

Almost. I've still to find my way to the seaview suburb of St Kilda where I'm booked in for a couple of nights. Someone points the way south, saying there's another eight kilometres to go. I follow his directions along bustling streets, passing the racetrack where just last weekend the first Grand Prix of the Formula 1 season had occurred. And then, at last, the Best Western on Acland Street that really did say journey's end.

In 1999, when I crossed America coast-to-coast, I'd pedalled into Key West and straight into the lenses of a waiting television crew. Later, I rode down Duvall Street to a small pre-arranged reception at the Hard Rock Cafe where the mayor of Monroe County pronounced me an *Honorary Conch*, an honorary citizen of the Florida Keys. Every retiring U.S. president receives this pleasing little accolade, but it has so far been awarded to only three Brits. The Queen; Timothy

Dalton during his short career as James Bond 007; and yours truly. At the time, I suppose I thought I'd actually achieved something. Americans certainly did.

The grand finale of the Oggy Oggy Ozzy Odyssey is somewhat different. The hotel receptionist asks where I've come from today. Seymour, I reply. He breathes out a low whistle. "That's a long way on a bicycle, mate".

"Yes. A long way".

"D'yuh take milk?"

"Yes please".

He hands me a small carton for the room, the same small courtesy I've had all along the way. Then he goes back to whatever he was doing before.

And that is that. If I expect anything more than the milk, I'm not going to get it.

Consolation comes in the form of a young lad called Tom Fell – the son of a woman in England for whom I'll always have a soft spot. Tom is out here taking the usual year off and is presently in Melbourne. We meet up in St Kilda for a few drinks and an outdoor dinner in the warmth of a summer evening. He is a very intelligent lad, good company.

Acland Street, St Kilda. It's like Islington's Upper Street; every second or third builing is a cafe, bar, restaurant. The words *No War,* repeated about 300 times completely covers the panoramic window of one establishment. Live music comes out of somewhere else. The narrow, colourful street is filled with strollers and posers. There's one bloke astride a sleek racing bike wearing all the Tour de France gear. He pedals slowly up and down the street; up and down, up and down, up and down again. Young women are cruising around in flimsy tops and tight-fitting shorts, their navels studded with cheap jewellery. Grinning men with shorn heads and tattooed arms observe their alluring body language as they strut along this relaxed neon-lit street.

Next day, I take a tram back into the city. The glass from tall buildings glints in brilliant sunlight. Silent trams move to and fro along pleasant downtown streets. I have been here only once before, 1961, a one-day stopover on the ship from Southampton to Sydney. I recognise nothing.

Melbourne would have been a very different place back in Ned Kelly's time; smaller, rougher, dirtier. A cop points me to Russell

Street and I walk up a long rise towards the Old Melbourne Gaol, a grim looking place that was modelled on Pentonville Prison in London. Nowadays it is looked after by Australia's National Trust, serving as a museum of penal history – an aspect that most Aussies would far rather forget. Whereas at one time in history a criminal conviction was enough to get you transported out here, now it will debar you from entering the country.

Inside, everything is as it was in the latter half of the 19th Century. Three tiers of cold, dismal cells and iron walkways line both sides of the building. The cells measure about seven feet by five wide. They have stone floors, brick walls, and arched ceilings. In one of them sits the dummy of a typical condemned man. He is remarkably lifelike, slumped against a wall, head in hands, with the letters PME stamped across his prison-issue shirt. *Prisoner of Mother England.* The initials explain how we came to be called Pommies.

Inside various cells are the death masks of hanged prisoners and a brief history of each man. Between 1851 when the gaol was built, and 1924 when it finally closed, 135 executions took place on a gallows at the far end of the second tier of cells. The gaol briefly re-opened during World War 11 as a military prison for Aussie soldiers who'd gone AWOL. I'll bet they wished they hadn't. This is no place to spend more than an hour or two. Victorian in the extreme sense of the word, the harshness of the times ooze from its cold yellowish walls.

Particularly inside the condemned cell where prisoners, Ned Kelly among them, spent their last hours. It differs from the other cells insofar as the unfortunate occupant could peer through a slit in the cell door and enjoy an unobstructed view of the gallows across an iron landing.

Enough to put anyone off the Last Meal.

I make the last walk myself; the same one that Ned Kelly and 134 others made from condemned cell to scaffold. It takes just three or four seconds.

Playing to the last on the Ned Kelly legend, the gallows are now occupied by four cardboard cutouts which, were they not so macabre, would be laughable. Kelly is on the trapdoor, a white cap on his head with a faceflap attached. His arms are tied just above bent elbows, the rope spread across his back between both arms. There is no way he can reach for the rope to halt his fall. The hanging rope is securely tied around an overhead beam, it's noose flopped on the wooden platform, awaiting the hangman to tighten it around Kelly's neck. Two prison guards in blue uniforms, one with a black moustache, the other with a dark bushy beard, look on. Facing the condemned man is a grey haired character in a short, dark, buttoned up jacket and pale trousers. He is the hangman – a prisoner himself, who has volunteered to do the job for a payment of five shillings.

What a mate. What an inmate. Can't wait to make his acquaintance. But the despatching of a fellow-inmate was apparently a common thing to volunteer for in this prison – representing the stark difference between those who were simply doing time, and those whose time was up. As cardboard cutouts go, this is one of the most chilling and realistic re-enactments you'll ever see; in its way, as bleak as anything you will find in Madame Tussard's Chamber of Horrors; the ritual of state-sponsored death, leaving nothing to the imagination.

What makes it worse is the sad fact that Ned Kelly's mother was in the same jail at the time of his execution, working in the laundry room. She was inside for what is largely suspected as a trumped-up charge of assaulting a police officer. You can only imagine her torment at the strike of 10 o'clock on the morning of November 11, 1880. One moment her son is alive, the next he is dead, wildly swinging at the end of a rope – until the swaying eventually stops and his limp body is left to dangle a few feet above the ground floor of the prison.

I walk back out into the lovely Melbourne sunshine, glad to be gone from there. I daresay that even Ned Kelly had such sentiments as he stood on the trapdoor. In a moment or two, the ordeal would be over. There would be nothing more that anyone could do to him.

"*Such is life*" he's reputed to have said as the noose was placed around his neck. Philosophical last words; to which I can only add that on the day that he died, a national icon was born.

Journey's end: Acland Street, St. Kilda

EPILOGUE
Return of the Boomerang

There is one thing I know for sure. Travelling through Oz, alone and on a bicycle, was the only way to have gone. If I'd opted for the comfort and speed of four wheels, I could not possibly have tuned into the Australia I was trying to find.

On a bike, you can only go so far at a time. With all the physical exertion that cycling requires, at the end of each day you are wherever you find yourself, like it or not. In this way, I was drip-fed Australia as it really is and wherever it is.

It was the little things that mattered: however trivial, they all connected to the bigger picture, like the pieces of a jigsaw. In no special order, here's just a few of them.

In *Playing Postie for a Day* with the bush pilots of Cape York Air I vividly recall that solitary Parks & Wildlife Ranger collecting his rations for the week from Lakeland Station's dirt airstrip – in itself nothing, but the expression on the man's face, his whole demeanour in fact, spoke volumes. That remote spot was *his* Australia, among the snakes and the crocodiles, where but for a few short minutes each week, the rest of humanity is but a faraway thought. To read about the outside world from his delivery of mail and newspapers is as close to civilization as he chooses to be.

In staying with the troubled Vietnam veteran in a settlement at the far end of a dirt track, where the local gossip was of the outside world creeping in on its 50-strong population, I got another view of remoteness – the concern of a lifestyle under threat from a rapidly changing demography in the shape of unwelcome incomers searching for second homes.

In Tin Can Bay, the *Yacht Club at the End of the Universe* – the port's one redeeming feature – I was gleefully reminded of Australia's wonderful sense of humour by the notice on the WC doors, *Inboards & Outboards*. And again in the tartan city of Maclean by the Bottom Pub landlord's description of his trials as a Down Under publican. And I remain amused and admiring of the bloke back up in Maryborough who tried to pass his house off as a boat by sticking a pair of outboard motors onto the structure. I can think of no other country in the world where that would happen. Ireland maybe.

But my chat with the garbage collector in Rockhampton was indicative of a widespread inertia syndrome when he claimed that 90% of Australians would love to do what I've been doing because of the 'freedom of it all'. He had completely failed to grasp that he too could ride a bike through Oz if that's what he wanted – instead of believing that he's trapped in Rocky and will never get out. Not included in this narrative were the many such gripes I encountered along the way from people who seemingly cannot see the woods for the trees. For reasons that escape me, they do not seem to realise that in this massive country of theirs, just about anything is possible.

For inspiration, they should note the sheer originality and inventiveness of David & Donna Lowe's *Forest Flying* enterprise, and their incredible underground eco-house. Their achievements told me that Oz is a land where you can still realise your dreams, be who you want to be and live the way you want to live, without too much interference from the outside.

Things began to change a little in New South Wales. The further south I pedalled, the more I came to notice the downtrodden male.

The morose pair of males sitting with their domineering partners at the Plough Inn on the night of Bulahdelah's annual 'bop' was not a sight I'd seen anywhere north of the border – yet had witnessed more and more as I moved ever further towards Sydney. Women wearing the pants is a major shift between today's Oz and the place I inhabited four decades ago.

The part-aboriginal street hustler in Sydney was especially revealing. He has honed his natural hunting skills by adapting them to modern urban use; persistence, menace, and charm in equal measures – eventually finding the one that would work on me. His is a hard lot, not fully of one race or the other.

In the interior, little has changed. The hospitality of the Rutherford family near Bathurst is a timeless tradition of the bush, as is an instant willingness to lend a hand whenever needed. The same sentiment goes out to that gruff old mechanic in Mandurama. If you are stuck, there is always someone ready to help you out in this amiable part of the world.

All of these little occurences, not much in themselves, help to form the big jigsaw that is Australia in the raw, and from which you can draw your own conclusions.

So when I went back to Buronga that day with Dick Holland – with most of the pedalling over and done with – I was so totally attuned into the people and the ways of this immense country, that to find myself back on a sheep station after a 42 year absence seemed as natural as breathing.

As for the purpose of it all, it was a fulfilling ride in every sense. From an editorial angle, even many months later, the *PedallingPom.com* website received thousands of hits each month so I knew that somewhere a chord had been struck.

On the personal side of things ... well, perhaps I'm a slightly improved human being for having done it, though probably not. Living astride a simple bicycle, pushing my way through a land that is by no means God's country – although definitely luckier than most – has had a cleansing effect comparable to clearing out the trash from an overloaded email site. In some manner, it has emptied all the junk from my mind and provided focus on a number of perspectives; it has cleared the way for whatever is left of my life by freeing up the inner-self, and creating the mental space needed for new thoughts and fresh ideas.

Some of that space has already been taken up with new projects. And some of it with a few more ponderables. So I'll sign off with this one final notion.

Everything we do or see is in some way interconnected. If you were to argue that there's no possible relation between, say, a bicycle tyre and an ocean wave thumping onto a Queensland beach, I would have to say that I'm not so sure about that. It seems to me that both play their part in the grand design of things – that very finely-balanced Master Plan.

Whether I'm right, wrong, profound or pathetic – you be the judge. But I'll tell you this about long-distance cycling. It doesn't half make you think.